Life in Kent
At the turn of the century

LIFE IN KENT

At the turn of the century

Michael J. Winstanley

DAWSON

First published in 1978

© Michael J. Winstanley 1978

Wm Dawson & Son Ltd, Cannon House
Folkestone, Kent, England

British Library Cataloguing in Publication Data

Winstanley, Michael J.
Life in Kent at the turn of the century.
1. Kent, Eng.—Social life and customs
I. Title
942.2'3'0810922   DA670.K3

ISBN 0-7129-0828-5

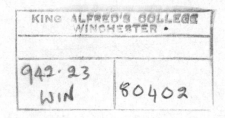
Printed in Great Britain
by W & J Mackay Limited, Chatham

Contents

To Melanie

Illustrations

Acknowledgements

This book is based on material collected for an 'oral history' project at the University of Kent from August 1974 to August 1977. It would not have been possible without the financial backing of the Social Science Research Council, and the help and encouragement of Professor Theo Barker and Mr John Whyman, the project supervisors. I would also like to thank Maureen Humphries who patiently transcribed nearly all the tapes and assisted with the administration involved in arranging interviews, Chris Rixson for typing the manuscript, Jim Styles for reproducing most of the illustrations, John Pell for drawing the maps and diagrams and Bob Seal of Dawson for his constant prods and words of encouragement. Above all, however, credit must go to all those people, only a few of whom are mentioned in the text, who allowed me into their homes to record their memories. Without them there would be no book. The achievements are theirs, the failings are mine.

I would like to thank the following for making available photographs for this book: Mrs Freda Vigden for nos 1, 6; Mr William Darby for nos 2, 5, 8; Mr Edward Carpenter for nos 3, 11, 12; Mr Charles Evernden for nos 4, 7; the Rothman Trust Picture Collection for nos 9, 13, 16, 17; the Douglas West Collection, Whitstable, for no. 10; the Faversham Society for no. 14; Mr James Medhurst for no. 15.

Preface

Be ye a hearer and bearer away of other men's talk.

Sir Henry Sidney to his son Philip (1566)

This book is not simply about Kent. Kent is the stage and backcloth on and against which the action takes place. I attempt to portray in detail the lives of some of its inhabitants—people often overlooked by contemporaries and historians alike because they rarely left any written records of their lives, folk who have not been considered sufficiently 'important' or 'significant' to merit attention.

Only one name appears on the cover of this book. The names of some of those who have contributed by allowing me to record their memories can be found in the text. They are the true authors. I have merely listened attentively to their recollections, recorded them and present them here with comments of my own, setting the scene, expanding on points they raised or explaining their significance. In many respects, therefore, apart from the introductory chapters to each section, this is a 'spoken book'.

No generation of people has witnessed a greater change in society than those born around the turn of the twentieth century. They are ideally qualified to comment on those years, not so distant in time but vastly different in lifestyle from our own time. Until comparatively recently, however, little interest has been shown in their memories. Distinguished people may have published their autobiographies but the majority of old folks' memories have been dismissed as nostalgic, distorted, selective or inaccurate. Grandmother's occasional lapses into yearning for her lost youth have been viewed as typical of the type of recollections which the older generation possesses. If this book has one overriding aim it is to disprove this unwarranted assumption by allowing elderly folk to tell their own stories in their own words. Through their memories, work patterns, many of which are now vanished, are brought once more to life. Values and attitudes which the present generation can only guess at are laid bare.

Unlike scientists or sociologists, historians have never been particularly concerned about creating their own evidence. They have relied almost exclusively on the scraps handed down to them by previous generations, scraps which they pick over, examine, and rearrange in an attempt to make sense of the past. Moving in literate circles, they have tended to assume that most important aspects of life would have been recorded on paper and preserved for posterity. Only primitive, illiterate societies have been assumed to rely heavily on oral transmission of historical material. This is simply not true. Documents automatically impose a definite slant on history. Their authors were invariably the exception rather than the rule in societies where the majority of people had neither time nor facility for writing. We will never know, for example, what a Roman soldier thought of Britain in 55 BC: we only have Caesar's account. Similarly, immense areas of life were never recorded because they were considered trivial or commonplace. The great mass of people rarely left any written record of their existence apart from the entries in parish registers recording their birth, marriage and death, quarter sessions records which laid bare their misdemeanours and, since the nineteenth century, census schedules which listed specific details which the authorities desired to have. Written historical sources remain silent on so many things.

With the invention of the tape recorder, however, we now have at our disposal a means of collecting and preserving some of the information which would otherwise never be committed to paper and would be lost with the death of the people concerned. 'Oral History', the unfortunate title given to the process of tape recording people's memories, has arrived on the scene with its own batteries of journals, jargon, technical problems, adherents and sceptics. This book is one result of an oral history feasibility project (financed by the Social Science Research Council), and carried out at the University of Kent between 1974 and 1977. During those three years, I interviewed over 180 people, about equal numbers of men and women, about their memories of life in Kent before 1914, and collected over 350 hours of tape amounting to nearly 8,000 pages of transcript (now stored in the library of the University). This book simply presents a fraction of the material collected.

There is still a fierce debate raging about the best ways of collecting, analysing and presenting oral evidence gathered through the tape recorder. Although this is not the place for a lengthy discussion about methodology, it is appropriate to say a few words about the road which these memories have travelled to reach the printed page.

All the interviews were carried out in people's homes. No questionnaire existed to channel the proceedings into preconceived patterns, because there was no guarantee that these would be the areas readily recalled by respondents, and because a specific list of questions would have had limited applicability for people selected from a wide range of backgrounds. An invitation to talk freely about what came to mind was the main approach and this was supplemented by prompts and questions from an interviewer eager to learn more about areas of life which he then knew little about. The recollections obtained, therefore, are a reflection of what people found important in their lives, comprehended and committed to memory—work routines, the minutiae of daily life, diet, clothing, entertainments, school, discipline, the home, street communities and so forth. Many of the events of political significance or national importance seem to have made little impression unless they directly affected the daily routines of life. Lloyd George is rightly remembered for his social reforms, but frequently wrongly assumed to have been Prime Minister before 1914. The Boer War is recalled for its exuberant celebrations, nicknames which it bestowed on people—Old Buller, for example, on boys who shouted a lot—and the rash of street names and christian names derived from places mentioned in the newspapers. Generally speaking, however, the concerns of the individual in the street were not those of the politician or the newspaper editor or even the majority of today's historians. He moved in a different world, and the interview technique employed recognised this and invited him to talk about it.

Once recorded, every interview was patiently transcribed. The words that appear in this book have been extracted from these transcripts, but they have been subjected to a certain amount of editing and rearranging to make them more palatable for the general reader. Speech is a vastly different medium from the written word. It is frequently ungrammatical, punctuated with unconnected digressions and ejaculations; it is repetitive and devoid of apparently natural pauses for full stops, commas or paragraphs. Since the interviews were unstructured, speakers were often asked to expand on areas covered during earlier stages, possibly elucidating them or expanding on them. The material did not arrange itself into any understandable, rational order. The pruning and reorganisation which has been carried out should make these memories more easily understood without destroying the patterns of speech employed by the people concerned. All of them would have wished to have presented their memories in a more ordered fashion had they known what areas their ignorant interviewer was going to ask them about!

This book, therefore, is about people, more specifically some of those who have been good enough to allow their memories to be recorded. It is offered in the hope that it will convince others that history is not the dry-as-dust academic study inflicted on them in their schooldays, but an essentially human subject involved with the lives of people like themselves. If it succeeds in putting over this view, the efforts of everyone involved in the germination and nurture of the book will have been worthwhile.

MICHAEL J. WINSTANLEY
Faversham, Kent
June 1978

Part I

Rural Life

Chapter 1

Kentish Agriculture

The first and most respectable of all the arts is agriculture.

Rousseau, *Emile* Bk. iii

It is appropriate that a book on Kent should begin with agriculture. In terms of land use, manpower and financial turnover, farming was without doubt the most important activity in the county before the First World War. Even though the number of men employed in it was falling in the late nineteenth century, nearly 50,000 were returned in the 1901 census, and the figure rose slightly in the next decade. In addition, several crops, hops and fruit especially, provided seasonal work for women and children, often on a large scale. With over 700,000 acres under cultivation, Kent, according to W. Little, the Assistant Commissioner reporting to the Royal Commission on Agricultural Interests in 1881, 'has a greater variety of produce, a larger amount of capital invested and yields a greater gross return per acre than any other county in the United Kingdom'. Its farmers possessed several advantages over their counterparts in other parts of the country. Little continued: '. . . within easy reach of the metropolis with its enormous population and its insatiable demand for dairy and garden produce, for green forage crops, hay and straw; with natural beauties which attract to it a large resident population

of wealthy consumers; with several popular seaside resorts; with a
variety of soils adapted for the growth of many products which cannot be successfully cultivated in many other counties, the farmer is
not dependent upon two or three commodities which everybody else
can grow.'
    Diversity was the hallmark of Kent's farming, different areas of
the county specialising in certain crops. The strip of land bordering
the railway and old Dover road from Rochester to Canterbury,
according to A. D. Hall in his *Pilgrimage of British Farming, 1910–
1912*, possessed 'a dusty, harsh businesslike look' which rendered it
'very unattractive' and certainly did not suggest 'agricultural rich-
ness'. As a fruit growing area, however, it had few equals. Hops
thrived in 'certain favoured districts' around the Medway valley and
its tributaries and on the rich loams of east Kent. The extensive grass-
lands of Romney Marsh were ideal for summer grazing for sheep,
although the young sheep were wintered 'up in the hills'. Thanet's
light soils and easy access to the London markets by water had meant
that it had long been famous for its arable crops, especially barley.
North-west Kent was developing a thriving market garden system to
cater for the growing demand of the sprawling London suburbs.
    There is a strong temptation to equate these important, but
localised crops, for which the county was rightly famous, with the
whole of the farming in Kent. This would be wrong. The Weald,
affectionately referred to as 'yellow belly country' by some east Kent
labourers, remained backward. In 1881 Mr Little found the west of
the Weald 'smothered in hedgerows and timber, and agriculture is
not advanced'. In the east, he encountered 'wet valleys and cold un-
drained grass lands'. Between Canterbury and Dover was traditional
sheep and corn country. Around Stelling Minnis there existed a large
body of smallholders who eked out a frugal existence. In fact, hops
and fruit rarely accounted for more than 10 per cent of the cultivated
land in Kent.
    The last quarter of the nineteenth century was remarkable for the
great changes which took place in British farming. The policy of Free
Trade adopted by the government allowed the imports of vast
quantities of food which led to a general fall in commodity price
levels, especially for grain. Wheat which had sold at 55s. a quarter in
the early 1870s had plummeted to a mere 28s. by the late 1890s. Hops
and meat were also particularly affected. Coupled with this dramatic
price fall was a series of inclement winters which hit the British crops
hard. No longer did the price rise in response to a shortfall of supply.
The farmers found instead their incomes drastically reduced.

The period soon earned for itself the title 'The Great Depression'. Two Royal Commissions were set up by the government to examine the plight of the farmers, one in the early 1880s, the other in the mid-1890s, and both came out strongly in favour of government help for farmers: by limiting imports, reducing rate burdens and improving leases for tenant farmers. Later historians, however, have tended to discount much of this evidence. The commissions consisted of landowners who were themselves undermined by the fall in rentals, and a large proportion of the witnesses were large farmers from the south and east of the country where arable crops were the predominant sources of income, rather than from the less affected northern counties. Much time was taken up by an airing of perennial farming complaints: the poor quality of the labour force and its excessive cost, tithe payments, the burden of local rates, the iniquitous railways companies who, it was claimed, gave preferential treatment to foreign produce landed at the ports, and the tendency for compulsory education to rob farmers of the cheap, young labour supply they had once been accustomed to. The period has since been referred to instead as one of adjustment rather than depression. Only those farmers lacking capital, expertise or business acumen went down.

Contemporary commentators seemed to differ in their opinions about the state of agriculture in Kent during this period. Many portrayed a gloomy picture. 'If you ride through the island,' wrote a 'Retired Agriculturist' of Thanet in the 1880s, 'you will find that on many farms the horses are not so good as they were, that the flocks have diminished, that there are not nearly so many yards of good fatting bullocks as formerly ... The fact is that Thanet is a corn growing district and it does not pay to grow corn at the price it fetches with the present expenses from the land.' The Isle of Sheppey, noted for its beans and wheat, was 'nearly all finished off', according to George Finn, farmer and land auctioneer, giving evidence before the Royal Commission on the Agricultural Depression in 1895. Rents there were a mere 25 per cent of their level twenty years earlier. Throughout the county, he insisted, 'There is scarcely any resident landlord ... the mansions are standing empty or let to others. You can sell everything you grow at less than it costs you to produce ... the millers have all gone to smash.' 'The series of unfavourable seasons', commented *The Kentish Gazette* on 12 October 1895, 'now unrelieved by any advance in prices, have exhausted the capital of tenant farmers and many of them cannot choose but go. Lucky those men who ten or fifteen years ago retired from agricultural pursuits while there was yet a balance at the bank.'

The Assistant Commissioners' reports on the Maidstone district of Kent and the evidence of several large farmers painted a happier picture, however. 'We cannot feel that we are so depressed as they are in many parts of the country where it is grass and cereals entirely,' remarked John Noakes of the Tunbridge Wells Farmers' Club in 1893, since he considered they were 'rather peculiarly situated'.

Aubrey Spencer, reporting to the Royal Commission on Labour, also in 1893, found that in the Hollingbourne area near Maidstone, 'The land appears as a rule to be in the highest state of cultivation, and makes a show of prosperity which is unfortunately at present lacking in many of the agricultural districts of England.'

The annual statistics collected by the Board of Agriculture reveal more precisely the changing nature of Kent's farming in the period (see Fig. 1). Arable farmland in the county fell from 435,341 acres in 1877 to 347,344 twenty years later and a mere 293,596 by 1914. Wheat crops especially declined considerably, from 98,697 acres in 1877, already down from a peak of over 105,000 acres in 1868, to less than half that figure, 42,993, by the turn of the century. Barley, however, held its own and actually increased in importance up to the 1900s before a general depression in the brewing industry reduced demand. This move away from arable farming was matched by an increase in livestock and dairy farming, fruit and market gardening. Permanent pasture increased from 302,722 acres in 1877, to 402,028 by 1897 and 429,166 by 1906. This was explained primarily by a rapid expansion of dairy farming, especially in the 1890s, the total number of cattle rising from 64,597 to 76,447 and 93,251 over the same period. Sheep farming, suffering from the more developed foreign trade in frozen lamb, a series of wet winters which increased losses and uncertainty about wool prices, actually declined slightly in the period. The number of horses remained relatively stable at about 28,000 despite the reduction in the number of fields under the plough.

Although this switch in farming practice was more pronounced than in other southern counties, many commentators tended to disregard it and suggested that Kent was a special case by attributing the apparent prosperity of the farmers to hops and fruit. Dr W. Fream, Assistant Commissioner reporting on the Maidstone district in 1894, remarked, '"Corn", I was told, "pays no rent," whilst hops and fruit have enabled many a man to weather the storm who might otherwise have gone under.' 'Hops', affirmed Charles Hoare, a large landowner from Staplehurst giving evidence before the Royal Commission, also in 1894, 'were the only things that paid and had any chance of paying.'

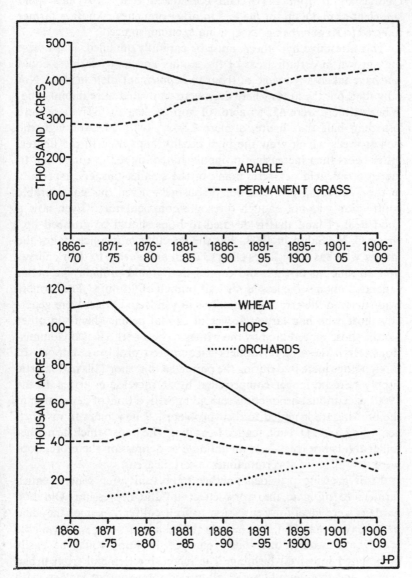

Fig. 1 Changes in land use in Kent 1866–1909

George Finn from Faversham considered that hops had 'paid sufficient to make up for the loss in other branches'. Another farmer referred to Kent as being 'exceptionally circumstanced'. This attractive hypothesis must be carefully qualified. Hops were only grown in certain areas of the county and many farmers could not have taken advantage of them to supplement their income. Not only that, but the areas where they were cultivated were diminishing. Whereas there were 45,984 acres of hop gardens in 1877 there were less than half that figure, a mere 22,626, by 1914. Although the richest areas which grew the high quality hops used in the lighter, bitter beers then increasing in popularity continued to thrive and to increase the yield per acre, many of the smaller farmers, especially in the Weald, were forced out of business. Even this considerable contraction was not enough for some commentators. 'Even now a good deal of land that is devoted to hops should be grubbed up,' wrote C. W. Sabin in 1908, 'but the speculative instinct makes the farmer who has a few acres cling to them and devote to their cultivation an amount of time and capital that would probably be better expended upon some less hazardous branch of farming.' The farmers who survived the erratic fluctuations in yields and prices were generally those who had large reserves of capital behind them—in other words, those represented by the witnesses before the Royal Commissions. Even these large farmers encountered problems. Imports of foreign hops increased during the period so that shortfalls in domestic supply were no longer compensated by an increase in prices. In the 1900s exceptional production coinciding with a time of depression in the brewing trade added to their problems. A newcomer to farming, according to A. D. Hall, tended to grub up the hops 'which he neither understands nor trusts'. As an antidote to depression therefore, hops were only effective at certain times in certain areas.

Fruit growing provided another opportunity for some Kentish farmers to mitigate the worst effects of the depression. Old hop gardens were ideal for conversion to fruit cultivation since they had been heavily manured. A relatively skilled labour force was available locally and women previously engaged in hops could be easily assimilated into fruit farming. The increasing demand from urban centres and from jam factories all tended to encourage farmers with sufficient capital and foresight to expand into fruit. From 1888, the first year when statistics were collected on this aspect of farming, the acreage grew rapidly, rising from 12,344 to over 22,000 in the 1900s, despite clauses in tenants' agreements with landowners which tended to discourage its development.

Fruit farmers, however, encountered problems too. The 1880s and 1890s were marked by crises of overproduction brought about by excessive speculation. Yields were often low because the growers lacked the necessary expertise in management and pruning. Marketing habits also left much to be desired. 'The slovenly way in which fruit is packed, thereby becoming bruised, battered and otherwise depreciated, is said to lead to a great diminution in value,' remarked Dr Fream in 1894. Twenty years later Hall noted the same fault, but considered its seriousness was compounded by the inefficiencies of the South-Eastern Railway. Farmers insisted on packing their fruit into returnable baskets, sieves and half-sieves: 'Of the adventures of returned empties on the South-Eastern Railway many lurid tales are told, of search parties taking the line section by section, of submerged trucks full of baskets that wash up in distant stations and there lie stranded in the sidings; but such is the force of long custom that the Kentish grower has not yet been converted to the value of non-returnable packages, which neither bring back disease nor mean idle capital.' As with hops, therefore, although fruit shielded many farmers from the full effects of the fall in prices, there were still several problems to be overcome, and only farmers in certain areas of the county were able to take full advantage. Outside the fruit and hop areas some commentators even thought that Kentish farmers were below average in their abilities. The overall situation is perhaps best summarised by Charles Whitehead, a farmer from the Maidstone area. Writing in 1899 in the *Journal of the Royal Agricultural Society* he observed, 'Without hops, fruit and vegetables, Kent would have felt the depression quite as much as any other county in England, as there is so much poor land within its borders, and excepting in districts especially well farmed, like the Isle of Thanet—many of its agriculturists who have neither hop nor fruit land have either succumbed or are in a sorry plight.'

A similar controversy raged over the condition of the farmworkers. Without exception, the farmers considered their labourers had benefited from the fall in agricultural prices from the 1870s, and official investigations agreed with them. Writing to the Royal Commission on Labour in 1893, the Assistant Commissioner for Kent, Aubrey Spencer, described them as 'better off now than they have ever been before' even though wages had fallen marginally, because 'the necessaries of life are cheaper now'. The labourer, complained Charles Hoare, had 'got too big a share of the cake'. Wage reductions were vital to the future of farming. Those involved in hop cultivation were rumoured to earn as much as £3 per week at certain seasons of the year.

These comments and the statistics supplied to support them need to be placed in their correct context, however. As F. E. Green astutely commented in his book on the agricultural labourer in 1920, 'the farmer, squire and parson . . . are inclined to take an exaggerated view of Hodge's income.' Always ready to take advantage of an opportunity to paint themselves as generous employers about to be ruined by their high wage costs, they invariably included inflated estimates of the value of perquisities which they supplied to their workforce—especially cottages at low rents, and occasionally food and fuel. As the official investigations showed, many of the smaller farmers did not keep records and could not be precise about their wage bills, and they tended to equate the labourer's potential earnings in a good week with his weekly average, although these were often wildly dissimilar, as the labourers themselves readily testified.

All the official enquiries into Kentish agriculture during the period concentrated heavily on the area around Maidstone, acknowledged by Dr Fream to be possibly 'per acre, the wealthiest part of agricultural England'. Here there was work for the whole family for much of the year, much of it on piecework. Hop digging, dressing, poling, digging round the hills—all these were added to the usual piecework tasks of grass mowing, corn cutting and tying, thatching, turnip hoeing and sickling, ticing and hedging, while the women and children carried out hop tying, pole shaving, and hop picking, to name but a few tasks. Although the rate for some of these jobs, especially hop picking, was frequently decided after the work had been completed, most men could earn above what they were normally paid on day work while their wives could add, according to Aubrey Spencer, up to £8 5s. to the annual family income, and more if they took their children with them. Elsewhere in the county, however, wages varied considerably, often from farm to farm. Spencer produced figures for a labourer in a non-hop growing area who had specialised skills in thatching, and despite earning up to £2 7s. per week at certain times of the year, his average weekly wage amounted to a paltry 15s. 5½d. Women's work outside these areas was also 'irregular and uncertain', often involving little more than the occasional stone picking. The Weald in particular had a reputation for low wages. Although it would be true to say, therefore, that there was a larger proportion of relatively prosperous farm labourers in Kent than there was in many other counties, it should be borne in mind that these were usually concentrated in certain well defined districts, and wages varied considerably depending on the skills of the labourers, the type of farming practised, the value accorded to perks, the weather, the availability of work for families and even local custom. Relative prosperity does not necessarily mean that the labourers were well off; to a starving beggar a man who possesses a crust of bread is rich. The labourers questioned in the early 1880s disagreed violently with the farmers who claimed that they were leading an easy life. 'I am trying my best to keep from parish relief,' replied one man from Milton. 'Scarcely pay my way' . . . 'A mean living' . . . 'Scarcely enough to live on'—these were typical of the comments Mr Little heard. 'Not a gay living for a large family,' explained one rather more forthcoming worker, '16s. 6d. per week, 2s. for rent, 2s. for fuel, 10d. for school, myself and wife and 7 children to live.' Spencer found similar grumbles in the 1890s. 'The men themselves did not admit that there was any considerable improvement of recent years,' he wrote. Some complained that they were not allowed to keep pigs or poultry because the farmer feared they would steal his grain. Others commented on the smallness of their gardens. Education, especially before it was made free of charge in 1891, was also a constant source of complaint. Not only did people have to pay for their children to attend school but it prevented them from supplementing the family income. Many continued to keep them away during busy seasons.

The standard of living enjoyed by farmworkers seems to have varied considerably and it would be foolish to attempt to generalise on the basis of the available evidence. Even oral recollections are contradictory. Some people recall a good living, others refer to frequent deprivation. Much probably depended on the size of the family, the health of the breadwinner, the area of the county where they lived, the opportunities for piecework and for women's employment, the extent of the garden and the availability of allotments, the weather and, possibly most important of all, the housekeeping ability of the wife. Only one thing is certain: there was no room for idle extravagance in farmworkers' lives.

That many men thought they could better themselves away from farming is clear from the census figures for the period. These show a continual decline in the numbers employed on the land up to 1901, and in common with other areas of the country Kent witnessed what became known as 'the Rural Exodus'. 'The general stagnation and in some cases, the marked decline in population', wrote Bavington Jones in 1901, 'suggests that there is something wrong with the villages.' According to the farmers this migration was not due to poor employment prospects in farming. Labour, especially good labour, was in demand everywhere because many of those who remained were of inferior standard and farmers had to rely on old men and boys to do their work. A glance at the age distribution of the labour force shows that there was some truth in this. Over 30 per cent of the 'farm servants' in 1901 were under twenty-five years old. Nearly 53 per cent were in this age group or over fifty-five. As the next chapter shows, the exodus was even more marked from certain specialised farm jobs. Many boys on leaving school were undoubtedly drawn into farming because they were too young to leave home and fend for themselves in the towns or the armed forces but once they reached adulthood they deserted the land in large numbers.

The classical economic interpretation of this exodus is that men were drawn by the higher wage levels in the towns. Well paid jobs in the Kentish towns, however, were few and far between. Unskilled labourers certainly earned no more than their rural counterparts, and it was in this group of workers that a migrant would initially be classified. Large-scale industry was restricted to a few areas. Although some undoubtedly ventured to London the official reports on the county's agriculture actually refer to Londoners who came down for hop picking begging to be allowed to stay on as farmworkers, so attractive and profitable did they find the life. The armed forces, a major recruiter of rural migrants, certainly did not pay well. Many old folk recall the shock they received when they enlisted.

Another hypothesis popular with farmers and some commentators was that young men were given ideas 'above their station' by the schools. Mr Allington Collard, a farmer from Herne Bay, wrote strongly to the Interdepartmental Committee on the Employment of School Children in 1902: 'I fear the robustness of youth is at times sacrificed for education which is serious when their future will probably depend upon manual labour . . . I consider raising the age limit tends to disassociate boys from the land, as they get out of hand for learning the detail of the work, in fact lose their apprenticeship; they think they are above agricultural work, and drift into the towns.' Almost every other farmer echoed his sentiments. 'I was always a very strenuous advocate of compulsory elementary education,' wrote a Mr Mannington from Yalding, 'but I think that free education is now carried quite far enough.' Since they had to contribute heavily through the rates to the cost of providing the education, farmers felt they had just cause to complain.

The facilities provided by the country schools were far from elaborate and their syllabi were limited and rudimentary. Farmers continued to retain a strong hold over them. School holidays were scheduled to coincide with the busiest times of the farming year. Boys were seconded for beating or helping with the hunting. Education probably influenced the child's outlook not so much by actively encouraging him to be ambitious or desert farming, but simply by increasing his awareness of the outside world, not only within the school walls but by enabling him to read the local newspapers or popular Sunday papers which were increasing their circulation around this time. Parents too, many of them uneducated themselves, viewed schooling as a means of giving their children advantages and opportunities which they had never had, if not on immediately leaving school, then as soon as they had contributed a reasonable amount to the family coffers. An aversion to farm work was certainly widespread amongst girls by the 1900s. Many viewed it as degrading and left for service. Many more, unimpressed by the prospect of devoting the rest of their life to slaving for a hop farmer as a condition of their husband's employment, undoubtedly persuaded their young men to seek work in the towns. Few girls who returned from service relished the thought of settling down to life as labourers' wives. The role of women in drawing men off the land has rarely been accorded its full importance.

The attractions of the town, its bright lights, theatres, numerous gaudy public houses and fancy shops must also have acted as a magnet for the more gregarious youth. Farmwork by the 1890s was not a social job. The fields were rarely crowded except at hop or fruit picking time. The introduction of the reaper and later the self-binder reduced the necessity to employ large numbers of people at haymaking or harvest time. Men often laboured on their own for the whole day, rarely seeing anyone, yet were clearly visible to all who passed, including the farmer. They lived a lonely but far from private life. Not only did a labourer live in a world where everyone knew his business but his whole existence was often rigidly controlled by his employer. He stipulated where and when he should work, how much he should pay for his house, the work his wife and children had to do, whether or not he could keep his own livestock, whether he had to attend church on religious holidays such as Good Friday. For the young men—waggoners, stockmen and occasionally shepherds—who lived in the farmhouse it would be true to say that their lives were not their own. Even the married men had few opportunities for escape. In the evening they could retire to the local pub, busy themselves with chapel activities if they were religiously inclined or huddle into the small cottage which their employers provided for them. The appeal of the town or even the armed forces was the crowd and the apparent anonymity which its members enjoyed. The rural migrant sought a society where he could lose his identity in the crowd, and perhaps also find it at the same time. He sought privacy in a crowded world and ran from a rural society where his personal affairs were common knowledge and his life was mortgaged to, at best, a paternalistic farmer. The exodus could well have been psychologically inspired.

It would be wrong to assume that farmers and labourers were the only country dwellers. This was simply not the case, but the whole basis of the rural economy was farming, and it is with various aspects of this work that the following chapters deal.

Chapter 2

All Jolly Fellows?—The Waggoners

So all you young men, wheresomever you be,
Take my advice and be ruled by me,
Never fear your good master I'll swear and I'll vow
That we're all jolly fellows a-following the plough.

Traditional song

The waggoner, or carter as he was often called in west Kent, was
frequently regarded as the most important worker on a farm. 'If he
is up to his duties', wrote Richard Jefferies in 1880, 'he is a most
valuable servant; if he neglects them he is a costly nuisance, not so
much from his pay, but because of the hindrance and disorganisation
of the whole farm work which such neglect entails.' The waggoner,
aware of his importance, usually tried to take a pride in his tasks, so
much so that his work has often been portrayed as intrinsically more
satisfying than that of the ordinary day labourer. It is tempting to
accept completely the picture painted for us by folksongs and many
rural commentators of brisk young ploughboys and jolly waggoners
being doubly rewarded not only with the 'fellowship of Nature' but
also by the superior material benefits of the job. The Kentish
waggoners were even more favourably situated than most of their
counterparts in Southern England. Richard Heath, who visited the

county in 1871, considered them 'rich as far as labourers go . . . well nurtured people in a well nurtured land'. Jolly fellows indeed. It is the intention of this chapter to outline some of the main aspects of the lives of Kent's 6,589 'farm servants in charge of horses' at the turn of the century and to take an objective view of the rewards and drawbacks of their job and lifestyle.

There were recognised advantages in being a waggoner. Along with the stockman and the shepherd he received higher cash payments than ordinary labourers. Farmers giving evidence before the Royal Commission on Agricultural Interests in the early 1880s expressed the opinion that he was too well off, 'in many instances better off than his employer', receiving 'much higher wages' for 'much less work'. Real wages remained steady despite the fall in agricultural prices in the last quarter of the nineteenth century so that by 1893 a married man could expect to receive from 15s. to 16s. a week, a free cottage, one or two tons of coal, 100 faggots and possibly some harvest or Michaelmas money each year. Although the figure varied fractionally over the county and between different grades of waggoners, by the early 1900s a total weekly income in excess of £1 was not uncommon, while the ordinary labourer received only 2s. 2d. to 2s. 6d. per day depending on area and season. The difference was enough to convince many men that the 'biggest shilling' was to be found with horses.

Waggoners and their mates were often hired by the year, an added advantage of the job because they were guaranteed their level of pay each week regardless of weather or sickness. The labourer, on the other hand, expected to be laid off if, for any reason, the weather not excepted, there was no work for him. Alfred Simmons, Secretary of the Kent and Sussex Labourers' Union, giving evidence before the Royal Commission of 1881, estimated that each man lost an average of 85 days each year due to inclement weather. Increasing mechanisation in farming during the late nineteenth century also increased the number of jobs performed by waggoners and regular farm hands at the expense of the casual labourer, seed drills displacing broadcasting and dibbling, mowers, reapers and later self-binders ousting bagging hooks and scythes.

The waggoners also considered themselves the elite amongst farmworkers. Although shepherds were respected for their skills they were never accorded the same privileged status as the horsemen, while stockmen were even looked down on to some extent. Dairying was still regarded by many men as women's work, a subsidiary rather than the major activity which it was gradually becoming during the period. There were also definite career prospects which encouraged dedicated youngsters to take up the work. Each team of four horses would be cared for by a waggoner and his mate, so that on a three team farm there would be a first, second and third waggoner each of whom would be helped by a mate. Each job was rewarded differently in pay and status. Leaving the stable or travelling along the road, the first man always led, the third man brought up the rear. If, as was sometimes the case on smaller farms, the waggoner also performed the role of bailiff he was definitely 'classed as a big man'. For every boy who took up work with horses, therefore, there was an apparently straightforward promotion guaranteed from third, second to first mate and then to a waggoner in his own right. Unlike the labourer, who would find it harder to obtain employment and more difficult to make up his income by piecework as he got older, a trained and experienced horseman expected to be handsomely rewarded for his years of training and accumulated expertise.

Doubts about this automatic progression up the farm ladder arise, however, when the age patterns of the occupation are examined. In 1901, just over 21 per cent of the total agricultural workforce (general labourers, shepherds, waggoners and stockmen), but nearly 30 per cent (28.8) of the 15–25 year olds and 24.4 per cent of the 25–45 age group were employed with horses. Over 40 per cent of all waggoners and their mates were under twenty-five; only 23 per cent were older than forty-five (compared to 43 per cent of shepherds and 42 per cent of casual labourers).

These figures suggest several things. First, a large minority, possibly even a majority of the boys who entered plough service, as it was often called, stayed only a few years. Possibly this was due to the treatment they received from farmers and waggoners some of whom were rumoured to be over-strict, even cruel, to their young mates. Possibly the appeal of communion with nature was viewed as a lifetime 'floundering around on the old farm' or 'up to the neck in mud'. Another probable reason for leaving, however, was the realisation that there were just not enough waggoners' jobs to absorb them all. A mate's pay was generally lower than that which he would have earned as a labourer, and he was in many cases paid only once a year. As long as he was assured of relatively rapid promotion to waggoner he was willing to forgo the financial rewards, but to spend any length of time as a mate was just not feasible if he hoped to settle down and get married. Since waggoners hoped to maintain their jobs for upwards of forty years it is obvious that, since they were matched by an equal number of mates, there were too few openings for the younger men. The unwillingness of many old waggoners to part with their trade secrets, a trait for which they were widely renowned, was soundly based. They were acutely aware of the fact that younger, stronger men were likely to be preferred by farmers if they knew as much as they did. Even so the census figures show that many waggoners left the work in middle age. Some undoubtedly were promoted to bailiffs or even became small farmers themselves but many suffered the indignity of being forced to take up labouring, possibly of a less demanding nature than that required in waggoning. Even expertise lost its value, it seems, when shackled to a body too old or deformed to work so that, after a lifetime of 'unceasing and protracted labour', the waggoner was likely to end his days in the parish workhouse or dependent on a munificent employer or kindly relatives.

Few old men could have endured the long hours expected of them. These were almost uniform over the county. The waggoner generally rose by 4 a.m. to bait the horses and get them ready for the day's work, breakfasting himself at about 5.30 a.m. after also waking his mate. They were then expected to be out of the stable at 6 a.m. whatever the weather. Ploughing in the dark was not unusual. Work in the fields then continued till 2 p.m. or 2.30 p.m., possibly with a short break mid-morning for a snack, or *bever*. After dinner the horses were fed and groomed and in the summer their green meat (hay, clover) was cut, the waggoner finishing his day's work at 6 p.m. while his mate had the privilege of baiting and racking up two hours later. During busy times of the year a two yoke system was often worked in east Kent, the team labouring from 6 a.m. to 10 a.m. and 1 p.m. to 6 p.m. or 6 a.m. to noon and 1 p.m. to 4 p.m. Both men thus worked at least a twelve hour day for six days of the week and on Sundays were still required to tend to the needs of their horses, morning and evening. Even this arduous routine was considered too easy by Mr Marshall. Writing in the 1790s, by which time this routine was common throughout the South of England, he called it an 'extravagant practice', allowing the waggoner, 'reposing in the hayloft', to grow 'as fat and as lazy as his horses' while the mate performed the evening duties.

These hours, which applied all the year round, were considerably longer, however, than those worked by ordinary farm labourers: ten hours in the summer and from dawn till dusk in the winter. Not surprisingly many men actually preferred to remain labourers rather than take on the extra responsibility and work-load involved with the care of animals. Several were astute enough to realise that the waggoner's hourly wage rate was actually lower than their own. In addition, as Albert Patterson (born 1892) commented, the 'weak ones' signed on for a year to ensure a guaranteed weekly wage, but the 'week ones' could at certain seasons take home much more especially during hay-making, harvesting, and hop picking. Despite this drawback, he and many others like him accepted the situation unquestioningly and still preferred to remain with their horses. Occasionally, as Percy Barnes (born 1889) recalls, they did receive extra money when they had a considerate bailiff or a generous employer, but most of them did not expect it.

'As a rule, at a lot of the places I worked at, we used to get what they called Michaelmas money. They'd give you thirty bob or a couple of pound and then you had to put in work along with the other men. Their overtime pay would be about 4d. an hour in them days, so same as I say, if you got Michaelmas money, you sort of worked for nothing really. I know one place where I was, we had a fresh foreman and he came to me when we were going to start hay-making and said:

"I understand you have Michaelmas money. I don't think that's quite right. You earn a lot more than thirty bob. You've been working all the hours that the other men are and when they leave off you've still got your horses to look after."

'I said, "Well, that's how it's always been."

"From now on", he said, "you'll have overtime same as the other men."

'Well, that made my pay a little bit better because we used to work long hours haying time till the hay begun to get dark with dew.'

Although the general practice in Kent was to hire by the year, some farmers were complaining that they were finding it increasingly difficult to find men willing to stay for the full duration of their contract, and half-yearly and even monthly contracts were becoming more common. For the married worker with a family the yearly contract provided highly valued security. Even if it was only verbal it carried the force of law. Men dismissed unfairly were entitled to compensation, often their full year's wage. Those sacked with just cause could lose it all. A worker who was unfortunate enough to choose a farmer who liked to drive his men, however, was stuck with him for the year. There was little point in him seeking alternative work in the neighbourhood; his only recourse was to run away completely. Many did, often being tempted to follow the drum and enlist, lured away by judicious advertisements in the local press offering 'Good Food, Good Clothes, Good Lodgings and Money to Spend Every Day . . . to active and steady young men between the ages of 18 and 25', or simply by the flashy and attractive uniforms of some of the local regiments. Taking a 'sub' from their employer, they went to town and never returned, only writing to their families to inform them where they were when well away from the area.

It was common practice, especially in east Kent, right up to 1914, for the single men who worked with animals to be boarded in the farmhouse where their employer could keep an eye on them. The treatment they received varied between farms although generally speaking they seem to have been well fed even if their sleeping quarters left something to be desired. Jack Larkin (born 1889) remembers his years in farm service with undisguised relish.

'There were just the three of us—the waggoner, myself as mate and the stockboy—lived in. We used to have our meals in the farmhouse and there was a bit of an old cottage attached to it and we used to sleep in there. The farmer always had a barrel of beer in and we used to have small beer for breakfast, ale for dinner and small beer for tea. The only time we had hot tea to drink was on a Sunday. For breakfast in the morning living with a farmer was a darn great lump of fat pork, half a loaf of bread, and, if they'd got plenty of milk, a jolly great bowl of bread and milk. That was something to go to work on! After I left that last farm, when I joined the service [the Royal Marines] at nineteen, I weighed twelve stone four pound. I hadn't been in the service three months and I went down to less than ten stone.'

By the 1900s, however, there were fewer farmers willing to share their family home with their men, and the task of boarding single men was often delegated to the married waggoner. For those with large families this must have created severe accommodation problems but many, like Jack Larkin's parents, welcomed them because the additional 9s. which the farmer paid them for their lodger meant that 'us kids lived a lot better when mother had a lodger'. If the waggoner's wife succumbed to the temptation to spend the allowance on her family, the unfortunate mate could often find himself sadly neglected, wondering, like J. H. Barwick who entered plough service on a farm near Eastry in 1902, whether he could stick it or not.

'I lived on fat pork for twelve months. That's all we had, bar Sundays, we had a beef pudding. Course I used to be allowed to come home one Sunday in a month and I used to get different then. But that's all I had for breakfast, dinner and tea—fat pork. Cor blimey! And sometimes it wasn't done properly and when the knife went through it you could hear it sort of crunch. Pork not done properly is awful too. The waggoner used to go down to the stable at four, come home at five, have his breakfast and back again at five-thirty. Well, when he went back he used to call me, but because his breakfast was all cleared away there was no telling what he had. No! We used to have to be out in the stable at six with the horses to go out in the field ploughing and stay there till two. That was eight hours. Do you know we didn't have a bit to eat or drink in between that time. She wouldn't lay anything out. She used to get 9s. a week for my board and lodging and she had the lot. But it was only for one year because that waggoner left and another one came and I boarded with him. His wife used to bring us tea and a piece of bread and cheese out if we were down at the farm. I was in clover! But that was pretty rough going that first year, I can assure you.

'There were three pairs of horses, the waggoner's and mine, and what they called the *allworks*. Well, the farmer was a bit of a market gardener as well and in the summer time the allworks used to go to Dover market every week regular. Sometimes they'd have two loads to go and they wanted an extra trace horse, well that used to be me. I used to start at eleven o'clock at night and get back about four-thirty or five o'clock in the morning. Do you know what I used to get for that? A pint of beer and a piece of pork and bread. No extra money, it was just that £12 a year flat. Used to get home and then I could go to bed but I had to be back at work at nine in the morning. I used to have to go out with one horse, the one that hadn't been out, but the horse that had been out all night, he had to rest all day. I had to go to work. It didn't matter about me.'

The gradual removal of servants from the farmer's home was indicative of a major change in his attitudes in the latter half of the nineteenth century. No longer did he consider himself to be primarily responsible for the spiritual and physical welfare of his men, and despite frequent criticisms that he was 'throwing away the advantages of the situation in which Providence had placed him, and neglecting to do the good which he can do and which the majority of mill-owners cannot', only vestiges of what was once a strict paternalistic system remained by the dawn of the present century. Lodgers could still be obliged, however, to dress up with a clean shirt for Sunday tea, to say grace and to attend church occasionally. Some were even forbidden to smoke. 'Prisoners free' was Albert Patterson's effective summing up of their position. The control exercised by the farmer would have been even greater had he followed the advice proffered by one 'Rural Rector' in a letter to *The Kentish Gazette* in 1850:

'First of all, when you hire a servant, be very careful to choose one who bears a good character. Tell him that you hope he will go to church regularly; not that you mean to *make him* go, but that you will feel disappointed if he does not go. Tell him that you expect nothing like bad language will ever be heard from his lips; that you wish yours to be a quiet well ordered household and that if he is willing to come to you on this understanding, you will be ready to take him. 'Then I have always felt that it would be very desirable that there should be *Family Prayers* in every farmhouse. You would not be able, perhaps, to assemble your servants in the morning, but you might do so in the evening. There would be little trouble in it, but a great blessing. You might ask your clergyman to provide you with a *very simple* form of prayers which all could understand; and so short, that none could be tired by them . . .

'Talk to them occasionally about the sermon they have heard, and ask them what private prayers they are in the habit of using, and press upon them the duty and comfort of *kneeling down* and praying to God night and morning, when they are in their bed rooms. It would hardly be believed how many offer up *no prayers at all*, how many repeat the most ignorant and unmeaning words, how many *never kneel*, and how few, alas, how very few, go to their Heavenly Father as children who need pardon for the past and strength and protection for the future.

'Show by your manner that you take an interest in your servants. Ask them about their homes, their parents, etc. Try to shew them that you are their friend. If there should be any fair going on in the neighbourhood, warn them of the harm they may get by going to it. A kind word of sober advice may just serve to check them in time when they are rushing into danger . . . a warm fire and a comfortable room would act as a great inducement to them to stay at home instead of wandering to the beershop.'

There were more effective ways of preventing farm servants frequenting the local inn. Not only were their evenings often devoted to racking up but they were generally penniless most of the year. Waggoners who did not board were usually paid weekly but single men only received a lump sum at Michaelmas, with possible advances at Christmas and Whitsun.

Old Michaelmas Day, 11 October, was the traditional start and end of the farming year; debts were settled, farms changed hands and hands changed farms. All work ceased at midday on the 11th until the morning of the 16th. Single men, changing employers, picked up their knife, fork and spoon; families loaded their scanty domestic belongings into the waggons and rumbled along apprehensively to new homes. Some waggoners rarely changed farms, others were almost gypsies, always anxious to move on, never able to settle. Two old waggoners at Challock are remembered for their quaint practice of changing places with each other every two years just to add a little variety to their work.

Securing a new position was at one time achieved at the notorious hiring or statute fairs which served as primitive job centres, the workers lining up in the market place to be inspected by prospective employers. Shepherds decorated their caps with bunches of wool or carried a crook to indicate their calling; labourers carried a *shining stick*, a short pole; the waggoners, some whip cord. Jack Larkin remembers seeing them:

'If a chap wanted to go to the hiring fair, he used to take his whip and what they called a *war-line*, that was a very long lead, all done up nice and neat, and he'd attach that to his belt and carry his whip over his shoulder. As soon as he'd been hired, he'd carry his whip like that—straight up. That was to say he'd been hired, and then he'd go and have a drink with his new boss then go and find out where he'd got to bed-in like for the twelve month.'

Hiring fairs retained their importance much longer in northern counties. In Kent, only the 'Jack and Joan' fair at Canterbury continued to attract any custom. In its heyday it had been the subject of much heated criticism but by the 1900s it was but a ghost of its former self. The columns of the local press, no longer filled with complaints of 'scenes of drunkenness and debauchery' by day and a 'riot of turbulence' by night, carried news of church harvest festivals and other more sober seasonal celebrations. The high spirits once associated with the fair were understandable. Since farm service provided little opportunity for entertainment young men, and at one time women too, flush with money, poured into the city to revive their capacity for laughter. For most of its life the fair was held on the site of the old cattle market just outside St George's Gate, the unfortunate cattle being removed to another site to make way for more valuable human stock. Complaints about noise and inconvenience from residents in St George's Terrace were instrumental in the removal of the declining fair to Rhodaus Town and the Agricultural Hall in the 1900s. Any resemblance to the celebration of the Christian feast of St Michael, the original function of the fair, had long since disappeared so the authorities of the cathedral city naturally regarded its activities with despair and, during the nineteenth century especially, were constantly seeking ways of eliminating the 'demoralising influences' which its celebration entailed.

Although the fair was still 'jolly good fun' right up until 1914, few waggoners or their mates considered it necessary or desirable to visit it to obtain employment. Less exciting ways were more common by then, three in particular. They could buy a local paper to scan the adverts—*The Kentish Express* seems to have been the most popular; rely on word of mouth, or spend a penny, the price of half a pint of beer, and visit the local pub where the landlord was ideally placed to hear of any vacancies in the locality. Farmers who resorted to advertising were often regarded with suspicion. Jack Larkin's father had strong views on the subject: 'My old dad always used to say never go to a farm that advertises for a man because he's no damn good. A good farmer always advertises himself, same as a good workman will always advertise himself.' Farmers and waggoners alike were able to form their own opinions of each other from the work which was clearly visible in the fields, and both good and bad men soon acquired wide reputations. References were rarely asked for and were unknown to many of the older generation. Albert Patterson knew of one old waggoner, unacquainted even with the word, who would politely meet any request for a reference with an apology and the offer of his father's if that would prove acceptable. When the term of service was as long as a year, however, both men found it worth their while to take note of local news even if it was only orally transmitted. Jack Larkin relates how it worked in one instance:

'My father's boss died and the people who bought the farm went to old dad and said,

"Larkin, you've got a jolly good character. I've seen your work, I've seen your animals and you please me very much indeed. I want you."

'My old dad looked him in the face and says, "Well, perhaps you do, but let me tell you, I know your character very well indeed, and you won't get me to work for you."'

The advantages of being a waggoner—greater security and a guaranteed wage—have to be weighed against the loss of personal freedom and opportunity for piecework which the job entailed. The appeal of the job lay rather in the scope it allowed for individual responsibility and self-expression. The successful maintenance of a team of farm horses for a full year was no easy task and the waggoner felt, with some justification, he was entitled to a certain amount of respect. It was the nature of the work, whether ploughing a straight furrow or dressing up the horses and waggons for road journeys, which allowed for personal creativity. It was the job itself which bestowed a certain valued independence on the man who performed it, inviting him at the same time to make it his life's work, often to the exclusion of everything else. The material benefits were paltry in comparison to this.

Chapter 3
Oxen

The old ox makes the straightest furrow.

James Howell, *Proverbs* (1659)

The horse is often regarded as the only motive power in pre-mechanised farming. The folklore, mystery, beauty and romance which surrounds the animal stands out in such complete contrast to the facelessness of the modern tractor age that he seems to be symbolic of all that was attractive and enduring about the old system of cultivating the land. It is not difficult to overlook the fact that this apparent champion of traditional ways was himself a comparative newcomer to the farms, and was the subject of much heated criticism and debate even as late as the nineteenth century. His defeated, and often forgotten, rival for the farmer's favour was the ox, usually portrayed as a dull, silent animal, the epitome of hard work and stupidity, or wrongly equated with the ungelded and often cantankerous bull. The ox proved a stubborn foe. Whereas the horse was universally superseded by the internal combustion engine within the space of fifty years, his displacement of the ox took several centuries.

It is impossible to be precise about when the ox first became man's most important agricultural assistant and, therefore, one of his most valued possessions. He has undoubtedly laboured in man's service for several thousand years and even after the invention of the traction harness and horse collar about AD 1000, his supremacy on the land was not seriously disputed for several centuries. The horse was not regarded as a working animal or bred as one. Heavy haulage or field work was considered too lowly for such a creature, prized as he was for his speed, good looks, social and military values. The ox, therefore, continued to be extensively used in many parts of Britain, and even as late as 1800 was championed by some highly regarded agriculturists. The Rev. Arthur Young in his *General View of the Agriculture of Sussex* (1813) considered that, even though oxen were employed at well below their full capacity, they were still far superior to horses, performing similar work with less expense and effort. George III reverted to oxen on his Windsor estate in 1799, and the government even went so far as to impose a tax on draught horses in 1801, much to the dismay of the farming community.

The ox as a draught beast possessed considerable advantages over the horse. He was cheaper to buy, feed, maintain and supply with equipment. He was generally a healthier animal, and well suited by strength and temperament to long, laborious work. He was more reliable and predictable. His slow, constant pull minimised wear on the more primitive wooden ploughs and made them easier for the ploughman to control. His manure was of much higher quality than the horse's and he gained in value with age while the horse depreciated, since, as Young remarked, 'the one at his death gives beef for mankind, the other is horse flesh for dogs'. The scales swung in the horse's favour, however, when the improved ploughs of the eighteenth century began to be widely accepted, although many farmers also employed horses on the older wooden implements. These new implements were more able to withstand the uneven thrust of the horse, and once the iron ploughs of the nineteenth century arrived, the ox, basically beaten for speed, was finally ousted from the field and farmyard. Improvements in horse breeding in the last quarter of the century dealt the final death blow.

Although the horse's empire extended throughout most of Kent as early as the 1790s, this 'costly, expensive animal' had made few inroads into the Weald, where oxen were still regularly used for carriage and ploughing work and for certain jobs for which they were ideally suited—putting bases in ponds, or dung stamping. They continued to be extensively employed on some farms well into the twentieth century, their continued use often being cited erroneously as yet another example of the backwardness of the area. Their popularity, however, was soundly based. Wheeled ploughs, especially the cumbersome Kentish turn-wrest, were ill suited to the heavy, soft Wealden soil and the foot or swing plough which continued to be widely used for breaking up the ground required greater efforts on the part of the ploughman to keep it straight and at a uniform depth. The slow, steady gait of the ox helped him in this. In an area where many farmers dabbled in hops it was important to possess an abundant supply of manure. Unlike other hop growing districts of Kent the Weald had no large towns to rely on, and suffered from excessively poor roads and a lack of water carriage which prevented easy shipments of outside supplies. The value of ox dung was thus greatly enhanced. The horse's speed had no advantage for road work either. The highways there were renowned as the worst in the country, and John Boys in his survey of Kent in 1794 warned that in winter 'it is extremely dangerous and frequently impracticable . . . to ride on horseback along the main roads'.

The red Sussex breed of cattle were naturally common throughout the Weald. Although small framed, they were excellent fattening animals and were reputed to be placid in temperament. Other breeds were also employed. Large numbers of young Welsh cattle (1–3 years old) were already being driven over to the Maidstone area in the late eighteenth century. In October, according to Marshall, 'the roads are everywhere full of them'. Some undoubtedly found new homes on Wealden farms. By the late nineteenth century they were the dominant breed in the area, favoured because they fattened more slowly and had longer working lives.

Despite experiments with collars and harness oxen continued to be employed chiefly in double wooden yokes fitted with hazel bows for looping under their heads. Although these were criticised at one time as possible restrictions on the animals' windpipes, they were still preferred by most farmers because they were cheap and easy to maintain and allowed greater freedom of movement—especially important in the summer months when heat and flies were troublesome. A chain attached to the middle of each yoke provided the means of connecting one pair of oxen to another. Most old photographs show them muzzled. It would be wrong to view this practice as any form of safety measure to protect the men who worked with them. Muzzling fulfilled two functions. First, it prevented the animals grazing while working, a common complaint in northern counties where muzzles had not been widely adopted on the grounds that this made them unstable and dangerous when yoked to a cart or waggon. Second, it enabled them to squash irritating flies and insects by merely moving their heads and trapping them between their face and the muzzle. Strong nets seem to have displaced earlier wicker basket muzzles during the nineteenth century.

There are few men alive today who can recall working regularly with oxen, and those remaining can only recollect the twilight of their reign when they were often used as a reserve draught power or in conjunction with horses. Although lacking the individualistic and often appealing nature of the horse, the ox is still remembered with deep affection by those whom it served faithfully and unquestioningly.

Although he spent most of his working life with horses, Percy Barnes has fond memories of the years he worked with oxen in the employment of the Cheesman brothers, first at Goddard's Green Farm, Cranbrook, and later at Sissinghurst Castle where he had the dubious privilege of living in the tower for a mere shilling a week. There is no doubt that, from the day he was introduced, as a carter boy, to his first pair of working oxen who were to replace the breeding mare in his horse team, he found a high regard for these often forgotten animals.

'I was set to work with two old oxen. I didn't know anything about them. I'd been used to bullocks and that all my life. I wasn't afraid of them, but I didn't know nothing what to say to them or do with them.

'Mr Cheesman said, "You go round to George Head," he said, "he'll tell you how to get on."

'He was stockman. He used to work them sometimes. Well, I went round the buildings and found him and we went out into the orchard, and as soon as we went in the gate the old bullocks, they began to saunter away up towards us. He put the yoke on one of them—that was old Winch, the one that worked the off-side—he held the end up and pulled the bow out and Winder, he come sauntering up under the yoke and he yoked him up.

"There," he said, "that's how you do that job! I never show anybody anything only once."

'I said, "All right."

'So I had the old bullocks out, had them up to the cart, and the off-bullock stepped over the *nib* and they stood theirselves in position. He went up between them and lifted the old pole up and put the plug in.

"Now," he said, "there's one thing you want to remember when you put that plug in. Tie it in with that bit of thong because that might drop out."

'However, I had these old bullocks and I had to go in the yard and cart some litter in there, you know, dirty straw and one thing and another. I know when I first went to go through the gate I got up against the post. I seemed as if I wanted to get hold of them like I did with horses, but that didn't work. So after that I walked through myself and they used to come through all right. They never run into anything.

'I don't think it was more difficult than with horses. For one thing they were more obedient. Horses, sometimes, are very self-willed, a lot of them—although I've had horses almost like human beings, they seemed to know pretty much as near as you knew yourself. But a bullock, if you treated him right—you didn't dare be unkind to him to make him nervous—I always thought he was more obedient than a horse. Then of course they knew their place. They knew their names. You always worked two together, and the off-bullock never had only one syllable in his name, hence Winch and Winder, Pink and Piny, and such names as that. Always used to say "yea" to them to come to you, and that off-bullock he'd always be the first one to come to you, and his mate, he knew, he might be back there amongst all the others, but he'd find his way up there. They was mates together and that was how they always worked.

'They're very easily subdued, you know. If you got a pair of oxen out roped to a post or something where you could get hold of them and get the yoke on them, then hook them on to something heavy that they couldn't move and hook the other oxen on in front of them, well, you had to more or less drag them about. If they had a day at that they were pretty well cobbled. They didn't want to cut up rough much the next day. They very soon used to get out of breath and hang their old tongues out. Sometimes we've had them sulk and lay down. We used to go down to a stream if we was anywhere near one and get a little old tin or a bottle, drop of water in it, put a few drops in their ear. They soon jump up. They didn't like that. And when we used to break them in we used to have a stick, about five or six feet long, and have a little spike in the end of it. When you said "yea" to them, you gave the old bullock a prick in the shoulder. Of course, that used to make him shoot forward. That's how they learnt that. They never forgot that either. I know when we've been harvesting sometimes we used to stick the whip in the back of the waggon and carry on picking up the sheaves, and if you wanted to start up just pull a straw out of the sheaf and you could guide them with that straw just as if you'd got a whip or a goad. They never forgot that spike.

'We never had no bother with them, unless in the summer time the warble fly was about [often graphically referred to as Nimble Dick, the prick fly]. That was the only time. You'd soon know if he was about! We never heard it, horses never hear it, but those bullocks do. All of a sudden you'd see one of their tails go up and be waved to and fro in the air. That wouldn't be long before the others, they done the same. Then you'd got to look out because they was very soon going somewhere! The only thing to do was to keep the off-bullock fastest so they kept coming round in circles. If you let them break away from you, you'd lost them. They'd make for a pond or a wood or anything —anything to get away from that fly. We didn't used to work them in the summer time when it was very hot so we never had much bother with them. Used to manage with horses.

'They came from Wales, those that we had. They were Welsh Runts. That is a breed of its own. They was a heavy bullock if you let them get their full growth before you started working them. Anywhere round about three years old, they used to be a good big bullock then. They are black. The insides of their mouths are black. Their eyes are black. They hadn't got a white hair on them that I know. They used to look ever so fierce, but they wasn't, they was quiet enough. Years ago they used to use almost any bullocks in an ox team. Some farmers used to take a pride in them and have all Herefords, white faced ones. Another one would have all black ones, and another one would have all red ones. Used to be a team at Glassenbury, at Goudhurst, they were black ones, and a team at Hawkhurst under the Pipers, they were red ones. We broke in two big old red steers at Sissinghurst Castle. Mr Cheesman bought four from Mr Pomfret's sale up here in the Park at Tenterden years ago. Lamb and Lion one pair was, and the other was Earl and Marquis, I think. They belonged to Mr Winch the auctioneer, and we had them to work on the farm to finish breaking them in. When they went back up there to his farm nobody would work them, so he fatted them out and they were killed, but we kept Lamb and Lion and they worked on the farm for several years.

'I think I would rather have a team of oxen than horses because they're steadier, and they've always got a bit of a sway. You got used to it, and it was easier really, because you always knew what they were going to do. Of course, a lot of those properly worked horses, they never made a mistake all day long, but I think I would prefer oxen. Eight was a full team. Yes. It was always thought that two of them would average one horse, but no horse could ever pull two of them away. They were far more powerful than any one horse. If they ever got more than they could pull they would kneel down and lay their chin on the ground. Then of course you've got to squat the waggon up and give them a tap on the nose and they'd stand up again.

'I remember once at Sissinghurst Castle I had to bust this piece of ground up for to plant kale. I had one of the old fashioned wooden ploughs—no wheels on it, just the foot—and I had the two old oxen, one bullock in the furrow and one out, and two horses out of the furrow. They'd walk along and follow the edge of that furrow. Used to always have the oxen behind on the plough because they were a bit slow and you had to give them time to pull out at the end. I ploughed all that Frogmead piece—oh several acres of it—with two horses and two oxen. They used to work all right together. Marvellous old things to work with.

'The only trouble with oxen was if the land was wet. Now where they took their front foot out they put their hind foot in. They always do that, and of course that trod the ground in such holes. We never used to have them on the land when it was very wet. We used to have them cleaning the yards out of all the manure after the bullocks had been in there all the winter. The farmers would always have you run on top of their *mixon* as we used to call it, to keep it tight so that it shouldn't ferment. Sometimes if that was left a day or two, when you went up on that, a bullock would go right down in up to his belly. Well, the only thing to do was to shelve the cart up, take all the weight off the neck and tell them to start. The one that was on top would pull the other one out. Of course if you got a horse down like that, that was a nasty business. You had to get his cart out of the way and more or less dig him out.

'They used to get pretty tired by the time night come. If they get too out of breath they always hang their tongue out. Always have to turn them round and head for the wind and let them stand there a while. Then we used to doddle off again. When you put them in the yard at night you went away and left them. Didn't have to go back or anything. You just gave them what they'd got to have, some roots ground up, hay, straw. Never had to groom them like horses. There was a lot of work with a team of horses. It was never done. Oh no, it was an easier life really with oxen. I never remember them being shod, but years ago they used to put little plates on them, just nail them to the outside of the hoof. You never wanted to join the claws together, you see, because when they walked they moved those claws. I've heard my old father say that the old oxen got used to it. When they used to go to the forge to be shod they used to have some straw down there and a lot of them would lay down to have these little plates tapped on them. I have sometimes ploughed up the little ox shoes where they've come off and they've lost them. Like little fish plates, three little holes round the outside.

'I remember when I was a boy at Cranbrook they told me one day to carry some hop poles down to the baker, Mr Dadson, down in Cranbrook. I loaded these hop poles up on the cart, half a cord, and you had to mind how you loaded them to get a half a cord of chopped hop poles on a cart. Anyhow, I sauntered away down there in Cranbrook town down Stone Street with these two old oxen, and I had to carry all them hop poles round into his bakehouse an armful at a time. That took me a long time. The old oxen, they stood out in the street chewing their cud. They didn't seem to worry about anything. I used to have plenty of room. Everybody was afraid of them because they had such great big horns, but they wouldn't hurt anybody. Yes, they was faithful old things. I always liked them. But of course these days, they wouldn't be fast enough. Nothing is fast enough today.'

Chapter 4

Horse Dealers and Higglers

They were all rogues. Horse dealers were all rogues. As long as they got them sovereigns and got rid of their horse, they was landed. There wasn't no law. You couldn't take a man to court for that job, not them days. You wanted to be a little twister, you know, never tell the truth.

Frank Kemsley

Unlike most rogues—outlaws, smugglers, gamblers, rakes—who usually attract some notoriety, even admiration, with the passing of time, horse dealers seem to have escaped the popular imagination. Perhaps their reputation is a little harsh. Some are remembered as 'genuine', 'reliable' or possessing 'lovely horses', but there were undoubtedly many not adverse to sharp practices, whose activities prompted potential buyers to approach them with more than reasonable suspicion. Some farmers avoided resorting to them by breeding their own horses, even though this usually resulted in one of their working mares being laid up for several months of the year. Breeding stallions, known appropriately—for obvious reasons—as *entire* horses, were frequently hired out by farmers or landowners or were driven around the country by horsemen who would put up overnight at public houses or livery and bait stables, which often doubled as their bases. Kent, however, has never been famous for its horse

breeding and many horse users, especially urban tradesmen, shopkeepers and professional people who depended heavily on the services
of good horses to carry out their daily business, had to give their
trust and their money to the local horse dealer.

It is not clear how many dealers there were in Kent at any one
time. The county directories list just over twenty in the latter years of
the nineteenth century and then there is a rapid fall in the first three
decades of the present century: fourteen in 1907, eight in 1924 and
only two in 1930. Although some dealers relied almost exclusively on
their dealing for a living, others engaged in a variety of business
pursuits. Hop growers, farmers, jobmasters, publicans, lodging house
keepers and even horse slaughterers were all listed at one time as
horse dealers. The turnovers and methods of doing business also
varied considerably. At Canterbury, the South of England Horse
Repository in Watling Street, run by George Slater, had regular
weekly auctions which were often advertised and reported in *The
Kentish Gazette*. On a Saturday in October 1895 he apparently sold
39 horses, a good proportion 'that had been working hard all season
at the neighbouring watering places and these were secured by farmers
and others at prices in the favour of the buyers'. Gypsies, on the
other hand, who as itinerants, were ideally suited to the trade, relied
on personal visits to farms and villages or made use of the seasonal
fairs and weekly markets. A few occasionally crept into the commercial directories. Tom Collins, listed in 1899 as a dealer at Ashford
cattle market, was probably the same man referred to by farmers and
labourers as far apart as Molash and Goudhurst as a traveller or
gypsy. He, like many others of his kind, possessed a good reputation
and was renowned as a good horseman. Several village shopkeepers
recall purchasing their delivery horses and ponies from such men.
Many of these itinerant horse dealers, however, escaped the attention
of the compilers of the directories which consistently understated the
numbers engaged in the trade.

One dealer never listed in commercial directories was Ted Kemsley
of Molash. He was always listed as a farmer but it is clear from his
son Frank's (born 1889) recollections that the farm was never more
than an accessory to his varied trading activities. Its thirty acres were
mainly devoted to pasture although some seven acres of oats were
planted annually to provide fodder. His advice to his son, who
managed and worked the farm when he was merely sixteen, assisted
only by seasonal, casual labour, to 'let your corn walk away', was
sound in a period of low grain prices. He had no established way of
doing business. A nine gallon cask of beer was always kept in the

farmhouse to refresh customers, but many of his contacts were made and his deals finalised in public houses which were open from 6.00 a.m. to 10.00 p.m. before the First World War. Like many others in the business, Ted Kemsley kept no records of his transactions. His word was his bond, and as his son recalls, 'he didn't dream about signing anything. Five out of six of them couldn't write. My father couldn't write his own name. I can remember when I was a little boy—that's going back some, isn't it—my father used to come home from Canterbury market or from town with a little old paper he gave a penny for so that I could read out to him what happened in the Boer War. I remember that well.'

His dealings were not restricted to horses. At least one local has referred to him as a higgler, an aptly named middleman who travelled round the country buying farm produce and livestock for resale at markets or to shops and wholesalers. Cottages and small farmers who lacked established outlets for their produce or had insufficient quantities to make regular visits to markets worthwhile were a higgler's main suppliers. In some areas of the country these middlemen played important, often specialised roles in the local economy. At Heathfield, just over the Sussex border, they were heavily involved in the poultry trade, buying from labourers and farmers and selling to crammers for the London market. When Richard Heath visited the area in 1871 he estimated that over 200 tons of fatted chicken passed through their hands each year on their way to London and half as much again to the seaside resorts of Brighton and Hastings. By 1910 the figure was nearer 1,200 tons. Elsewhere, however, higglers were not particular about what they dealt in so long as they obtained speedy and adequate returns from their transactions. Their activities were frequently considered to be the major cause of the decline of smaller local markets. Edward Jacob, writing as early as 1774, considered that Faversham markets were 'mere skeletons of what they formerly were' and he had no doubt that one cause of this 'lay in higglers being permitted; for they go all the country over, purchasing the above named articles [poultry, eggs, butter] off farmers at their houses, giving them as good prices as can be got by sending the same to our market'. Ted Kemsley collected poultry for Webbs of Canterbury and for the London market, bought pigs and bullocks to fatten for market, supplied ferrets for shipment to France, and sold milk in the village and Whitstable whelks at local fairs. He even found time to run a small hire service taking local residents to and from the station at Chilham and provided transport for weddings and funerals. It would be wrong, therefore, to consider him as a mere farmer, or even a straightforward horse dealer, although the latter trade certainly seems to have occupied a large proportion of his time and interest.

Frank recalls:

'Trades-people came to him from Faversham, Canterbury, all round, for him to find them a pony or horse to do their business with a cart. My father used to tell them the truth and he gradually got a good name for genuine business. He wouldn't send a horse to a man if he knew it didn't suit him. If he got one that wasn't genuine he used to send it to a man at Folkestone we used to call Slippery Joe and he generally give him what it cost so he didn't lose too much money. That was agreed between them. I think these horses, what you couldn't recommend, were shipped over to France. They eat a lot of horse meat in France, see.

'Father used to go and buy these ponies off farms or dealers—oh, wherever he could hear about one. Say it come through the grapevine to my father, that perhaps Joe Norris had got a pony for sale. My father would slip up.

"Got a pony for sale, Joe?"

"Yes," he said, "have a look at him, try him."

"Warrant him?"

"Yes, every way."

'If father knowed the man he'd know his warranty was good. So they'd put this pony in harness and drive him up and down the road. My father had all manner of tricks. He'd say, "Drive him by me," and he'd whip a white handkerchief out and shake it. If the pony didn't take any notice he wasn't a shyer, see? "Drive him by his farm," he'd say—his house where he'd stopped. Now nine horses out of ten, if you tried to drive them by where their home was they'd pull in, you know, try to go in the yard. But if you just touch them that side with the whip gently, they'd go straight on. They knowed if they didn't, they'd have it slashed up their ribs quick. Horses were very sensitive. Us boys used to have to ride them to see if they're safe to ride or drive them on the road. You'd never believe what horses can do if they're not broken properly when they're young. We've had them . . . oh wicked! I've been bitten all over! Never was kicked. I always looked out and give them plenty of room for the legs.

'We had a lot of horses out of London. Only lasted two years in London, you know, them days. They used to put two ton behind one big horse and it didn't want no pulling only stopping and starting, you see. That took it so much out of horses' legs, the front legs used to go over like that, bent. We used to buy them. They used to come back on the farms and they used to recover. They were only six or seven years old, you see. We used to get them used to farm work and then sell them to farmers around about. There were chaps up there at the London mart used to bring them down. For other buyers too. Walk them. Perhaps two or three of them used to come down together with about a dozen old horses out of London. Stop at every pub. Time they got down here they was pretty near boozed!

'Gypsies used to come in and ask if they could stop for a day or two on our land, especially when the fairs were on. We didn't mind them. There were some bad gypsies and some good gypsies. Well, we had one lot, name of Collins, used to come and see my dad, and if they'd got a decent pony they used to bring it and sell it to him. I remember one day they sold him an old, grey horse starved of life. He could hardly walk. Father give him a fiver for this horse and we nursed him up, got him to be in good condition. We sold him to Earl Sondes. About three years afterwards, I was about eleven or twelve, father had a letter from a woman named Baker-White, Street End Farm—they've still got it. She was going to Germany and she wanted Lord Sondes to have this horse back because she didn't want to sell him. She wanted him to have a good home all his life.

'He said, "No, I don't want him. You send him to Ted Kemsley. He saved his life. He'd like to have him."

'So she wrote to my father. We went over there to see her in the pony cart.

"Now," she said, "I'm going to give you that horse on the condition you never sell him. You keep him till he dies or have him put down. You can have his cart and the harness and everything with him."

'She told her groom to put the horse in the cart and put all the tackle in it, nosebags and flynet—you don't know what it is, I expect: a net they used to throw over them to keep the flies off. I brought it home and we kept that horse eleven year. He was a beautiful horse. That's the old horse we used to drive people to the weddings with when I got older. When he got too weak to work, he got very lame, and winter was coming.

"Don't like doing it," my father said, "but we shall have to put old Buller down."

'We called him Buller after a man in the Boer War. General Buller, wasn't it? I couldn't go and see him killed. I never went.

'Kindness. That's the main thing with horses. Plenty'd talk to you if you had them long enough. We never used to keep them long though. Perhaps we only had a horse a week. Sometimes he hadn't only got one; sometimes he'd got four. Never had the same two

horses together long. I used to be out on the farm to work with a pair
of horses and he used to come along with a man to see this horse
work. He used to sell it to him, and we used to take it out and go
home. He used to pay for it and take it away.

'We never sold horses for hunting. The old farmers used to hunt
their own horses. We used to have the Yeomanry every year—I think
it was in April. Farmers' sons used to hire a horse off father for to
ride. They used to go up for a fortnight's training, so my father used
to get quite three or four horses about. Buy them purpose for the
job. Charged them £5 for the fortnight. It was a lot of money, but
perhaps the horse wasn't much good by the time they done with it.
Me and my brother had to make sure these horses would take a
saddle. Some horses didn't like people on their back. They'd never
had anybody on their back. Father used to bunk us up on 'em and
off he used to go. Sometimes we fell off. Sometimes we went off and
didn't know how to stop. Had all manners of capers. I was riding one,
one day. I walked him down the field and galloped back and there
was this sheep hurdle in the middle and the bloomin' thing went
straight for this and jumped it. Cor, it pretty near jarred my inside
out when he landed. I wasn't very old, about fifteen. Father said,
"He'll do." That were just the horse for the Yeomanry, you see!'

Frank Kemsley portrays his father as an honest dealer. We will
probably never know how typical he was in this respect, but most
people, even his son, seem to have had poor opinions of most dealers'
trustworthiness, especially those who frequented markets. 'If you
went to market to buy a horse, you must expect to be had' was an old
saying that rang true. A buyer, like a modern motorist planning to
purchase a second hand car, was advised to know what to look for.
William Allen (born 1891), who is still a coal merchant at Lydd,
recalls how careful his father was when buying a horse.

'They used to have horse sales at Romney Marsh fair (21 August).
It was a great game that was because you had to watch what you were
doing in those days. Oh yes, they were very sharp. Course it's like
everything else, if they're selling a thing they don't cry stinking meat.
My father, he was very keen, he knew what a horse was. For one
thing he'd look in his mouth and see how old he was. Then he'd feel
his legs and tendons, to see that he'd got no *bog spavins* and that sort
of thing. Then he'd get a man to trot him up and down and my father
used to stand and watch them. If he showed just a slight limp, he
knew he was a bad egg. They used to fire some of the horses if they'd
got weak tendons and were a bit lame. They'd get like a red hot poker
and run it up and down their leg to burn it and strengthen the tendon

so they could sell them. After you'd bought one and he'd gone lame you hadn't got a leg to stand on! Some of these fairly decent, straightforward dealers would say, well, have him on trial. Then of course you'd got to pay for it, have him on trial and if it was all right, well, naturally you'd buy it.'

The ideal customer, from a dealer's viewpoint, was one who could recognise a good horse when he saw one, but be fooled by a poor one. There was no market for overworked, lame or headstrong horses; a dealer who found himself in possession of one, therefore, often resorted to chicanery. Even those who allowed horses on trial periods sometimes sent out unsuitable horses in the hope that customers would return them and then be persuaded to part with additional money for a more reliable animal. Albert Patterson, a trained horseman in a dealer's employment, recalls that he took one horse out to seven different customers, each one returning it and spending more money on his next visit. He also learned to cultivate a taciturn nature and to turn a blind eye to much of what went on in the stables.

'Somebody'd come in—poor wretch—wanting another horse. Well, I didn't used to take much notice. They used to say, "What's this one like?" "Don't know." "Well it looks a nice horse. How old is it?" "Don't know." They didn't used to stop with me. They used to see the old man, the man who was dealing. You've got to be careful what you say when you're with a dealer. You might trip him up and not be aware of it, but he'd know, wouldn't he? Oh yes, there's a trick in every trade. I've seen some of them. They used to bleed them up in the forepart of the mouth. That used to keep their heads up! And they always put Welsh shoes on them. Ordinary Kent shoes are round, a Welsh shoe is buckled, so when they run they've got to keep their feet out, throw them. Oh yes, they was patched up. You put a patch on trousers, once that begins to go it falls off, doesn't it? Well that applies with old horses.

'If you wanted to get rid of an old horse you'd send it to Maidstone fair. That would go. Run them up there, get them trimmed up, they looked all right. People didn't know. There'd be gypos an' all I've seen there, scrapping over a pony or something, having a set-to. The police would have a busy job sometimes. Canterbury fair used to be nice. There used to be some money changed hands there. I've seen as many as forty horses go up Wincheap. Two men, that's all, a lead each side and the others would be haltered and tied to the horse's tail in front. Away they used go go. Old Georgie Lee from Ashford was the fairest man I knew about sixty odd years ago. He was a genuine dealer. If a man hadn't got quite enough and he wanted to buy a horse, he'd say "Look. Take this horse. Pay me within twelve months. That'll be all right." He was for the working man. There wasn't many in those days for the worker, you know, only for what they could get out of him. "If I don't get the money you don't get the horse," and they were usually only old crocks what they'd got.'

Rogues or not, no economy reliant on horse power could have continued without the valuable services of these colourful middlemen.

Chapter 5

The Steam Thrasher

We had nine to ten men with each machine . . . They were
principally old South African soldiers but they were good
fellows to work.

Harry Gambrill

Thrashing or threshing, the act of separating the grain from the straw
and chaff, has rarely received the attention accorded to other aspects
of farm work despite its importance in the agricultural process. Its
neglect is understandable for it is difficult to find anything romantic
or attractive about its methods. Its unpopularity is aptly illustrated
by the various other meanings associated with the word thrash: to
solve by exhaustive discussions, to chastise or to work at what is un-
productive and unprofitable. Beating the grain with flails or frails,
primitive hand-held instruments, was the most common method even
well into the nineteenth century. It was a long and arduous process,
noisy, dusty and inefficient, but it did provide employment for farm
workers through the long winter months, often on a piece-work basis.
The lengthy, labour-intensive, yet repetitive nature of the work
supplied considerable incentive to those searching for alternative
methods. They were successful for thrashing was the first agricultural
process to be fully mechanised.

Machines of dubious effectiveness consisting mainly of revolving flails seem to have existed as early as 1636 but the real breakthrough came in 1786 when Andrew Meikle, a Scotsman, produced the prototype of later machines based on the employment of a concave drum and beaters. The next thirty years witnessed various improvements in his design, and machines, often produced locally by small craftsmen and operated manually or by horse power, were installed in barns throughout the north of England and Scotland. Despite the numerous advantages claimed for them—economy of labour, shortening of the process allowing earlier marketing, cleaner separations of the grain— they were slow to spread in the southern counties. A variety of reasons can be found to account for this. Farms in the south were often smaller than their northern counterparts, so that as J. S. Mill rightly observed, 'It may not answer to a small farmer to own a threshing machine for the small quantity of corn he has to thresh.' Some commentators claimed that the widespread use of the scythe which laid out the corn less regularly than the sickle or bagging hook also hindered their introduction by making it less manageable for feeding the corn into the machines. Those farmers who did employ them may have tried to economise by using smaller machines which performed the job less well, thus increasing other farmers' suspicion of them. The chief cause, however, seems to have been that labour was more plentiful in the south and farmers were only too well aware that by failing to provide their men with adequate winter employment they would be pushing them on to the parish which would inevitably lead to an increased poor rate. Rather than support them while idle they continued to employ them in hand thrashing. At times the machines provoked active hostility, the most famous incidents of which originated in Kent in 1830.

On Sunday, 28 August 1830, a gang of labourers, reputed to be over 400 in number, destroyed a thrashing machine at Lower Hardres, just south of Canterbury. Although there had been outbreaks of arson and rioting in west Kent during the previous few months this was the first reported case of machine-breaking and it was treated seriously by the authorities. Two of the county magistrates and several special constables went out from the city to wait for the gang's expected return in the evening, accompanied by thirty of the 7th Dragoons who were to lie in wait until the mob had overpowered the civil forces. The mob, however, did not reappear, and over the next twelve months there were at least forty-eight reported cases of machine-breaking in the county (the number varied from newspaper to newspaper), most of them by gangs, but some of them by the farmers themselves.

Whether the machines were the major or merely a contributory cause of the riots and disturbances which then spread throughout the south is not clear. Many of the uprisings were concerned with wages, tithes, and political issues rather than the comparatively mundane issue of thrashing machines. As early as October 1830 correspondents in a local Canterbury newspaper were quick to distinguish the arson and riots elsewhere from the machine-breaking in east Kent. The former was the work of 'ugly outsiders', inflamed apparently by the successful suppression of smuggling, who directed their anger against those magistrates who had been instrumental in the campaign, while the machine-breaking was motivated by the distress of the Kent people. The nature of the outbreaks apparently supports this distinction, although whether the smuggling allegations were correct is debatable. Machine-breaking occurred almost entirely in the corn growing belts of the eastern part of the county, and there were few reports in the Maidstone area or the initial hotbed of trouble, west Kent. They were most common too in the areas where small farmers sympathetic to the aims of the labourers predominated: Wingham, the Elham Valley, Lower Hardres, and Sandwich.

These disturbances further delayed the introduction of thrashing machines into southern England but the invention of steam-powered portable machines in the 1840s—Ransome's first steam portable thrasher was displayed at the Royal Agricultural Show of 1841—overcame two of the major obstacles to their use, capital outlay and mobility. These machines were owned either by a group of farmers who shared costs between them or by an outside contractor who hired them out along with a couple of operators. They were hauled from farm to farm by teams of horses, usually supplied by the farmers themselves. So successful was the application of steam power to thrashing that horse-powered machines were dropped from the Royal Agricultural Show after 1867, and by 1870 about 80 per cent of thrashing was estimated to be carried out by steam, although older equipment lingered on in some parts even into the present century. With the perfection of self-moving traction engines in the 1870s even the portables were superseded and the pattern for the next sixty years was established.

Although these developments ended the drudgery associated with flail work and brought thrashing into the open farmyard and fields, there was still little to excite the imagination about the job. The group of men, between nine and thirteen in number, who worked the thrasher and the steam engine failed to inspire the imagination of agricultural commentators to the same extent as migratory harvest

workers or sheep shearers had done, while the almost total exclusion
of women and children robbed it of any cosy, familiar connotations.
It remained dusty, dirty work but it was now performed by men who
had few other connections with the farming community, outsiders
who followed the machines around the farms. Except on the very
large farms, labourers found themselves excluded from the process.
From being a major winter activity it had ceased to provide them
with work or income. The virtual exiling of thrashing from the yearly
cycle of jobs performed by farmworkers themselves is symbolised
today by the enthusiasm with which traction engine devotees have
accepted it as within their sphere of interest and by its relative absence
from books dealing with farm life. Its importance to the agricultural
community remained undiminished, however, and for some men it
became a way of life in itself. One such man was Harry Gambrill.

Young Harry, as he was known for much of his life, was born in
about 1890 (he is unsure of the precise year), at Stone Street, Petham,
only a few miles away from where the first thrashing machine had
been destroyed sixty years previously. His father, T. H. (Old Harry)
Gambrill, was miller, baker and agricultural contractor, although by
the time Harry was old enough to be involved in the business his
father had suffered the misfortune of seeing his mill burnt down and
had consequently decided to abandon his bakery too. The agricultural
contracting had been started by his grandfather before he emigrated
to Australia in the 1880s, a move he was later to regret. Although they
performed some haulage work—coal, wood, furniture, bricks—and
carried out some steam sawing in the local woods, the Gambrills
always felt that 'Agriculture was our chief subject. We were always
very happy at it.' In Harry's youth, his father once possessed seventeen self-binders, eight grass mowers, two Aveling plough engines
and tackle, two Fowler and one Aveling thrashing engines, and two
Marshall and one Ransome thrashing machines for hiring out. His
father also acted as agent for Frost and Wood, a Canadian firm who
specialised in mowers, reapers and hay rakes, Bluebell Binder Twine
and One and All Manures, and carried out general repairs on farm
machinery of all descriptions either in his yard at Stone Street or
occasionally on the farms themselves. The business was small compared to those of their local rivals, Holman's of Canterbury or the
Wingham Engineering Company, but until the coming of the tractors
it provided a comfortable living for the family. Tractors were more
suited to a wide range of farm activities and were more likely to be
purchased by farmers than their predecessors, the traction engines.
Indeed, had steam been more successfully applied to other aspects of

farm work contractors like the Gambrills might have died out much earlier than they actually did. Harry kept the business going until 1948 when he sold his last engine 'for a song'. The life was in his blood, however, and he continued to attend traction engine rallies until just before his death early in 1977.

Although thrashing was only one aspect of their work it was an important one providing continuous employment and a regular income for engines and men for a good eight months of the year— inclement weather and slow-paying debtors excepted. By the 1900s nearly every farm in Kent relied on a visit from a firm like the Gambrills' to carry out their thrashing, but, as Harry recalled, the old systems were still in evidence even then, although they were not too popular with farmers or their men.

'Long before I was hatched out, they used to do it all with what they called a frail on a wooden barn floor and knocked the corn out that way and then shook it out of the straw. If they were pushed and we couldn't get there perhaps for a few days and they wanted corn for the animals, they'd thrash it with these frails. They're like two long sticks fastened together with a thong which made it like a wrist joint. They used to swear at us. They'd say, "Why the devil did you keep us waiting for?" We couldn't help it. Perhaps the weather had hindered us, something like that.

'When I were quite young they still had a threshing machine that was driven by what they called a horse gear. That was a *crocodile*. It was a stump down to the ground and it had got two pinions. There was a round set of gear and it had got a casting at the top and a four inch pole about ten foot long and they used to attach a horse to that. He'd got a small bar of iron come from his mouth to the pole so that he couldn't get out of the way and he couldn't go the other way, so he used to keep going round and round. The horses got used to it. They didn't want no handling. They used to put them in and they walked round and round for hours. Some had got two or three horses depending on the size of the machine they'd got and how much pulling the corn wanted in the drum because the longer the straw was the harder the pull. The same happened with an engine, but of course you'd got the power there; an extra shovelful or two of coal, two or three pounds of steam, a bit of stick and you was away. I can remember one farm, Stelling Lodge, they'd got a tremendous big machine and they had a big roundel built on purpose and had four horses in it all coupled up to these poles. It's still there but they don't use it of course, it's a dairy place. Anyway, this shaft used to drive the threshing machine. You never heard such a rattle in your life—clutter bump, clutter bump. No hum or anything.' Course as the steam tackle came in all such things were scrapped but they continued to use them for drawing water out of the well where there was no water laid on. They used to let a bucket down by hand, couple a horse to the pole and he'd walk round driving a windlass up the top with a rope on it. There were double lids on these wells and as soon as the bucket came up and rattled and the lid went bang, the old horse would stop. He'd gradually ease back and this thirty-six gallon barrel would settle down on the lid. They also used to use them for cutting chaff, not many years ago in fact. It would cut chaff, pulp wurzels and turnips for cattle—a wonderful affair really. Nothing regular about them. If the old horse got in a hurry it went fast. If he got lazy, well it hardly worked. Some farmers even had them on the road. Woollett, at a place called North Leigh, Stelling, he had one with a horse and he ran about from far to farm.

'Portables came in next. My grandfather had Wadden Hall Farm and Lime Tree Farm and he had thirteen sets of portable tackle and used to thresh all the way from home to Dover. We used to have to deliver them to the first farm and when they'd done at that farm the farmers had to use their own horses to pull them about. They used to put two on the portable engine, I've heard my father say, and two on the thresher and they had to set them in the farm yards with these horses, get the engine to within a little, and square it up with the thresher drum so that the belt ran true on the flywheel with men using crow bars under the wheels to throw it about front and back. Some were still operating when I was a boy. Thruxted Farm and Burnt House Farm down in the village had a set of his own down there for many years and he used it right up till he died. An old fellow by the name of Clover was in charge of it, he growed up with it and knew all about it.

'My father gave all the portables up when he had a Fowler compound engine in 1884. Of course gradually other people got traction engines, well they had to, because once one had got one the other farmers used to say: "If you'd got one like old so-and-so, we shouldn't have to fetch your tackle with our old horses." So the owners either sold out, packed up or bought a traction engine. Holman's had quite a few portables at Canterbury and they went in for tractions about the same time my father did. He used to buy them up at Fowler's; they were a good firm and they'd got a good representative. I remember as if it was only yesterday. His name was Jim Gausney and he'd do business with anybody. He used to travel Kent, Sussex and Hampshire. I know the second engine my father bought, he bought out the bedroom window. It was very hard weather and I can just remember it. We were only little kids and we were fidgety wanting to know who it was. That was delivered to a show at Tunbridge Wells, then Fowler's people brought it as far as Lenham and then it was passed satisfactory and passed over to my father. Two of us went to Leeds to fetch another. It took three weeks, three days, and seven nights to drive home. A lot of people used to fetch them. It was rather better than having them on rail; sometimes they got hung up and you didn't get them when you wanted them. Although Aveling's were the quietest engines of the lot and Fowler's were very noisy—like a lot of bells ringing the gears were—we always like Fowler engines. They were always a masterpiece of an engine—one of the best.'

Like all contractors, the Gambrills preferred to deal with large farmers. To set up the tackle in the farmyard was no easy matter and farmers who could provide only half a day's thrashing were not popular customers. Not surprisingly they sought work on the extensive farms of Thanet and resented attempts during the wars to allocate farms to local contractors in an effort to make the most efficient use of the available machinery.

'The majority of our thrashing started in the Isle of Thanet the middle of July. That was winter barley which was very early, and spinach seed, perhaps some onions, turnips, that sort of thing. We generally used to say we're finished at the end of March, but some used to keep what they called overyear corn to early spring and it might be June or July when that was threshed. That was an awful, dusty, old job, but they used to say the corn was better kept like that for the stock than what it was if they'd threshed it and stored it. Thanet was one of our big places. Walter's Hall, Monkton Court, Monkton Parsonage, Acol—I can't remember all the names of the farms but they were some of our biggest. When I was a lad they used to cut all the corn at Walter's Hall and it averaged forty white corn stacks, three pea stacks, four bean stacks and a barn full of barley. It used to take at least six weeks' work there, but we didn't do it all at once. Perhaps we'd go and have a week threshing a lot of wheat, then in a couple of months they'd want to thresh again and they'd have all oats. That's how they went on till they got the lot cleared up.

'Now up on Stelling Minnis they were all little farmers there. Half a day's thresh, perhaps two hours, you could do eight or nine farms in a day and you hadn't done anything much. It was wicked. My father used to do a little for one or two of his friends. An old miller there, old Davidson, he was a pal of the old chap's and they used to get together, the old millers. There were one or two others but they were very patient. They used to say, "Whenever you get a chance, little broken time, come up. Let us know the night beforehand and what men you've got." The best of them were all like that, but none of them had got a day's work there, but of course a lot of them kept pigs and they wanted the corn. A good many other firms—Holman Brothers—they wouldn't go up there for anybody, but if they were patient we used to get to them. But you couldn't earn nothing and the chaps with you couldn't earn nothing.'

Following the drum meant a nomad's life much of the time. Visits home were limited to weekends when Harry and his father were working out at Thanet. Enginemen are often portrayed in the interwar periods as cyclists arriving each morning in the farmyard from quite some distance away but although Harry bought himself a bicycle when he was eighteen, his father consistently opposed them, insisting that they would 'ruin your legs'. He walked everywhere. Journeys home from Thanet or Eastry would involve several hours of walking to arrive home at near midnight on Saturday, leaving again in the early hours of Monday morning to get back and start up the engine.

The day's work was long and the life associated with it was rough. Harry's first job was far from his liking but he soon learned that the work had its compensations, not least of which was the company of the men who travelled regularly with the thrashing machine. Between nine and thirteen men were needed to ensure an efficient operation, but only two of them were paid by the contractor—the driver and the feeder—both being considered skilled men. Farmers were responsible for finding the rest of the workers and although large farmers occasionally supplied sufficient men and even hired out their men in slack periods to smaller neighbours who had helped them in busy summer seasons, many of them relied on the motley crew who followed the machine and were known personally to the driver and his mate. This suited both parties; the farmer was relieved of the responsibility of finding additional labour for an unpleasant job and the contractor was assured of a group of men who knew their job. The men matched the job they had to do. They were rough and ready, refugees from the mainstream of society, running away from wives, families and responsibilities they did not care for. Their life style would not be envied in an age where increasing emphasis is placed on the material comforts as the most important ingredients of the quality of life, but Harry has fond memories of these men and the life that they led. Although the nature of the job dictated that he was 'never at home with it' he felt that he was 'always at home at it, they were such a jolly bunch of men'. While he acknowledges the unpleasant aspects of the work, the quality of life was obviously far from being a simple matter of money and possessions.

'It used to be 3s. 6d. an hour for the engine, machine and two men —driver and feeder—who had sixpence an hour each out of that. There were quite a few done quarter work. My father did two big estates, eighteen pence a quarter all round, but when this insurance job came in and they said that the owner of the tackle was responsible for the labour, they packed it in and wouldn't do anything, only hour work since the farmer was responsible for all the casual hands. We had nine to ten men with each machine. They would carry the straw and chaff and caving, look after the stack, cut bonds, stack the straw and work on the ricks, pitching the sheaves to the thresher. The farmer used to pay for their labour and they got, when I first started, 3½d. an hour, ten hours a day, but we always used to draw the working men's money off the farmers when we'd finished at the farm each time and pay them. The men always used to look to us drivers to pay them. Sometimes the farmers might give us a tip for taking the money and paying them, keeping count of their hours every day.

'We used to have to start some farms at six o'clock and every Monday morning you'd got to go and light a fresh fire. Someone would be detailed to go off, perhaps at 3.30 a.m., because it used to take a couple of hours pretty well to get steam up because of the dead coal. Ordinary mornings, if you'd been working the day before, the flue tubes were clean and it wasn't long, about three-quarters of an hour, before you got enough steam to turn the wheels. Sometimes they used to bank them up, chuck in a lot of fire, put a drop of water in the ash pan and a wet sack over the top of the chimney. Most times all you had to do then was lift your ash pan lid up for draught, take your wet sack off, and poke the fire up. It used to draw up like that. Farmers used to give them a pint of beer at nine o'clock and a pint of beer at three in the afternoon. If they had to work after six they used to give them a sandwich or two and another drink to encourage them to finish a stack so we could get away, otherwise it meant two hours the next day and no more work. We didn't get no lost time money whatever and all we got extra to our wage was a shilling shifting from one farm to another. If it was here to Margate we only got a shilling and if it was only across the road we got a shilling. There was no wet weather money. If it rained we used to hang about, but once three o'clock came we'd shut the engine down, put the top on the chimney and that was the end of it. We'd go and have a warm up side the fire, a warm and a bit of food, then get into the barn and have a rest.

'My first job as a youngster was carrying water to one of the engines and I had eighteen pence a day. I was about fifteen. I went home at night after we was finished and paid.

'My mother said, "You don't look very happy."

"No," I said, "I'm not. I worked harder than any of the men with two buckets on a bit of wood on my back from the pond to the engine and my shoulders are very sore."

'So anyway, I had to pull my clothes off and showed mother and they were raw where this wood had worn my shoulders, because these buckets had nearly half a bushel of water in each. They were heavy old buckets and I used to dip right on the duck board as we used to call it in the middle of the pond, then hook the chain on them, walk up to the engine and tip it in a big packet. Anyway, mother got some boracic water and bathed them, I put a clean shirt and fresh jacket on and had my food. Father came home.

'Mother said, "Have you seen Harry's shoulders?"

"No," he said, "what's the matter with him?"

'So mother pulled up my shirt and said, "Look there, and he only got eighteen pence a day."

"Well," he said, "he's only a boy. If a fly set on him it would bite him. He's got to get used to it."

'Next morning I wouldn't go. I said I wasn't coming anymore. They'd shifted to another farm that night.

"Well you'll have to do something," father said. "You can't put your feet under the table if you can't work."

'I said, "No. I'm going in the Army. I won't get messed up with a job like this."

'So I didn't go. Mother gave me a job chopping some wood, digging up a few potatoes, pulling weeds out of the cabbage patch and all that for a week. Father shifted again to another farm.

"Now look," he said, "Are you coming threshing Harry?"

'I said, "Yes, I'll come if I can have a man's money but I ain't going doing a man's work for a boy's money any longer and getting a sore back."

"All right," he said, "you can come with me and you can go on the stack and have a man's money."

"Fair enough," I said, and I come.

'We used to have nearly the same men every year. Now and then you might get a stranger come along, one of them might be ill or left and we used to put him in his place till the other one got better, on the understanding that when Jack or Joe came back he'd have to go. That used to work all right. Lots used to come to see if there was any chance of a job; be there early in the morning to see if anyone was missing. Sometimes there have been eight or nine besides the gang we'd got all waiting to see if there was a chance. It was terrible to see them, big able fellows and nothing to be earned. They'd got no dole and some had only got 3s. 6d. a week on what they called parish relief. Some of the farmers'd say, "Terrible thing. Good working chaps and can't get nothing to do. Well, you can spread dung." "Ain't got no forks, master." "Never mind about that. I've got twelve acres wants spreading. I'll find you some forks. You take care of them and you can have your money when you're done." They got 3s. 6d. a hundred for spreading dung, a hundred lumps.

'Sometimes we used to get men that they'd stood off on the farm, but you always found the farm worker a good able chap. You hadn't got to show him anything because he knew.

'The men were rough. They were principally old South African soldiers but they were good fellows to work. Now and then they used to have a fit of saving up a bit of money, perhaps for three months, and then they'd have a turn of being drunk. The Compasses, Sole Street, that comes in Crundale but it's just out of Waltham, that place in particular and opposite the Granville, Street End, they used to get so drunk there sometimes it was a week before they could use the tackle. Drivers and all, all laying about anywhere. They'd have about a week, spend out, then they'd go off to work and work like niggers, no trouble to nobody until they got round the country back to Sole Street, the two big farms there, then they'd have another drunken fit. Father used to say, won't be much work done up there. Some of them used to get a tidy bit of money from their parents to keep away from them, because a lot of them used to come from well-to-do people, you know. We had one, he was a parson's son from Birmingham and he was with us about eight years. He had about £11 every two or three months to stay away. And another one, he was a solicitor's son from Redhill, Surrey. When he was cleaned up he was quite a smart man, but he travelled about here for many years with us all through the winter months and then in the summer he went to work for the farmers in the fields, doing anything. If he didn't know anything they'd show him because he would work. Yes, they were trustworthy till they went on the randy as we used to call it. Bad boys really, you know, but all right with us and the farmers used to like them because they used to say, "Oh, they'll be back when they've spent out."

'After the First World War all we got then was people that didn't want no work but come off the dole. You couldn't make nothing of them. It got terrible at the finish, 1918, you couldn't get nobody wanting work. They wouldn't work. They didn't want it. They were some of the laziest whelps you ever did see, almost too tired to eat their dinner. But the old rough chaps, well they'd work night and day if you wanted when they was all right. If they'd been drunk and laid out all night, they'd work the next day no bother. Many a time they'd come round of a morning, first thing, been laying out all night with frost on their back. We used to boil a kettle in the furnace for them and they'd have an old tin pot they used to chuck something in, put their old hands round it and drink it. After they'd had a good drink of this hot water and whatever they'd say, "Well, get them wheels going, don't earn nothing if they don't go."

'They all had nicknames, you know, all the lot of them except my father, they used to call him Old Harry. There was Crooked Nose Charlie with a crooked nose who'd got hurt in the South African War. Ally Sloper another old boy was—he'd got a long nose. Then there was Doings, a rough and ready herbert, but a nice fellow. He went in the Chequers and got boozed up. My father had got one of the big chimneys off his engine and this chap come out of the Chequers, came in the yard—well next door to the pub—poked his head in the chimney and was raking it about. All at once he came out and laid along side of it, proper boozed up. So my father got some whitening and he done his cheek, his forehead and his nose and he kept on saying, "Curse the flies. Don't matter where I go, they won't let me alone." Then my father got some soot and he blacked him as well. Well, he had a sleep for a matter of an hour and half or more and then he said, "The old flies have been tormenting me, Old Harry." "Yes," he said, "there's a lot of them about, it's the warm weather, you know." Time come—the pub was open all day then—he gets up and he goes in again. Gawd, he looked a state! He was the laughing stock of all the people there. Doings *was* his nickname but they called him Old Spotted Leopard after that. He was an old soldier, time-serving man, spent his life out in India pretty much.

'I know I was very queer when I was about sixteen year old. It didn't matter what I had, I couldn't stop diarrhoea. I was very weak but I kept getting about. What mother give me wasn't no good.

'The old boy said, "You ain't very grand, young Harry."

"No, I ain't, Doings," I said, and I told him what was the matter.

"Well," he said, "you'll have to do the same as we did out in India. You go up along the hedge and find some yellow blackberry leaves. You get three of them and roll them up tight like a pill and swallow it. Then about an hour afterwards take another one. I'll guarantee you'll never be troubled with it no more."

'And I never was.

"Wash them if you like," he said, "but we never used to. Screw
them up tight, get them back and they'll rough up your inside."
'It was a funny thing, though, but it worked all right. Of course
they knew, didn't they. Poor old boy.
'A few of the men that used to booze were bad off. They'd got no
clothes any good, ragged and dirty. I know one come to work one
morning and he'd been earning good money with the thresher; my
father knew justly what he'd had. He come this Monday morning,
his knees was out, his sleeves were nearly out, his old shirt was black.
The old chap got hold of him, he pushed him down on the ground,
knelt on him, got a piece of chalk out of his pocket and chalked all
those places round where everything was worn through.
"Cor, old Harry," he said, "you'll kill me."
'The old man said, "No, I ain't going to kill you, mate, but I've a
good mind to chuck you in the pond, if you don't come with some
different clothes on next Monday morning."
'He would have done too, because father was ever such a hefty
man, he didn't care about none of them or how rough they were.
But he came with new cord trousers, a new corded waistcoat and
a fresh jacket and clean shirt and a handkerchief thing round his
neck.
'The old man said, "You just saved yourself, mate, from having a
ducking. You weren't fit to live coming to work like that."
'He kept himself quite nice for some years after that.
'But most of them were spotlessly clean. They used to wash every
night unless they laid out, and sometimes before they went out to the
pub we used to give them a bucket of hot water out of the engine and
they'd have a wash and put a clean shirt on. They'd have an old bag
and had always got two or three shirts, and they'd put one on, a fresh
wrap around their neck and off they'd go. They shaved every other
day, and they had no looking glass or anything. They used to make
the lather brushes out of the self-binder string off the sheaf.
'I said to one of them one day, "Do you want me to bring you a
lather brush?"
"No, young Harry, we don't use them."
'I said, "Why's that?"
'He said, "Well a lot of people have had skin diseases on their face
from using lather brushes. The hair they're made of contracts all sorts
of complaints. No bounds what maggoty old bullock or horse it
come off. If you make them out of string," he said, "that's all sterilized
stuff, it'll never mark you."

'So they used to get a lot and tie it all together and bind it up tight, then cut it off and that's what they used to use. Then they'd hang their old strap on the wattle gate-head or on the gate itself and sharpen the old razor two or three times. A lot of them had got their old Army razors with numbers on them. Then they'd just have some hot water in an old tin, a little soap, lather theirself, and then they'd hold their nose and you could hear the razor pulling the whiskers off. They never used to make no bother about it. If they wanted to have a wash down properly they'd get a great old bucket of hot water and go down along the hedge or under a bush where they'd take everything off they'd got and with an old flannel and soap they'd wash theirselves all over, and do their hair an' all, put a clean shirt on and bring the bucket back. They looked quite smart. "Ah," they'd say, "that feels better."

'Sometimes they'd have a sing song round the fire. They were allowed to have a bit of rough wood and they used to cook their food and have some of the songs they used to sing when they were out in South Africa. 'Course, us young ones, we used to sit and laugh. We couldn't help it. And they always used to have a sing song at the pubs. If there was eight or nine of them, they never thought of having a pint of beer in them days, it was all glazed cream quart pots and they'd have one each and a little tiny glass, then if they knew you they'd say, "Here you are, have a little drop of my beer." Then about nine o'clock—used to shut up at ten at night—one would have a sing song. One big fellow, Spratty we called him, used to say, "Well it's time we had a song." He used to sing—I can remember if it was only yesterday:

> I've been a wild boy to my parents,
> And daily I roam about
> To earn a small mite for my shelter tonight,
> God help me, I am cast down.

'Well he'd have that all through—I don't remember it all—then he'd say, "Now look. Nobby's going to give us one now. Peace and quietness so we can all hear him."

'They'd go right round the lot, and perhaps go home singing to the farm. If it was late, they shut up. They never disturbed nobody round the farm. Some of the farmers used to say to me,

"Some of your mates will be big headed this morning."

"Why?"

"Well, they were singing coming up the road last night but it shut up all at once. I suppose they come round and went to roost."

'They were very helpful to a young fellow, because I was quite a young man when I had some of them with me.

'They used to say, "Do you want some coal up in the tender, young Harry?"

"Yes," I'd say, "I have to put it up a little at a time."

"Oh, I'll put you some up."

'They'd get hold of a hundredweight at a time, chuck it up in the tender, get in there and pull the sack off.

'They'd say, "There you are. See you again presently."

'Covering up, packing up of a night, keeping the tackle clean, they were very helpful. They'd get whisps of straws and rub the thresher all down and some of the old boys would shine your brass up if we were going to shift.

"We'll look a bit smart on the road," they'd say. "Where's your old brick dust?"

'They used to have a bit of this with a drop of oil in it, and a bit of rag and polish the old brasses and shine them all up.

"There," they'd say, "you're fit to go on the road now."

'It was a marvellous turnout.

'It was a wonderful job really. If we wanted some food somebody used to go into Ramsgate or somewhere and get some rashers of bacon and some eggs if the farmer hadn't got any. We used to get the old clinker shovel, make it hot and then wipe it out with a bit of paper, put the rashers in it, put them in the furnace and wait a second or two, bring them out and turn them over, slap it on our bread and away we went. Some of the farmers were very good, they used to say, "I'll set you up with a few eggs. Do you like them?" They used to be very nice. You used to do them in your clinker shovel, and make an egg fritter. Cracked them all, put them in it, then cut it in pieces and share it.

'We used to get a bit of a laugh sometimes. We was at a farm called St Nicholas, and an old Scotsman had it, a little, short, fat man. One morning we couldn't start. It rained and he wouldn't let us fetch the thatch off so we all got down a big chalk hole which is still there I think today. Father was there and some of the chaps had got hold of some eggs from out the farm and they was having a fry up on a camp fire.

'Mr Smith, the Scotsman, come down, and he said to my father, "I can't make it out, Mr Gambrill."

'So my father said, "What's the matter, sir?"

"Well," he said, "as soon as the drum comes the hens cease to lay. It must be the smoke from the engine."

'He knew what was happening. He knew the chaps had had them but of course he didn't find no fault, but he knew.

'Another thing we used to have was swede turnips if they let us have some. We used to scrape the rind and that off, wash them, cut the tops off them about three inches, and put them in the smoke box of the engine at half-past ten. Then about half-past eleven used to turn them over and when twelve o'clock come and we stopped for lunch, we used to take them out, put them on a clean sack, have an old dandy brush that they used to groom the horses with, brush all the old soot and that off them to leave a nice polished skin, and we used to cut them open and put a bit of butter or margarine in. Anyway we used to live and do well. They say poor old times, but they were good old times. The food was nothing and it was good. Even if you wanted a drink of beer along the road, it was twopence for a pint. If you wanted a bit of tobacco, threepence ha'penny for half ounce. Bread was only twopence for a two pound loaf, penny ha'-penny for a stale one. They'd put you twelve stale buns in a bag for a tanner. And meat, the best of joints of pork were only sixpence a pound. Tea was fourpence a quarter, I think, and sugar penny ha'-penny a pound. We used to buy bones in a little place here at Petham nearly as big as an ordinary ham bone but a good ten inches across the top and that used to be eightpence. It was very seldom that cottage people bought tinned meat, but the old soldiers that used to follow the thrashing machines, they used to be very fond of bully beef. 'Cause they'd always been used to it, they used to love it. They used to say, "We're going to have a treat Sunday—bully beef stew." They'd empty the tin into a drum with some water, and boil it all up with some vegetables. That's how they used to live.

'Some had got an old attache case, some a little sack, a sugar sack, what they'd bought at a grocer's shop to carry their stuff in. Yes. They used to roll up their old Army blankets and tie them in a bundle and they poked them in the old machine wherever we was going. They'd say, "We're going to the pub. When you get the other end just lay them out on the draw-bar of the old machine so's we can pick them up." I had to lay their bundles of bed clothes out. If it rained they'd say, "Well put them in the cart lodge, we know where that is" —because they used to come to the farms many times, you know. We used to lay them on the old cart rods or if we couldn't find nothing else, used to pull a bit of string and tie them to the beams. All sorts of capers. Some of the devils never got back to the farms till the early hours of the morning.

'Lots of times we slept in the barn. Now and then perhaps one of the farmers had got a nice matchboard granary and he used to say, "If you boys don't smoke you can go in the granary and if you want to warm the sacks just put them under your engine sail." So we used to do that, get the sacks nice and warm, get in one, pull another one up round the shoulders, stuff the top up, put it on our head and pull it over our back so the muck didn't get down our neck and then fall back in the straw. We used to call them Twyman's blankets after the Canterbury firm that hired them out for years to farmers. That's how we used to manage. You could lay there as warm as toast. It didn't matter how cold it was outside. All but hay. We never laid in hay. Never seemed to get warm in hay. Oat fly was beautiful stuff to lay in. You never laid an ache. It was nice and soft, lovely and warm, never itchy. A lot of farm chaps used to get the other chaps working with the machine to fill up little old bags with this oat fly or chaff, and they used that for filling ticks for beds. Father used to have it. Perhaps every month he'd take it out the garden, take the old lot out and put a new lot in. It was very handy if you'd got small infants. Then perhaps they'd have a tick for a full size bed and they'd have a lot of clean wheat straw cut up short to fill this tick. That used to be renewed about every three months, but of course they used to shake it up like you would feathers. After a while they used to be very dusty. When you went to turn them, the dust used to come out of them and would make you sneeze. Palliasses were all made up in factories and filled up with straw. There used to be a wheat called bearded wheat and it used to have whiskers on it. It grows with these long oils on it like a shrimp—we called them oils but some people called them hairs. They used to use that for these palliasses and for straw hats. They used to make quite a lot of money from that. Bearded wheat was its proper name, some call it rivets wheat, but we used to call it brustly wheat. It growed like a tree. It would grow on very poor ground and they used to leave it in the field till it had shed its oil, then we'd thresh it and we didn't have to knock it about because these people that made straw hats used to buy it. It was all tied up properly, what was left of the ears, and they were all put away with two straw bonds round them. That was cruel stuff. If you got any down your neck it was like a fret saw. You'd have to take your under vests off in the daytime if you got a bit down your back. You couldn't rest. Oh, it was wicked stuff.

'Barley would itch too, but mayweed was the worst problem after it was dry. It used to get harvested in the corn and tied up and most of the time the stuff was in full bloom. When you came to thrash it you'd sneeze all day long because it's a nasty sharp smell and it makes your eyes sore, oh, for days afterwards. The seed of it was very small, and you had to be careful when you was up on the old machine feeding it, otherwise a big bit would go in and the seeds would fly all over you and you'd get some in your eyes and they used to burn. We never had goggles in those days. Another thing, if there was a lot of poppy and you had a day or two in an old fashioned barn, the dust from the poppies would nearly drive you to sleep. There was laudanum or something in it, they used to tell us. That was wicked stuff. It would make you very drowsy. Another aggravating thing was blue moor thistles. They stuck all in your hair and round your face if you hadn't had a shave. The latter part of my time with the thrashing they used to have a piece of cloth that came up and tied round the back of their head, over their nose and mouth. Of a night when they'd finished these were filthy where they would have breathed all this stuff in. But we never had them much. We didn't take much notice of it, you know. Where they had carried corn too early and it had gone off, which they call heated corn, oh, that was another wicked one. It was so rich, the smell of it, that it used to make you really sick and bad sometimes, especially if you was in a barn and you were shut in.

'Lots of the old thatched barns years back were very infested with fleas. You was lucky if you didn't get some. You was itching, scratching, scrubbing perhaps all day long. If you hung a jacket up, a coat you were wearing perhaps to go to work in the morning, if you weren't careful where you hung it, I bet you'd find some mice in it. Been through your pocket, the devils. Some of the farms had lots of cats, but they never done away with the mice because they used to live and breed in the ricks. God, there used to be thousands! They'd get in your clothes and many of the men used to get them in their trousers, so they used to tie the bottom of our trouser legs up. Dirty little devils they were. I remember going home one night just before we give the engines up. I had a wash, turned my shirt collar up and sat down at the table. It was a nice bit of beef pudding with a bit of kidney in it, lovely it was with a drop of gravy. I felt something prick my collar so I put my fingers down there and out jumped a mouse on the table!

'You'd catch as many as eighty rats a day out of a rick. Some farmers would put wire netting about six or seven feet away from the stack, then get the thatch off. Ever so many would jump out and the chaps used to be in there with sticks getting them and chucking them out. They used to put faggots down on the ground and the rick on them so when we'd got the stack nearly finished, down to the last sheaf or two, some of the farmers would say, "Your time will still go on, boys. Pick them faggots up and make a long bundle the other side of the fence." As you picked them up there was little ones and big ones. Oh, it was a regular game! The old farmer always used to give them perhaps some extra beer, or if they were teetotal farmers they'd give them an extra copper or two.

'I remember once being up at Bockholt Farm, Waltham, and they'd lost some sheep, some little Southdown sheep which died of some disease, and they chucked them in the barn and stacked corn on them. Anyway, we didn't know it, busy thrashing, got down to the last row of sheaves and found the carcasses of these sheep all rotten. Rats! You've never seen anything like it in your life. There were hundreds. We killed a tremendous lot of them. Some of them got away. A bloke said, "There's a hole in that tall door post and there's rats in there." The bailiff bored a hole quite a way up then he got some hot water out of the engine in the water can and poured it down, and they got eighteen of the biggest rats you ever saw out of that hollow post. They was squeaking and hollering and some of the chaps gave them a clout—because they're filthy things, you know. Most of them will go for dogs and bite them. Some of them are very big old sandy things, all sores up their tails. Cor, I used to hate the sight of them.

'One man was very amusing. I'd got nine men with me and there was a tremendous lot of rats.

'When we finished the rick he said to me, "Those men are lazy. They won't catch rats."

"No," I said, "you must tell them about it, governor."

'So he said to one big burly fellow, "You might just as well have caught them rats than let them get away."

"They're water rats, sir," he said.

'He couldn't make it out so he come to me. I said, "Well you know what they mean, governor, don't you? You don't give them nothing for catching them."

"Oh," he said, "if that's the trouble I'll pay them."

'After that he might give 1½d. each for the rats and that's how he used to get rid of them.'

Their heavy investment in thrashing equipment meant that the Gambrills came into contact with farmers as equals rather than mere employees. Tact was needed by both parties if a satisfactory working arrangement was to be maintained. They had to fit their customers into their rota as soon as they were able to, or they might lose them to competitors, while the farmers had to plan ahead, ensure that there were adequate coal and water supplies for the steam engine, and then stand back and leave the actual process of thrashing to the con-tractor's men. The thrashers rightly felt that they knew more about their machine and its capabilities than the farmers did and Harry, for one, was ideally placed as the owner's son to teach demanding or meddlesome farmers a lesson. Dealing with such a variety of farmers, Harry and his father were also well situated to judge the prevailing economic climate and to form their own opinions of farmers as a class.

'Nearly all the farmers, if they wanted father to do anything they'd come and find him. Now and then one would write if he was a long way off, but the majority used to come and see the old boy, explain to him what they wanted. If they wanted a thresh they'd ask how he could fit it in.

'He'd say, "Well, I'm busy with my tackle for about a week, but I can let you have one in just over the week. Do you want me to let you know?"

'They'd say, "No, we're all ready when you come. Bring as many men as you can. We've got plenty of coal, you've no occasion to be in trouble."

'They used to find their own coal you know. That's how it used to go on.

'Some of them was very cantankerous, some was very nice, but he wanted a lot of pleasing, a farmer did. I expect he does today. You were a lucky man if you could make one smile, especially when the pay time came. I've had them cry. I've had them swear. I used to laugh at them.

"I don't know why you don't chuck the business up, mate, don't have none. If I get as bad as that," I said, "and I hope I never do, I hope I drop down dead before I get as miserable as you."

"There's two worst things in this world," my father said to me one day.

'I said, "What's that, dad?"

"Well," he said, "a dissatisfied farmer and a discontented woman. If you can find anything worse than that for heaven's sake come and tell me."

'They used to get on his wick sometimes, you know, some of the farmers. Of course some of them was very good, there was no getting away from it, but they were few and far between. A lot of the old devils that went queer were always out on the booze with an old pony cart, never at home looking after the business. The pub was their place and that's where the money went, I suppose. Then they used to go bang, and creditors had to suffer.

'Lots of them turned bankrupts, years back, right up to the 1914–18 war. Then there was plenty of money about. I don't think there's many of them that have turned their noses up since the 1914–18 war. It was very bad in the thirties but they managed all right. Corn and that was worth nothing, but a lot of ground was laid down and with having a lot of sheep, they held their own. They pulled through all right. But in my early days, if they had a bad year, it used to take them a long time to get over it. There was no help in those days from any government source. They got no help from anyone. They wouldn't get none from the banks if there were no deeds or anything to lay in there. If they'd got a bad year, a wet season, stuff spoilt and that, they used to say it took seven years to get over it. I've heard my old father say old Baker White had a bad year, I think he said it was 1893, and he'd got several farmers that hired farms off him. When the time come to pay the rent they hadn't got it, but he quite understood because he was in farming himself, so rather than not settle or turn them out, he let them off with half the amount of the rent for that year. Of course that helped them along. But there wasn't many of them done it. When they went bang a lot of them, where they owed money, they used to give the old boy a tidy knock, you know. I remember one, he owed father £58 and he got 58d. That's all he got. Couldn't have no more. Of course he wasn't the only one, there was a lot more beside. I used to go what they called money hunting for my father when I was quite young. A pocketful of bills in an envelope. I'd go and find them and they'd say, "Tell father I'm ever so sorry, young Harry. Tell him I've got little money." Sometimes they'd send a couple of pounds off a £20 bill. You couldn't have no more, they hadn't got it. Mind you, I remember a lot of them, they was only scoundrels. They was always on the booze and messing about. They were never at home looking after their business. They used to leave it to other people and that's how it is they came to grief.

'There was one farmer at Thanington, Wincheap, we'd never done anything for him, but he'd had Holman's, he'd had Wingham Engineering Company, and they weren't right, so he come and found me. I was thrashing at a place called Milton Chapel along the bottom of where that bridge is along the Ashford Road.

"You're often down this way aren't you, young man?"

'I said, "Yes, I've been coming to Mr Talbot here for quite a few years."

"I wonder if you'd like to do something for me. I would like to thrash in about a fortnight's time."

"Well," I said, "I'm not the owner, I'm only the son, but I'll ask my father." So I did. I asked dad that night.

'He said, "Well, I wouldn't put nothing in your way but he's had

Holman, he's had Wingham Engineering Company and there's something wrong somewhere. They're monied people, you know. I won't put anything in your way. You go and see what you can do. I'll leave it entirely to you. I'll take the best of your men along with me so's you don't lose them," because he didn't want any hands, only driver and feeder.

'Anyway, we draw in one night, seven o'clock. The bailiff bloke come out, "Can you start six o'clock in the morning, driver?"

'I said, "All right, governor. Can start now if you like."

'He never said no more. Six o'clock we started, he'd got all his own men there, thrashing away till nine o'clock. He came round.

"How much wheat are you getting in an hour, Gambrill?"

'I said, "Four quarters sir."

"I want more than that," he said.

"Well, you can have it," I said.

"Put some more men on the stacks so that I can get it quicker, and some more men on the straw so they can get it away. You can have it just as you like it."

'Anyway he did, and I put my finger up to my mate on the machine and instead of him opening the sheaves up he just knocked them in the drum. We'd been running about an hour and we was getting six and a half to seven quarters an hour, which was a lot more. The bailiff came round to me,

"Have you been round the straw rick in front?"

'I said, "No. Don't want to. They ain't my men."

"No, but have you seen the wheat underneath it. You go and have a look."

'I said, "No, I ain't going to."

"Cor," he said, "there will be something the matter when the governor comes out."

"Well," I said, "there will have to be."

'Out he come—he'd got his stick on his arm and his felt hat on one side—and the first thing he done, he got his old stick and he worked it away and he saw all this wheat. Beautiful stuff. Come back to me.

"Have you seen all that wheat round that straw rick, Gambrill?"

'I said, "No. The bailiff said there's some there, but you can't help it, you know."

"What do you mean?", he says.

'I looked at him straight. "Now look, governor, you ain't satisfied with nobody," I said. "There's only two ways to do this job, properly and anyhow. Well, we're doing it anyhow now and if you don't want any wheat to come down there you'll have to let us go back to the old style."

"Oh, like that, is it?"

"Yes," I said. "You couldn't find none at four or four and half quarters an hour, the machine's got time to shake it out, but as it's going on now it's in and out. Fellows haven't got time to do anything with the machine."

"Oh well," he said, "you'd better go like you was."

'So we took the other men off the stacks, some out of the straw, let them clear up and we jogged along. I never had no more trouble with that man at all. See if Holman's chaps gave him any sauce he would go and complain to Holman's which was a bigger firm and they'd give them their cards or pay them off. But I wouldn't get the sack. My father always said that they sent a demon of a driver from Wingham there—because Holman's and Wingham were thick buddy pals—and the old chap reckoned they sent a rough driver there on purpose, so he shouldn't want them, see. He swore they nearly set the place alight!' 'Course, this farmer, he'd been to college and his father—a different type of farmer, an old type, a very wise old fellow—had left him quite a bit of money. Nearly everybody used to take the mickey out of him. But he found the wrong party when he had a go at me.'

Even while Harry was still learning the business the ultimate threat to his family's way of life was being perfected in the Canadian prairies—the combine harvester which cut and thrashed the corn in one operation. Introduced into Britain in 1926, it made little impact on depressed British farming before the Second World War but spread rapidly afterwards. Unlike the thrashing machine which would be in employment all the winter, this monster was needed for a short crucial period only. Farmers would not, indeed could not, delay their harvesting to fit the convenience of an outside contractor. Faced with a buoyant market and an increasing labour shortage, they tended to purchase their own combines, and within fifteen years the old thrasher and its large troupe of followers had virtually disappeared from the agricultural scene.

Chapter 6

The Great Work: Hop Picking

No other branch of agriculture gives anything like the same
amount of employment as the cultivation of the hop.

John Marsh, *Hops and Hopping* (1892)

Hop cultivation had no parallel in farming. It was, according to one
authority, 'not really farming at all'; to Hall, it was 'more like
manufacturing'. Not only did farmers need to invest considerable
capital into the elaborate equipment required to grow hops but they
had to carry large financial reserves to carry them through the
frequent runs of bad years. No other crop demanded so much
attention all the year round—digging, poling, wiring, training,
shimming, manuring, weeding, washing—and unlike grain crops,
which were increasingly harvested by machine, hops continued to be
handpicked right up to the 1950s. Little wonder that hops 'maintained
the most numerous and best-paid body of labourers in the countryside'. George Finn produced figures in 1895 for his labour expenses
during the previous year. On 250 acres of pasture they amounted to
£78 13s. On 240 acres of arable land, about ninety of which were
given over to hops, they were £3,010. Many farmers were not slow to
quote similar outgoings when arguing for protection from foreign

imports. 'If any article deserves Protection, hops do,' remarked one in 1893.

Hop picking was the operation which required the most labour and, since Kent, despite its diminishing acreage, continued to supply over 60 per cent of the national crop before 1914, it had to draw on a variety of sources to supplement local supplies. Widely regarded as 'light and easy' work, hop picking attracted women and children not only from the immediate locality but from neighbouring towns and from London, in hordes which defied accurate enumeration. Contemporaries put various figures on the total seasonal labour force, ranging from 80,000 up to 150,000.

The pickers came for a variety of reasons. To some it was primarily a holiday. 'What the banks of the Riviera are to the children of the aristocracy, the banks of the Medway are to the children of the poor,' wrote John Marsh in 1892. Hop picking, even for many local children, was 'the only holiday we ever had . . . picnicking every day'. Others had different views. Kids, especially boys, 'had to be knocked into picking'. Many remember mother hurling clods of dirt at them whenever she caught them slacking: 'Mother never used to let us run round. We had to sit and pick all the time.' Although 'kids made fun of it', they recognised that 'it was darn hard work.' Some disliked it intensely. 'It was a rough time. Although people used to say how lovely it was out there in the hop gardens, I didn't like it when I was a youngster. It was a case of having to like it. I was never sorry when it was finished.' Money was apparently of secondary importance to Londoners since 'they didn't seem to care if they went back with nothing.' A 'vast proportion' was spent on drink.

Despite misgivings about the unhygienic living conditions in the gardens, people also regarded hopping as good for their health. It gave them 'marvellous appetites . . . we used to eat like horses.' London children who came down as 'poor, puny things' after five or six weeks 'would go back as brown as berries, full of life'. The smell of the hops was reputed to be conducive to sleep too, and folk returned home supplied with enough of them to make into hop pillows for the coming winter.

For the majority of 'home' pickers, however, it was the money which attracted them to this repetitive and monotonous task. Seebohm Rowntree and May Kendall, who carried out a survey in 1913 on *How the Labourer Lives*, discovered in every part of the country they examined that families relied on charity for their clothing. Had they ventured into Kent they would have reason to qualify their generalisation. 'After hop picking we all had new clothes for best, and the previous best we used to take for school, so we were better off.' 'We didn't get any money as children out of hopping because that all went on our winter clothes.' Almost without exception local people picked to rig themselves out for winter. How much they earned depended on a variety of factors. Picking was always paid on piecework on a five or six bushel measure, but the rate, or tally, varied with the quality and size of hops, the current state of the market and the speed with which the farmer thought his pickers ought to work. Since the market was prone to extreme fluctuations in price and the pickers' wage comprised such a large proportion of the total costs of production, farmers preferred to delay their decision until paying-off day. Such an arrangement did not always suit the Londoners who were not averse to striking to obtain an early and acceptable tally. Apart from this, the skill of the individual picker, the number of child helpers which she was able to recruit, either her own or those of friends, her positioning in the hop garden, and her working relationship with the measurer all played a part in determining her total income. In east Kent, where the hops were picked into five bushel baskets, the pickers attempted to make the hops 'hover', to get as few as possible into the standard measure. An unfriendly measurer who gave the basket a sudden jerk could cause the contents to settle and justifiably demand that the volume be made up. In west Kent, however, they picked into bins, large canvas sheets draped between two horizontal poles, and here there was even greater scope for dispute, since the measurer used to scoop up the hops into a bushel basket to measure them. The number of hops required to fill the basket varied with the pressure which he applied to them. Hoppers persistently implored the measurer to be generous and scoop them up loosely. If moral persuasion failed they resorted to picking dirty hops, leaving leaves and twigs on them, in an attempt to increase their volume.

With the tally set variously at between 10d. and 1s. 4d. for five bushels in the 1900s, a woman and her children could hope to earn £6 to £8 over the four to six week period. Individuals found the work less profitable. Jack London, the author better known for his tales of the Canadian Arctic, spent some time living in the East End of London and wrote up his experiences in *The People of the Abyss* (1903). He travelled down to try his hand at hopping with a friend. He found it 'simple work, woman's work in fact, not man's', but despite becoming 'as expert as it is possible to become' within an hour or two, he soon realised that 'living wages could not be made—by men . . . For it is the woman and the half dozen children who count as a unit

and by their combined capacity determine the unit's pay . . . where-
upon we both lamented our negligence in not rearing up a numerous
progeny to help us in this day of need.'
Although their families participated in picking the farm-hands
themselves did not. They were employed at other related tasks. Some
were binmen or pole-pullers, hoisting down the hop bines for the
pickers to work from, checking that they picked clean hops, moving
the bins and baskets when necessary, carrying the pokes, ten bushel
bags full of hops, to the oast houses for drying. The measurer, the
man with overall responsibility for the hop garden, who visited each
of the pickers in turn with the bookie, or booker (frequently a local
school teacher) to tot up the pickings, and the men who worked in the
oast houses drying the hops were also recruited from the farm-hands.
Drying the delicate hops at the right temperature for the correct time
was a skilled and demanding job, and the head drier usually distinguished himself as 'the high priest of the oast' by donning a red
tammy-shanter. Depending on the size of the oast, he would be
helped by a second man and a number of labourers who performed
odd jobs like fetching and breaking the coal, clearing the hops off the
hairs on which they were laid above the fire, and pressing them into
pockets for sending off to the hop factors or to market. It was a
round-the-clock job, and men lived in oast for six days of the week,
snatching a few hours sleep when they could, cooking their own food
outside to avoid tainting the hops with smoke, and sustaining themselves with the beer supplied by their employer. Oddly enough, they
seemed to thrive on this extended labour and put on weight over the
period.
The pickers were a motley crew. Along with the women and
children from the villages there were those who walked out daily from
the neighbouring towns and others from further afield who stayed in
the huts which the farmers provided for them, or in stables, lodges,
cart sheds, barns and even converted pig sties. These working-class
people were supplemented on the one hand by 'respectable' ladies
who would cluster round bins and baskets and pick for charity or for
church funds, and on the other hand by gypsies, diddikais and
tramps, 'the most dangerous and disorderly section of the hoppers'.
The latter group received a mixed welcome. Respected for their
expertise at picking they were nevertheless feared for their violent
tempers, and distrusted for their 'love of chicken and linen'. For the
Poor Law Unions throughout Kent, but especially in the hop growing
districts, autumn was a quiet time. Mr Davey, a Local Government
Board Inspector reporting in 1889, found the workhouses 'empty of

Life in Kent

all but the very young, aged and infirm persons'. He found no able-bodied women in any workhouse. Even the children were often sent out hop picking. At Faversham, for example, the Guardians regularly took them into the hop gardens. This not only helped to reduce the rate burden but they made use of the extra income to inculcate thrift in their charges and to give them a treat. In 1905, 'It was decided that 5s. should be placed to the credit of each of them at the Post Office Savings Bank and that they should have 3d. to spend. This will absorb £8 18s. leaving £12 10s. for the annual excursion to Herne Bay next summer, the cost of which is always defrayed from their hopping money.'

The largest and most boisterous group of pickers, however, was the Londoners. They poured into the areas which lacked sufficient local supplies of labour: the Weald, especially around Paddock Wood, Yalding, Marden, Hunton, Horsmonden, Goudhurst, and the hop growing belt between Faversham and Canterbury around Selling, Chilham and Molash. Evidence presented before the Royal Commission of the Housing of the Working Classes in 1885 showed that they came from all over London but especially from the East End: Barbican, Stepney, Mile End, Stratford, Grays Inn Road, Commercial Road, Whitechapel. They travelled in any way they could. Some walked, some, especially costermongers and their families, brought their horses and carts. The railways laid on specially chartered hopping trains which consisted of low standard rolling stock and which ran, often with lengthy delays, through the night. Many more went back by train than came down, possibly because they were flush with money, more likely because farmers often paid for their return fare home. Freda Vidgen, a young girl before the First World War, remembers them descending on the farm in Chainhurst, near Marden, where her father was bailiff.

'The London hop pickers had from January on been writing post-cards to book hopper huts and bins for the coming year, so we children in the winter evenings used to address the postcards and put "Hop picking will commence . . ." and leave it until my father had been in the hop garden in the autumn. Then we had to get these couple of hundred postcards out and send them off to London and book the hopping train. Then the farm waggons used to be got out, the horses were dressed over all with *catis*, which is coloured coarse ribbon, and brasses, and they went three miles to Marden station with us country children running behind them all the way. Two vans went for luggage, and a dung cart went for old people. They had a sieve basket, which is a bushel basket, a wickerwork basket that they used to pick apples in and they would throw it up in. Most of the old ladies weighed about twelve, fourteen, sixteen stone for the porter they used to drink in London made them so stout. So the waggoner would put the basket down, put his shoulder under their bottom and heave them up into the dung cart. All the children would sit up on top of the luggage. Then coming down Pattenden Lane, the horses would stop and the families would undo bags and tip out two or three children. They had put children into sacks so that they shouldn't pay the fare down, taken them out on the train and then put them back into the sacks to get off.

'Then they had their huts, and they all renewed acquaintanceships with children from last year. We'd got all the huts ready. The farmer would get stones, faggots and straw for their beds and we would whitewash the huts. Then the waggoner went round every day and put two faggots outside each hut for firing, and so that nobody would pinch them the children would be sent home early to put them in the huts and get the fires going to boil their kettles and billy cans. They did all their washing and that was draped along the hedges. They never did any ironing because there wasn't anywhere to heat irons.

'They were real characters, these Londoners. My father, he was in the Territorials, and he had a bugle, and he used to come into my bedroom, open the window, and blow this bugle for the people to start work. Then in the afternoon he would call "Pull no more bines" which meant that everybody in the hop garden pulled another bine because they wanted to get some hops in their bin to start in the morning! And paying-off day was a marvellous day because they subbed during the week and most cottage people had an extra allotment where they grew potatoes and dahlias to sell to the hop pickers. We told them time and again that chrysanthemums would travel better, last longer, but they loved the brilliant colours of the dahlias. We never minded if the hens hatched pullets so long as there was enough cockerels to sell to the hop pickers. Then the final day the farmer would put boxes of apples in his farmyard with one of the farmworkers to share them out because he knew that if they didn't give them apples they would pinch them. They then used to come to the door and say, "Ha'porth of apples and pennorth of taters." They wanted the bigger potatoes and the small apples. We made quite a lot of money.'

Not everyone portrayed the pickers in such an attractive light. To Jack London they were 'an army of ghouls' which poured out from the 'slums, stews and ghettos' into a countryside which did not want them: 'They are out of place. As they drag their squat, misshapen bodies along the highways and byways, they resemble some vile spawn from the underground. Their very presence, the fact of their existence, is an outrage to the fresh, bright sun and the green and growing things. The clean upstanding trees cry shame upon them and their withered crookedness, and their rottenness is a slimy desecration of the sweetness and purity of nature.' Others, like A. D. Hall, saw them 'in the main' as 'respectable families who are engaged year after year on the same farm, and there obtain good wages and a health-giving month in the open air,' an acceptable but 'not always an easy team to drive'. Just how the indigenous population viewed these newcomers who, whether they were 'ghouls' or 'respectable families', certainly represented a different way of life, makes an interesting study. The answer cannot be sought through direct questioning: 'What did you think of the Londoners?' Such an approach elicits non-committal replies: 'not too bad' . . . all right' . . . 'a bit rough but they were sociable', and so on. Only through an examination of the active responses of local communities to this annual invasion can their response be understood. The rest of this chapter is devoted to this reaction.

Almost every section of local society gave the pickers a guarded welcome. Farmers could not have managed without them. Shopkeepers and publicans had a bonanza, a 'mad rush', taking more in a week than in a month during the rest of the year. Traders bought in goods which they did not otherwise stock, especially large quantities of cheap but flashy hardware, clothing and home-made sweets. Publicans cleared one room out especially for the visitors, and those with small farmsteads attached often killed a pig or two to sell off. Bakers worked a seven day week cooking joints and puddings for them on a Sunday. Cottagers, who also helped out with the cooking, sold them vegetables and flowers. Itinerant traders roamed the gardens selling kippers, sweets, hot rolls, 'hokey-pokey' ice cream and lollies which the women bought to bribe their children to work harder. Everyone tried to persuade them to part with as much of their money as they possibly could while they were still in the area.

The locals were only too well aware, however, that the Londoners did not always feel inclined to pay for the goods and services they required. They were 'rather light-fingered', inclined to 'pick up anything', unable to leave anything alone. Farmers hired men to patrol the orchards which still had to be picked. Few of them considered hiring the visitors to do the picking—hops were not likely to find their way into the family pudding but apples were.

Shopkeepers too had their reservations. 'Hopping used to be good for business if you could stop the stuff from being pinched.' 'You had to be careful where you left stuff laying about the shop, otherwise you'd lose it.' Ernest Stanger (born 1900), a grocer from Tenterden, recalls an incident his uncle had at Goudhurst. 'My uncle had a shop at the top of the hill there and he'd just had some of these big cheeses delivered. All of a sudden one morning, someone put his head in the shop and shouted, "Mr Walters! Come and look after your cheese." When he went out, they'd put one of these on end and it was rolling away down the hill and they were trotting behind it. They were all Londoners. All sorts of tricks they got up to.' Some traders erected wire barriers around the counter and moved all their stock behind it or tied everything left on display into place with special knots. Londoners were often segregated from locals and even shopkeepers preferred to view them through little cubby holes which they erected on the counter. Few traders considered allowing them any credit. 'It was a case of cash on the nail. Some of them were very good, but a lot of them, if you allowed them credit, that was it!' Despite their capacity for drinking, possibly because of it, some publicans decided to ban them from their houses. Others insured themselves against loss by charging a deposit, in some cases as much as 6d., on glasses.

Their moral failings were a constant source of worry to religious and philanthropic organisations and to the police who were entrusted with the maintenance of law and order. Drunkenness and sexual immorality, symbolised by hopper marriages carried out by extempore priests, and the effects which close proximity to such activities might have on children were special causes for concern. Those who were called upon to provide better accommodation or who were likely to be most hard hit by regulations affecting child labour in the hop gardens, the farmers, were not always among these 'large-hearted Christian people' who campaigned, not always effectively or with the hoppers' approval, for their cause. The following view, expressed during the proceedings of the Interdepartmental Committee on the Employment of School Children in 1902, is an example of this attitude: 'I cannot commend the moral effect but I should answer the question by asking another. Is it better in London?' 'I suppose there is a good deal of immorality?' continued the earnest questioner. 'We hear more of this from the London papers than we see,' replied the farmer, undaunted.

The campaign some of these reformers waged was almost a crusade in its scope and motivation. The Rev. J. G. Stratton, rector of Ditton, near Maidstone, was a leading light in the movement and instrumental in establishing in 1866 the Society for the Employment and Improved Lodging of Hop-pickers which, in collaboration with a few large hop growers sympathetic to their cause, pressed for 'decent lodgings'. Despite an act of Parliament in 1874 allowing local authorities to make bye-laws to ensure that these lodgings were provided it is clear from the recollections many people have of conditions at the turn of the century, and from continuing fears expressed in official circles, that the problems were not eliminated. Nevertheless, the attempts to raise hop pickers 'morally as well as physically in the scale of social life', which were carried enthusiastically into the hop gardens themselves, meant that John Marsh was able to report that owing to the 'efforts made by Christian ladies and gentlemen' hop pickers 'exhibit a degree of improvement which is both gratifying and important'. Some of these activists actually travelled down from London where they spent the rest of the year engaged in similar pursuits, while others were locally inspired. Missions, coffee houses, evening schools, temperance clubs, refreshment booths and even hospitals were established by these kind-hearted and well-meaning people. By 1905 the Church of England Temperance Society, based at 64, Burgate Street, Canterbury, one of the organisations, according to *The Kentish Gazette*, 'in the forefront in providing for the spiritual and temporal wants of hop-pickers', had forty full-time workers throughout Kent, from Wingham in the east to East Peckham and Paddock Wood in the west. This body distributed literature, held services and lantern lectures, provided Sunday Schools for the children, nursing for the sick, and coffee and groceries for the workers, and visited the huts to talk individually with the hoppers.

If one word could be singled out to describe most effectively what the villagers thought of Londoners, it would be 'dirty'. Cleanliness amongst country folk was a matter of pride. It endowed a person, however poor, with respectability. It was the one characteristic of their lives which many people could maintain without cost to themselves and as such it was a status symbol. They could at least look down on dirty people. Londoners, therefore, were a class apart because they seemed to place little value in this quality. Although they may have been 'all right as a rule', 'sociable people', 'tremendously good hop pickers' and full of fun, many villagers had as little as possible to do with them as they could. While recognising that the conditions under which they lived were not conducive to cleanliness, locals still held the Londoners and any other pickers who resembled them in low esteem.

The measurer in particular went in constant dread of becoming infested by fleas. Mrs Vidgen recalls the council issuing free diarrhoea mixture to the locals to protect them from the unpleasant side effects of the habits of the Londoners. Then, 'Every dinner time when we came home from the hop garden, my mother would put a piece of white sheeting on her lap and we would kneel in front of her and she would have a tooth comb, a double-edged, very fine comb, and she would scrape it through our hair to get these nits off the strands of hair and shake them on to a newspaper and burn them. That was done morning, noon and night so that you shouldn't get these nits and have to have your head shaved. Your greatest shame was to go to school after hop picking with your head shaved.' 'Officially', she was not allowed to mix with the London children.

Other people have equally unsavoury memories. One lady from Laddingford, near Yalding, recalls, 'They were dreadful in those days. Oh dear! They were poor and dirty too. After they went back we always used to pray for good rain. Oh, terribly dirty! The sanitation was dreadful. Especially the Brighton pickers, they used to be awful, dirtier even than the London people.' Allan Wise (1894–1977) used to pick at Goodnestone, near Faversham, his home town, when he was a boy. 'We didn't know them. No! We was too classy for them. Well, we thought we were. What used to annoy us, they wouldn't stop in their own garden to do their "business" they used to come in our garden to do it. If you didn't mind out when you got a load of hops and you dragged them along, you'd drag them through it. They were devils.'

Jack Larkin is able to portray his experiences vividly, with unusual turns of phrase and effective similes. Here he recalls his first real encounter with the Londoners while he was a young lad working as a waggoner's mate but still living at home.

'When I started work, I used to have to go to either Selling station to pick up the hoppers and their luggage, or if they came from Folkestone and Dover they used to go to Chilham station. But when the Londoners came down, I can tell you this, when we got back after unloading, our mothers wouldn't have us indoors until we'd changed all our garments outdoors. We used to be as lousy as cuckoos. They used to bring all their dirty bedding down. All their dirty, filthy, stinking bedding, they used to bring all that down for to put in the huts. And bugs! Oh Lord, bed bugs! There was plenty of them. Our mother used to make us hang our garments up and give them a good shake, and she used to disinfect them with some powder and she wouldn't have them indoors. We had to undress ourselves in the lodge, and the next morning too. We kept them clothes until we finished, like.

'Then going back, they used to leave all their stinking bedding behind. And the straw, the farmer wouldn't have the straw back in his yards because of his animals getting the fleas and the lice. We used to burn all the lot as far away from the huts for safety. Going back, we used to look forward to taking the hoppers back again, because outside Chilham station was a pub and they used to go in the pub, and Selling station there was the Sondes Arms. 'Course, us chaps with the horses always used to get a drink. Plenty of beer then. Then some would give us a bob, some a tanner. That was jolly good money in them days, you know. We used to dress our horses up and the waggons. It was about dahlia time at the end of hop picking and we used to put dahlias and all Michaelmas daisies all round the waggon, dress them up and make a proper gala day of it.'

Dirt was not the only problem. The high spirits of the Londoners, which locals welcomed to some extent because it put a bit of life into their otherwise mundane existence, were also manifested in bad language and fights. Village children were kept away from the visitors as much as possible, 'because of the language'. Weekends in particular, when the husbands came down to see their families, were 'not very pleasant'. Lacking comfort in the huts the pickers naturally retired to the pubs for a 'good gargle' and 'jollification'. The result was often amusing, and locals often aided and abetted them in their drinking, as Freda Vidgen recalls.

'On Sundays, outside the Pig and Whistle was like cup final night. We had clothing stalls, billy cans and hurricane lamps, all the things they would want to buy for a camp. It used to be so crowded, so chocker-block, that my father used to collect all the children and we would have to have a crocodile through them to Sunday School. We children used to be afraid of them really because they were all singing.

'Well, during my childhood the licensing hours were altered and the pubs closed at 2.30 p.m. My aunt, a very enterprising woman, lived in the cottage next door to the pub and all the washing baths which were about, I should think fourteen to sixteen gallons of water, the galvanised baths we did our washing in, they all hung in the shed but hop picking time they hung on the wall outside her house. She knew, about just before 2.30 p.m., men would come round and hire the baths for 6d. Sixpence was quite something in those days and she had three baths so she had 1s. 6d. The men would have a whip-round and go in the pub and buy five, seven gallons of beer, whatever the baths held, so they could stay outside and lay over the road on the grass verge and drink until the pubs opened again at six o'clock. They drank from tin cans, billy cans, enamel mugs, and you've never seen anything funnier than a man who is already half drunk trying to drink beer from the pook of his cap . . . We as children were frightened of all this noise and carrying on.'

Generally speaking, however, they let them get on with it. Fights were regular occurrences and once the beer started 'talking' offence was soon taken to a couple of words out of place. Women too 'could fight just as much as the men could. In fact, sometimes more.' The local policemen stayed well out of the way. They were, as they all realised, comparatively helpless in such circumstances and knew it was better to let the high spirits be worked out naturally. The sight of a blue uniform tended to incite them to more violence—'regular dangerous they was.'

Despite the life, money and new popular songs which the Londoners injected into the quiet rural society, therefore, they were always a long way from being integrated into it. The complete disruption which they brought with them, the high spirits, bad language and above all their dirty habits ensured that there was always a cultural barrier between them and the locals. They were a necessary but unwelcome intrusion. There were sighs of relief all round when they left. Everybody, admitted one lady from Marden, was 'always glad when they went back'.

Part II

Fishermen

Chapter 7

Fishing and Fishermen

It was a wonderful life out there. I wouldn't have changed my
life as it was out there for anything. The variation! Wonderful
life.

Sonny Stroud, Whitstable fisherman

Over-fishing, pollution, poaching, illegal fishing by foreign boats
inside territorial waters, the improper use of undersized mesh in nets
—one could be forgiven for imagining these were comparatively
recent problems facing the fishing industry. Far from it. All of these
topics were raised regularly by fishermen or their representatives at
official enquiries throughout the nineteenth century. One of the many
attempts to exercise tighter control over fishing activities was the
passing of the Sea Fisheries Regulation Act in 1888, which permitted
the newly formed county councils to establish Local Fisheries
Committees. The committees had power to make bye-laws to restrict,
prohibit or control any form of sea fishing off their coasts, to prevent
'the deposit or discharge of any solid or liquid substance detrimental
to sea fish', and to authorise the laying of oyster beds. Fishery
officers, with the same authority and status as police constables, were
appointed to enforce these measures and supply the committee with
information. The Kent and Essex Sea Fisheries Committee, jointly
staffed by county council members and representatives of the

professional fishermen, was set up in 1890 with jurisdiction over the coastline from Dungeness in the south to Harwich in the north. It is clear from the evidence which members of this, and other regional committees, presented before the Departmental Committee on In-shore Fisheries in 1914, that they found their policing role a difficult one. Not only had they a long stretch of coastline to supervise, but they had to contend with very disparate fishing communities, employing a wide range of fishing methods and landing a regular farrago of fish. The actual statistics and commentaries for each of the Kentish fishing stations which the committee supplied to the Board of Trade clearly demonstrated this variation. They form the basis of much of the following survey.

Of the thirteen fishing ports listed each year in their official statistics, Ramsgate undoubtedly had the strongest claim to be called the foremost port in Kent (see Fig. 2). As early as 1878 a commentator had described it as 'the most important fishing port on the east coast between the Thames and Plymouth', and little occurred to disturb its dominance before 1914. Only Whitstable presented any serious challenge to it and even then could only match the value of the Ramsgate catch in exceptionally good years. In addition, while Ramsgate maintained a steady or slowly rising income, Whitstable's fluctuated wildly. In 1891, for example, Whitstable's catch, comprised almost exclusively of oysters, was valued at £98,004, as against Ramsgate's £66,128. A mere four years later, however, Whitstable was in the depths of depression, its oysters netting only £27,081. The value of Ramsgate's catch only once fell below £70,000 during the rest of the 1890s. The boats which operated from the port were almost entirely deep sea trawlers and they worked all the year round. Some inshore drifting for mackerel, herring and sprats did develop on a small scale in the 1900s, and dredging for whelks, which found a ready demand in the local seaside resorts, accounted for about £1,000 of its annual catch. But, as Dr James Murie of the Sea Fisheries Committee remarked in 1914, the bulk of the fleet consisted of 'an enormous number of vessels of the deep sea'. All the boats which plied from Ramsgate before 1914 were sail powered, and of the 174 belonging to the station in 1903, 160 of them were engaged solely in trawling. The majority of these were large boats, 138 of them first class vessels with keels in excess of 45 feet. They fished the North Sea for upwards of a week at a time, possibly even landing their catch elsewhere if the weather prevented them returning to port, or if the market opportunities for their fish were better elsewhere. The lifestyle was rough and the smack owners had no qualms about using men

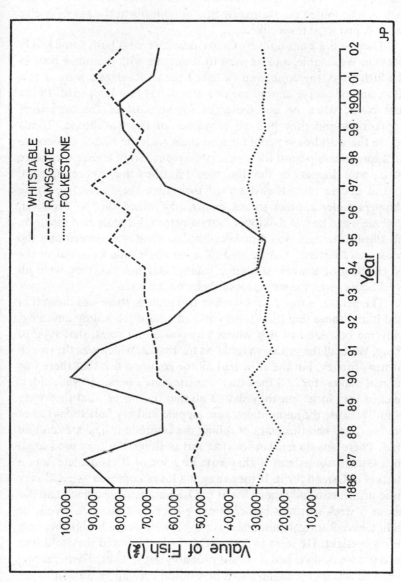

Fig. 2 The value of fish of all kinds landed at Ramsgate, Whitstable and Folkestone 1886–1902

and boys who had certain pressures put on them to sign on. Robert Dale (1891–1975), a Whitstable man, remembers being told by his father, who joined the Ramsgate fleet voluntarily at the age of twelve in 1878, just what it was like.

'There was a boat built by Collar Brothers, who built some lovely boats in Whitstable, and he went to Ramsgate with their new boat as the fifth hand, the cook, and he fished out at Ramsgate a week at a time, and of course he told me of a few things that happened. In the first place, when he got there, he found most of the men were apprentices and they had all come out of the workhouse. That's where the workhouse people placed them with the smack owners on an apprenticeship until they were twenty-one. So of course they were pretty well skippers by the time they'd finished their apprenticeship, and of course after they'd served their time they were free to be skippers under another smack owner. My father, on one occasion, told me when he was a skipper, only nineteen, his mate was nineteen, his third fisherman was nineteen, his deckhand was sixteen and the cook was fourteen, and he said all us young chaps were out in the North Sea for a week at a time fishing. But he said, they were all workhouse boys, the whole lot of them, but he wasn't.

'The people in those days were in two groups, there was those that had it and those that didn't. So you had a hard job selling anything, only the best kind of fish which was plaice and soles, that type of thing. Well, all the prime was sold on the market which was the smack owner's money, but the crew had all the common fish that there was no real market for. All the other was the crew's perks. It was sold, it fetched very little, but they shared all that on top of what they were paid—because the apprentices were all paid and my father was too of course. They had this extra of selling the common fish, skates and all that. There was no market for that sort of thing, but they used to go into Ostend sometimes if they caught a lot of it, and there was a market in Ostend for it. If they caught a lot of common fish and very little prime, naturally they took it to Ostend, then came back and did about a week's fishing before coming back to Ramsgate. Well, he didn't leave Ramsgate until he was about twenty-two, I think, because of his eyesight. He went to Moorfields in London and they told him he'd got weak sight and it would probably get weaker. Then, fearing when he was on the night-watch he wouldn't see all he wanted to see and endanger the lives of the others, he decided he'd come back to Whitstable. Luckily, the woman he lodged with at Ramsgate persuaded him to put his money, instead of leaving it in his room, in a Post Office Savings Bank, and he saved so much—I don't know he got it, but he got it off that awful fish as they call it, the fish that had no value—and he bought half a boat with his brother, it was only £100, a second-hand forty foot cutter, and a house, a £165 cottage, new.'

Mr Dale's account is substantially correct. Ramsgate, in common with several other deep-sea fishing ports, almost exclusively on the east coast, relied heavily on apprentices from workhouses for its crews. Unlike Hull, Lowestoft, Scarborough, Harwich and Yarmouth, however, where the apprenticeship system was beginning to die out by the 1890s, in Ramsgate it continued to thrive. In 1893 there were 150 ex-workhouse boys and youths under the age of twenty-one serving apprenticeships on the Ramsgate smacks. Only Brixham and Grimsby had more, and the latter port experienced considerable difficulty in holding on to the boys. A substantial proportion were committed to prison for breaching their indenture terms, while others successfully absconded and fled to Hull where they could earn much higher wages as weekly hands. Ramsgate, however, had taken great pains to ensure the continuation of the system and to comply with the provisions of the Merchant Shipping (Fishing Boats) Act of 1883. This act had fixed a lower age limit of thirteen years for apprentices, restricted their employment to boats over 25 tons, encouraged the extension of social amenities for the boys when on shore, and appointed superintendents in each port to deal with violations of the terms of indenture. The outcome was a drastic reduction in the number of prisonable offences. While some 10 per cent of apprentices were committed in 1878 for breaches of their terms, there were scarcely any by the 1890s when offences were invariably settled in a 'domestic fashion'. A report on the system in 1894 was generous in its praise. 'Earnest and successful efforts' had been made in Ramsgate, it said, 'to improve the condition of the boys by keeping them under supervision when they are on shore, by carrying out the provisions of the Act of 1883 in a sympathetic spirit, and by the establishment of a well equipped and kindly managed fisherboys' home.'

Although the life was unquestionably a hard one for young boys, all those involved tended to agree that the apprenticeship system had much to recommend it. For Poor Law Guardians throughout the country, the fishing industry provided openings for boys who 'at the age of 14 or 15 and who from having been brought up among vicious surroundings or from some defect of character are not fit for domestic service'. Writing to the compilers of the 1894 report, the superintendent of Edmonton Poor Law Schools remarked that 'It should be borne in mind that it is only the stronger, rougher lads that are sent to sea from these schools, boys that it would be very difficult to do anything else with.' Fishing, however, provided them with a trade, board and lodging with the job and an opportunity for those 'sufficiently steady and skilful' to progress to successful skippers or even smack owners in ports where the majority of the vessels were still relatively small and not controlled by large, capitalist concerns. Fishermen, once qualified, were capable of earning exceptionally good money. The authors of the 1894 report could think of no trade 'where so much money can be earned by men of average skill, without capital . . . Many of the most prosperous smack owners started off as Union apprentices.' The master, willing to cater for the daily needs of the boys, was also rewarded with a relatively cheap, stable and skilful crew. Despite these apparently indisputable advantages, however, and the continued support of official bodies, the apprenticeship system in fishing, as in almost every other craft and trade, continued to decline steadily in the 1890s and 1900s.

The emphasis placed on prime fish and plaice at Ramsgate was reflected in the annual fishery statistics. Although varying amounts of skate, ray, soles, dogfish, whiting, turbot, brill, cod, lemon soles, dabs, and conger eels, to list but a few of the species, were regularly landed on the quayside, none of them rivalled the quantity of plaice which passed through the port, upwards of 20,000 cwt in most years just before 1914.

Folkestone was the only other Kentish port involved in deep-sea fishing to any extent, and the only one capable of matching Ramsgate's diverse catch. The annual value of the fish landed, however, was generally little more than one-third that of Ramsgate, and consisted of a much larger proportion of lower priced fish. Plaice and prime fish such as brill, sole, and turbot were only landed in small quantities. Dogfish actually comprised the majority of Folkestone's catch in some years, and there were fluctuating amounts of mackerel, herring and sprats. Nevertheless, fish to the value of about £30,000— no mean sum—were consistently landed at Folkestone during the pre-war years. Deep-sea trawling was practised on a much smaller scale than at Ramsgate, and usually only for the early part of the year. More common were inshore trawling and drifting which only involved day trips from the port. In addition, lines were frequently used for catching wet fish; whelks, lobsters and crabs were collected in basket nets and pots, and even the occasional oysters found themselves dredged up and brought into the railway owned harbour. Folkestone's fishing fleet was some 95 in number in 1903 but the majority of the boats were noticeably smaller than those at Ramsgate, and consisted mainly of second class vessels between 26 and 45 feet long, and unclassified third class boats. Only five were designated as first class and none of these matched the Ramsgate trawlers for size.

No other fishing station, with the exception of Whitstable, came close to matching the value or variety of fish landed at these two ports. Dover, despite the commercial importance of its harbour, paid little attention to fishing. It is true that variable but usually relatively small quantities of fish of all descriptions amounting in value to between £4,000 and £7,000 were landed here each year, but much of this was accounted for by boats from other ports who fished the Channel and put into Dover in bad weather or when their catches were too small to justify returning to their regular base. Dover, therefore, was primarily a meeting place for fishermen from elsewhere. There were rarely more than twenty fishing boats belonging to the port and although they engaged in trawling, drifting, long lining and even seining for mackerel and mullett on occasions, their owners were always quick to spot more profitable pursuits. In 1910, for example, the local fishery officer reported that 'recently local boats have given up fishing as they have found better employment in attending to the fleet. Very little line fishing has been done. No sprats or mackerel were caught locally in the drift nets. The boats usually employed in this mode of fishing have been engaged in salvage work in connection with the German ship *Preussen*. The landings of escallops were considerably below those of previous years.' The last trade was apparently being lost to Newhaven which was nearer the beds.

Between Dover and Ramsgate were the fishing stations of Deal, Walmer and Kingsdown. Despite persistent references to Deal in tourist guide books as an old, important and definitely quaint fishing town, it was by this time comparatively insignificant. Deal owed its continuing reputation not to its professional fishermen but to its angling connections. It was, indeed it still is, a mecca for the amateur, pleasure-motivated angler, and was already a headquarters of the British Sea Anglers' Society in the 1900s. By 1914, according to Dr Murie, anglers thronged on to the pier 'in great numbers' and local boatmen, always quick to exploit the situation, naturally found taking paying anglers out in their boats a more profitable and less precarious pursuit than fishing. The result, claimed some local fishermen, was that Pegwell Bay was being ruined as a fishing ground 'just to give the Cockney an idea of what sea fishing is'. Kingsdown was the least thriving of the three stations. Not only did the value of its catch decline steadily but the number of boats engaged in fishing also fell. Fishermen complained bitterly of the poor rail facilities for transporting their fish to market, while the local fisheries official commented frequently on the 'large amount of traffic near this station' which impeded fishing operations. Even potting for crabs and lobsters, once a regular occupation off the coast, declined drastically. The value of the fish landed at the other two stations rarely exceeded much more than £1,000 a year, however, even though the three places together could boast a small flotilla of boats, some 165 in number, in 1903. With the exception of just three, all the boats were less than 22 feet long, and, being on the exposed east coast, they were frequently prevented from putting off by rough seas. When involved in serious fishing, most of them drifted for mackerel, herring and, most especially, sprats. Edgar's of Deal, a well known tinning factory, was their main customer, but since the fishermen relied so heavily on this one outlet whose demand was dictated by its processing capacity, they found that when sprats were available in abundance, prices were liable to plummet. Many fishermen thus kept their boats on the beach even when they were confident that there were plenty of sprats available for the taking.

Margate and Broadstairs are more usually portrayed as holiday resorts, but both of them supported a modest fishing trade. Broadstairs was much the smaller of the two with only twenty-four, small, mainly unregistered boats fishing from there in 1903. They employed a variety of fishing techniques—drifting, long lining, and even shore nets for prawns and shrimps during the summer—but they were mainly engaged in potting crabs and lobsters for the local market. The quantities of fish despatched inland by rail appear to have been negligible. The trade was never particularly developed here nor were the fishermen very keen to extend it. According to Dr Murie, they consisted mainly of 'old men' who made 'a living, fair and moderate but quite satisfactory to them'. There were about 50 boats at Margate during this period, almost all of them small, third class vessels, which were used for a wide variety of fishing, encompassing the inshore practices of the east coast ports and the approaches of the stations along the Thames estuary which relied to a much greater extent on shellfish.

Although there was a certain amount of inshore trawling and lining for wet fish and sprats in the Thames most of the fishing communities along the north Kent coast owed their existence to shellfish. The increasing pollution of the coastline, caused not only by London effluent but by the discharge of sewage from the north Kent towns, thus posed a serious threat to their prosperity and none of them was able to avoid entirely its harmful effects. Gravesend, once a thriving fishing port, was in rapid decline, although there were still twenty boats based there in 1903, mainly using trawl and hose nets for shrimps and stow nets for sprats. The annual value of the fish landed in Gravesend, however, had already been quartered in the 1890s and by 1914 only a few shrimpers were left. Queenborough, too, found it increasingly difficult to maintain its fishing industry, although it was still ranked as the fourth most important port in Kent in the late 1920s. The town's famous oyster fishery slumped dramatically. Only a small portion of the extensive beds belonging to the Queenborough fishery was being cultivated by the mid-1890s when Dr H. Timbrell Bulstrode visited the town to compile a report on the cultivation and storage of oysters for the Local Government Board. Even this area of the Swale, known as Long Reach, was not operated by the company but leased to a private oyster merchant who imported Portuguese and French oysters to lay on the beds each April, and then dredged them up for market as required. There was no attempt to cultivate young oysters or keep them over the winter, and the storage pits on Queenborough Causeway and at Long Reach had already fallen into disuse. The scarcity of brood and halfware, which had affected all oyster fisheries in the last quarter of the century, probably accounted for this depressed state. Dr Bulstrode's report of 1896 gave the town a clean bill of health. The badly polluted Milton Creek, over four miles away from the oyster layings, was then considered too far away to be a potential hazard. Nevertheless, whereas an average 1.8 million oysters were dispatched each year from Queenborough between 1902 and 1906, the figure was as low as 66,000 by 1912.

After a relatively prosperous period in the 1890s, the East Swale station, which included Faversham, experienced a similar slump in the 1900s. Although oysters and other shellfish—especially cockles, whelks and periwinkles—formed the bulk of its trade, this was also once an important centre for all sorts of fishing: inshore trawling, drifting, dredging and shrimping with beam nets. The long established oyster fishery, incorporated into the Faversham Oyster Company in 1840, had never enjoyed the same success as its close neighbours at Whitstable and was only in business on a small scale at this time. Nevertheless, the value of oysters and shellfish collected here regularly topped £4,000 each year in the 1890s and was even as high as £12,800 in 1899. This can be partially explained by the fact that two other concerns were based here. The East Kent Oyster Company operated some beds just west of Harty Shore Ferry and others north of the

Whitstable company's ground, and the Anglo-Portuguese Oyster Company imported oysters for laying on the beds in the Swale. All the oyster layings were considered safe in 1896, although Dr Bulstrode warned in his report that 'oysters laid down or dredged up near the mouth of Faversham creek would run risk of pollution from the untreated Faversham sewage'. Within seven years the damage was done. In 1903 the fishery officer explained that oysters 'on examination, were found to be contaminated. The fishermen allege this is caused by the local sewage being discharged into Faversham creek.' In subsequent years the value of the fish landed rarely reached £2,000. 1910 was an equally disastrous year 'owing to the pollution of the beds by sewage'. An average number of 423,610 oysters were landed each year between 1902 and 1906. The average for 1907–11 was a trifling 89,860. Even a revival in 1912 was only short-lived.

Two major fishing communities remain to be examined to complete this brief survey of the county's fishing: Whitstable, 'one of the most curious places on the coast of Kent', according to one local tourist guidebook, and Dungeness, an equally curious place but one accorded far less attention than it deserves. These are dealt with in greater detail in separate chapters in the rest of this section.

Nearly all these Kentish fishing ports received a huge fillip in the latter half of the nineteenth century from the spread of railways and the boost to consumption provided by the steadily improving standard of living throughout the country. Although fishermen along the Thames had been sending a large proportion of their fish, especially their shellfish, to London by hoy or barge for well over a hundred years, many fishermen had relied on disposing of the bulk of their catch through local outlets: at markets like Folkestone, to itinerant salesmen, or to fishmongers in the towns and seaside resorts. Local outlets continued to be favoured by many fishermen well into the present century: they received prompt payment, they could deal directly with the buyers and they reduced the risk of wastage. Although refrigeration and ice box facilities were becoming more common in central markets it was not uncommon for whole trunk loads of fish to be rejected on arrival at the London market, especially if they had been delayed in transit. Smoking still remained the predominant method of preserving fish. Indeed, for many country dwellers, fish was synonymous with the bloaters which they bought from travelling salesmen. The local markets, however, were incapable of absorbing the increasing quantities of fish being landed, and, despite the fears the fishermen harboured about the integrity of distant salesmen in London who acted on their behalf, the magnetic pull of Billingsgate increased, and special fish trains were laid on to cater for the traffic.

By the 1890s every fishing station except Kingsdown had a rail head, and judging by their repeated complaints about marketing facilities, the fishermen there undoubtedly recognised their lack as a major disadvantage. Prior to 1899 when they came to a working arrangement several ports were served by two rival railway companies, the South Eastern and the London, Chatham and Dover. Ramsgate men invariably used the latter company's more direct line with the capital along the north Kent coast. Those at Whitstable, however, still patronised the South Eastern's short branch line to Canterbury since it was directly linked to the harbour, but the figures for the 1890s show a marked shift in favour of the rival company despite the fact that its station was much further inland. A trifling 6 per cent of the catch was dispatched by this route in 1885. The figure was as high as 24 per cent by 1890, 29 per cent in 1895, and, in 1897, an exceptional year, it even topped 57 per cent. Apart from these two ports, and Margate, Dover and Gravesend, the rest of the county's fishermen were reliant on one or other company. In addition to using their local rail head, some fishermen chose to dispatch their catch from other stations. The bleak terminus on the Port Victoria branch line was a popular and easy alternative for the fishermen from Queenborough and the Medway and several hundred tons of fish were annually put on the rail there. Sittingbourne, too, handled between 200 and 300 tons each year.

Despite the annual reports, frequent enquiries and voluminous statistics about the fishing industry, scant attention was paid to the fishermen themselves. On only two occasions during this period did the authorities show a major interest in their welfare. Although the Ramsgate apprentices, the subject of the 1894 enquiry, were not typical of the rest of the county's fishermen, they merited examination because they were in effect juvenile hired hands, and, in common with their policy towards the employment of children in factories, workshops and from 1886 even retail premises, the government felt responsible for their conditions of work. As 1914 approached, the government became increasingly concerned about a possible diminution in the number of fishermen in the country. Their concern this time, however, was with national security, not working conditions. The arms race with Germany, especially in the naval sphere, was foremost in their minds. Fishermen had always comprised a large proportion of naval recruits, and even those who stayed at their jobs often joined the voluntary Royal Naval Reserve. Of the forty-four men in the R.N.R. at Whitstable in 1913, exactly half were fishermen. The proportion was even higher at Folkestone and just over the county border at Rye.

Fishermen expressed a similar lack of interest in their relations with official bodies established to oversee their affairs. Although they were allotted half of the seats on the Kent and Essex Sea Fisheries Committee they rarely attended. To do so would have involved them in considerable expense, robbing them of valuable fishing time. Their representatives were usually oyster company directors or fish salesmen—in other words, their employers and the men they perpetually regarded with an element of suspicion. They adopted a pragmatic policy in their dealings with any official body: they ignored it except when they thought it could be a useful ally in a struggle to achieve a specific objective such as the expulsion of foreign boats from territorial waters. Then they were not backward in demanding effective action. Otherwise they tended to go about their work unmolested and unconcerned about officialdom. The fact that they were probably frequently overlooked by the census enumerators on their decennial rounds would not have worried them. There were undoubtedly more fishermen based in Kent in 1901 than the 1,235 listed in the census returns.

Despite the diversity of fishing practices, there were remarkable similarities between different fishermen. With the single exception of oyster dredgers, who carefully nurtured their stock on protected grounds, all fishermen were essentially hunters. Apart from an awareness of the need for conservation and returning young or undersized fish to the sea, there was little to distinguish their practices and attitudes from those of primeval men. They simply pursued their prey, often in packs, armed with an arsenal of meshed and hooked weapons, improved and modified over the centuries but still primitive in their origins and functions. Their work routine was not effectively dictated by any legislation. The few attempts that had been made to control their operations could not be enforced effectively. Fishermen were still almost unique among occupational groups in completely ignoring the clear cut distinction between day and night. Natural forces like the weather, the state of the tide, the life cycle and movements of their prey were the primary influences on a fisherman's life style. The bitter complaints fishing communities hurled at each other occasionally, or the hatred different types of fishermen in the same locality often felt for each other, were not far removed from tribal clashes over hunting territories. Drifters, therefore, complained about the harmful effects which trawlers had on the sea bed; oyster dredgers railed against whelk trappers for littering their grounds with whelk pots which fouled their dredges; boat fishermen detested the body of men who filled the shoreline with stake nets; Kentish men resented Essex men coming over to fish off their coast; everyone protested about the foreigners who dared even to approach the British coastline. Bonhomie was maintained only when fish were plentiful.

The universal system of dividing the proceeds of the catch among the crew also paralleled the practices of the early hunters. Sometimes each man received an equal share, sometimes the junior member of the crew or the boy received less. In every case the owner of the boat and equipment took an extra share to cover his costs, but that was his his only perquisite. If the boat needed a crew of four the catch was divided five ways. A good and profitable season, therefore, did not result in the boat owner increasing his share of the proceeds. The members of the crew were, in effect, working for themselves. They were not paid a flat wage. This system had another important consequence. Fishing communities where the share system operated were almost classless. There was no antagonism between the boat owner and his crew: their interests were identical. Threats to their welfare came not from internal disagreements but from the activities of rival groups or outsiders like the middlemen to whom they frequently sold their catch. Since the boats which they used were still relatively small, it was feasible for every crew member, given reasonable luck and a degree of thrift, that all-important Victorian virtue, to aspire to own his own boat. Similarly a run of poor seasons, or the loss of his uninsured boat, could quickly reduce a boat owner to a simple fisherman again. This state of affairs, involving a host of vulnerable entrepreneurs who required a low capital outlay and who not only worked in conjunction with a small group of other men but shared the profits with them, differed immeasurably from the system operated in farming and most manufacturing industry. It engendered co-operation rather than fostering class antagonism.

One other factor was common to all fishermen's lives—uncertainty. Not that the job, unpleasant and hazardous though it often was, was particularly dangerous. Fatal accidents were not common. Boats could not put off in bad weather and experienced fishermen usually acquired a good knowledge of weather lore which they willingly passed on. The precariousness was financial. However skilful he was, a fisherman might be prevented from working by the weather. Mending nets and repairing the boat, although useful and necessary tasks, did not bring in any money. In addition, he could spend days, weeks, even a whole season, fishing regularly but catching very little.

Acquired skills might have enabled him to choose the most likely spots to cast over his nets, but he could never guarantee a specific return. In some seasons the fish simply failed to materialise and the fisherman was helpless to do anything about it. His income could vary considerably over very short periods. One Whitstable man's books for the summer of 1912 show a variation in his weekly share earnings from a high of £2 9s. 6d. in late March to a mere 10s. 9d. in September. By late December he was receiving little more than 4s. in some weeks.

This irregularity in their income, therefore, forced fishermen to take a long term view of their financial positions. They did not talk of weekly amounts but of annual averages. Robert Dale's father, back in Whitstable after his ten year spell at Ramsgate, hoped for £50 per year, much of which he aimed to make from trawling for Dover sole in the summer. The rest of the year he eked out a living where he could. Some men abandoned fishing completely during certain times of the year, others simply changed their methods, alternating between drifting, trawling, seining, or even potting. Despite this variable income few fishermen saved regularly in a bank, unless it was a Post Office Savings Bank when it was easily accessible. Most seem to have kept their money at home as cash. To maintain a constant standard of living throughout the year required sufficient willpower to keep back some of each week's earnings during peak periods and the assistance of one or both of two people, a wife who could keep within a strict budget and a willing creditor, usually one of the local shop-keepers, who would provide short term help in bad times. Many men, however, willingly accepted this drawback to the job. For them, the attractions far outweighed it. They valued the variety, independence and possibilities for bettering themselves which could also be found in fishing.

Chapter 8

Whitstable and its Oyster Dredgers

It is literally true to say that the oyster beds at Whitstable are as
carefully prepared and maintained though always under water,
as if they were flower beds on the shore.

A. O. Collard, *The Oysters and Dredgers of Whitstable* (1902)

Whitstable has long been renowned for the quality of the oysters
which were once cultivated and dredged up off its coast. The 'Royal
Natives', so called because the Whitstable Company of Free Fishers
and Dredgers had obtained a royal charter from George III, were
exported the world over and valued as a special delicacy. In terms of
quantity too, Whitstable was the foremost oyster town in the
country, despite the fact that the grounds were only a few square
miles in extent. The two companies which operated there at the
beginning of the century regularly supplied over half of the national
catch. In 1912, for example, by no means an exceptional year, just
over 33 million oysters were landed in England and Wales, over 19
million of them at Whitstable.

For the oyster loving pilgrim, however, a visit to this highly
esteemed place in the late nineteenth or early twentieth century
would probably have been a little disappointing. During the 1880s
when local oyster 'spat', or spawn, was scarce, the greater part of the

grounds was laid with young French oysters not only 'far inferior to the genuine British bi-valve' according to one author, but even worse, 'even few of these are retained for the consumption of visitors or inhabitants'. In the 1900s although the quality of the oysters was once again improving, visitors to the town remained unimpressed by their place of origin. 'It is at first sight a singularly unattractive place, and the more you see of it, the less you like it,' wrote Charles Harper in his book *The Kentish Coast* (1914). 'The streets are narrow and mean, without the saving grace of picturesqueness, and the seafront adds to the squalor by being occupied by the railway station and a very coaly dock.' Charles Igglesden echoed his views. Instead of finding the air 'pregnant of that delicious, fresh, though faint, salty odour that his majesty "the Royal" emits', he was 'rather overcome with coal dust up by the station, which lies near the harbour depots where colliers unload all day, and sometimes all night long. And when you leave that end of the town you come past black huts that smell of pitch and wooden buildings that smell of paint and tar, for boats that go out to sea are built here.'

The truth of the matter was that there was much more to Whitstable than oysters. 'The average boy that was brought up here then went in for about four different things,' commented Arthur 'Sonny' Stroud, who was born in the town in 1900. 'Either shipwright, and of course they had to go apprentice to them for four years down one of the shipyards here. Anybody what I call a little better off, say with only two in family, or a skipper of a ship, well, they could put their boys to apprenticeships. The same with the builders. There were about eight or nine big builders about here. They went either as carpenters or bricklayers. But the biggest thing was the sea.' The local economy, therefore, was not totally reliant on oysters. The harbour, built in 1825 and connected by railway to its commercial centre, Canterbury, as early as 1830, was the hub of the town's commerce, and ship building naturally sprang up in the immediate vicinity to cater for the local but very mixed trade. The building boom was of more recent origin. Several farms and estates had been sold off in the 1890s to speculative builders who attempted to develop new residential suburbs on them. Many were abandoned, and the countryside around Whitstable is still dotted with grand-sounding cart tracks and private roads which lead nowhere, but the Tankerton estate expanded rapidly in the 1900s after a shaky start and many smaller terraced houses were also built near the centre of town just off the High Street. Even the sea provided a variety of occupations and many local men joined the Navy or became seamen on the coastal vessels which plied from the port. Nor were the fishermen solely oyster dredgers. They trawled for soles and plaice, dredged for mussels and starfish, went shrimping and spratting, picked periwinkles off the shore, raked for cockles, and engaged in trotting and dredging for whelks. There is no doubt, however, that the majority of the town's fishing community relied to a greater or lesser extent on being involved at some stage with oyster cultivation.

Oyster dredgers had more in common with farmers than they had with other fishermen. They tended and cared for their oysters on protected grounds, clearing them of weeds and vermin, watching over them to keep away poachers and harvesting them systematically when they reached maturity. They collected young oysters, known as spat, brood or half-ware depending on their age, and deposited them on their own grounds just as a farmer would sow his ground. The oysters grew better under some conditions than others, and the situation off Whitstable was ideal. The sea bed needed to be clean but with plenty of cultch (a bed of hard material), stones and shells for the oysters to cling to, and never completely uncovered by the tide and thereby exposed to dangerous winter frosts. In addition, as Edward Johnson, a Whitstable dredger, explained to the Sea Fisheries Commission when they visited the town in 1865, an ideal oyster bed 'should be near the mouth of a river where the fresh water and the salt water join. It should also be in such a position that you can work it continuously and keep it clean. Then again, it is necessary that it should be sheltered as much as possible from heavy sea. Heavy seas rolling in upon oyster beds would do them a considerable amount of injury.' All these attributes were to be found just off Whitstable.

The successful farming of oysters, however, required that certain fishermen be granted exclusive rights over sections of the sea bed. The Whitstable oyster beds were originally leased to companies of fishermen by the Lord of the Manor who owned the foreshore. In 1792, however, Thomas Foord, the new lord, sold his rights to the fishermen who then formed themselves into a self-governing co-operative the following year under an Act of Parliament, the Whitstable Oyster Fishery Act. This allowed them to elect annually at a Water Court, a foreman, deputy foreman, water bailiff and twelve jurymen who then managed their affairs and organised the cultivation and sale of oysters. At Seasalter, the Dean and Chapter of Canterbury leased the grounds to a body of fishermen until 1859 when they were taken over and run by a private concern. By the 1900s both organisations had been incorporated into shareholding companies, the Whitstable Oyster Fishery Company and the Seasalter and Ham Oyster

Fishery Co. Ltd, and were run like any other company employing men to work for them.

Recognising the benefits which accrued from the intensive cultivation of oysters on protected grounds, the Board of Trade recommended in the 1860s that potential companies should be able to obtain licences to take over specified areas of the sea bed which were traditionally common ground. One of the first companies to be established was the Herne Bay, Hampton and Reculver Oyster Fishery Company in 1864. This company was granted exclusive rights over a large area of ground off the coast, some six by one and a half miles in extent, considerably more than either of the companies based at Whitstable. In common with all speculative ventures it was very optimistic in its prospectus, aiming to provide continuous employment for upwards of 2,000 men, five times the number then engaged at Whitstable, and referring to oyster stocks to the value of £5 million. Unfortunately the promoters were unlucky in their timing. For reasons which remained a mystery to all concerned, oysters simply ceased to produce spat from the mid-1860s and many oyster companies all over the country experienced considerable difficulties. The Herne Bay company never really got off the ground. A Board of Trade representative sent to enquire into its operation in the early part of 1876 found it in a sorry state, and concluded that its licence should be revoked, at least for part of the ground. The company employed only two or three boats on a regular basis by 1874 and the grounds were never properly cultivated or cleared of vermin—mussels, dog whelks and five fingers (starfish)—or harmful sea weed and mud. Much to the relief of the other local companies, which had previously dredged over the grounds off Herne Bay for young oysters to lay on their own grounds, the company failed soon afterwards.

All-important for the successful cultivation of oysters was an abundant supply of oyster spat or spawn. Oysters spatted in the summer months and were not considered fit to eat during this time, hence the belief that that should only be eaten during months with an 'r' in their names. Each spring, therefore, the fishermen examined the grounds with magnifying glasses to look for the tell-tale white clouds in the water, and as soon as they appeared they ceased to dredge oysters for market. The only boats allowed on the grounds in the summer months were involved in cleaning them, or in moving oysters from one section of the beds to another. The oyster, much to the dismay of all concerned, was not always reliable, however. In some years spat was produced in vast quantities. In others it never appeared. Even the fishermen could only hazard guesses as to the reason. Hot sultry weather seemed to encourage its production, but local attempts to artificially re-create similar conditions to stimulate the process met with no success.

Whenever possible the oyster companies relied on spat which originated from their own grounds but since it floated down on the tide it was deposited all along the Kent coast towards Margate on what were known as the Kentish flats, or the common ground. From there it was dredged up by flatsmen, men who engaged in a variety of fishing and relied on selling young oysters to the companies as well, and brought back to the beds for laying. In years when the local spat proved insufficient brood and half-ware were imported from elsewhere: Essex, Falmouth, Jersey, Ireland, France, Portugal, indeed from wherever it was available. Although these foreign oysters proved to be tasty specimens if they survived the winters off Whitstable they could not strictly be marketed as the prized 'natives' since they did not originate from the locality. They could also be easily distinguished by their shell markings. Whenever possible, therefore, the oyster companies preferred to buy their stock from local fishermen like Sonny Stroud who explains here how it was done.

'When I first went on the water there was a terrific lot of spat here. It was a good year, and I don't know if you know this but spat floats and it went down with the tide and fell down off Herne Bay. There was so much there they called it "The Confetti Bed". You had to go down there and you caught everything to do with oysters—brood, small or large. Every one was 5s. a wash. That was just over five gallons, 5¼ gallons. You fancy, a shilling a gallon, and most of the oysters was only as big as shillings themselves! Now you fancy how many shillings—five pence pieces now, isn't it?—how many you can get in a gallon measure. That's all the companies were paying for them. Mind you, the four of us in the boat were getting a lot of them. On a good working day, a jolly good working day, possibly sixteen to twenty wash. But I've seen some arguments! We sold ours to the Seasalter and Ham Company and they used to have a foreman down there. Now this here wash measure used to be a little tub and of course, if you had a wash measure of water it would be level, wouldn't it? Well, with oysters it wasn't. It had to have a round top! He used to say, "A few more on", and you used to have to put a few more on. So we used to put them in these here long thin bags, pull them up high and let them out so they used to hover.' Hop pickers would undoubtedly have appreciated the problem and the ruse employed to overcome it.

Plentiful spat was, however, a mixed blessing to the flatsmen. The companies worked on the principle that one good year was sufficient to stock the beds for several seasons. During the 1900s when spat was abundant they eventually ceased to buy from the flatsmen. W. P. Coleman, the flatsmen's representative before the Departmental Committee on Inshore Fishing in 1913, explained their plight.

'. . . For some reason in 1909, they declined to buy and the flatsmen had to work only what they could eke out, a partial living by the mature oysters, whelks, herring and anything else that they caught. Then in 1910, in consequence of that—and it is likely to happen again—the fishermen put in a memorial to the Board of Trade asking them for a grant of the sea bottoms in order that they might form themselves into a Cooperative Society, pretty much on the basis of the Whitstable Oyster Company.' Nothing came of their petition.

Flatsmen, in fact, had frequently been obliged, long before 1909, to leave Whitstable during bad winters to seek employment elsewhere. Robert Dale's father, a flatsman after his return from Ramsgate in 1888, soon found himself forced to travel to find work.

'My father went to Stranraer in Scotland for the season of 1890–91. My mother was expecting me and she went with him and I was born in Stranraer on 9th March 1891. It was better than Whitstable apparently because he had a wage up there. I don't know exactly what he got but when I went up there as a fisherman in 1909 at the age of nineteen for a winter on my own to see where I was born, I had 25s. a week standing wage for six hours a day on the oyster grounds. My father's elder brother spent a long time up there. He was kept on all through the close season, in fact, he was foreman up there when I went up there. His family were born up there, a boy and a girl, and his son came back to Whitstable because the fishing was all right here. I suppose that would be somewhere about 1902. Then we had a depression in Whitstable in 1909 and he went to Aberdeen and was skipper of a trawler from then all through the First War. But my father only went once to Stranraer. My mother wouldn't go any more. She had me up there with no proper midwives and struck a bad patch and so she said, "No. Never any more are you going to take me down there. If you want to go down there in the winter, you go alone. I'll stop here." So he didn't go any more. He hung the winters out in Whitstable.'

Once the young oysters had been laid on the beds of the respective companies they were carefully nurtured. The number of men employed on a continuous basis was, however, quite small, just sufficient to provide watch over the grounds and keep them clean. When additional workers were required to work on the beds dredging up oysters for market or clearing them of exceptionally large numbers of starfish or mussels, the flatsmen were taken on and paid a flat wage for their day's work. Sonny Stroud explains.

'When they had enough oysters, they wanted boats to catch their own oysters on the beds to sell them, so they'd what they called lay it in. They wouldn't buy any more oysters. They'd make you go on their beds to work. There always used to be a foreman on the oyster beds. The oyster company paid him. He was just a workman really. His job, mostly, was to tell you what you had to do when you got out there and what time you all had to start work. You might have to turn out anytime, say three o'clock in the morning, and you worked six hours on the grounds. There wasn't much water on the beds, only about two fathoms and a half, and they were all cut up into squares. They'd have poles all over them. One might have one painted piece of canvas on it. Another might have two. Or it might just be a square or there might be a hole cut in the middle. One of these squares might have just brood on it, little bits of oysters. Then they'd have three or four grounds all fit to sell next year. It was all organised. You had orders to go and work one of them grounds. You had to go and work where you got your orders. They might turn round and say, "Go up on number four ground and catch ten bags," twenty bags, whatever it was. We used to have to work six hours on the ground then but we had to sail out there in our own time. When we'd worked three hours we was allowed ten minutes, a quarter of an hour break to have a snack. When we'd worked six hours the foreman would put a flag up or a bag on a pole and then there'd be a proper race to get home.

'You weren't allowed to go on the grounds at any other time, though. They even had watchmen living aboard boats out there. They were allowed home one weekend a fortnight. They came home Saturday morning and went back Monday morning. The next week they used to come ashore Saturday morning and go back the same day. When they weren't there they sent a relief off. There always had to be somebody there so nobody could steal their oysters. If you went anywhere near them and they thought you was dredging, they'd come and chase you away. Report you. The Essex men used to come across. They had more trouble with them than they did with us. But all the summer, from May to August, when they couldn't sell anything, every mortal boat apart from these watch boats which had to go cleaning up as well, every mortal boat was off the oyster grounds.'

Although the men were paid for only six hours on the beds they were often away for much longer. If there was no wind, they had to row. If there was too much wind they might be called in early and paid less. If high tide was well before daylight they might have to go off early and moor out on the beds till they could see to work. If the weather turned and they were far enough away from the shore they could find themselves in trouble. Robert Dale relates some of his experiences.

'You didn't know how long you was going to be gone. It all depended on how long it took you to get there and how long it took you to get home again. If you had a fair wind out there and could get out of the bay at daylight, then you could start right away. You couldn't get out of the bay at low tide after a certain ebb so often we had to go very early, then if the wind happened to be against you you'd have to tack all the way in, or if it was calm you had to row the big boat in from the little boat. That's how I learned to row. To tell you how much I rowed, one day we had orders to go out there, and it was a fog and calm. Couldn't see very far but the watchboat would ring and let you know the directions to help you get there. We could generally judge it very well. Well, we rowed out there and there was no wind when we got there. We rowed for oysters for six hours in the boat. Three men rowing and one man with a dredge shooting it over the side. At the end of six hours' work out there we had to row ashore again and pull the big boat in again or push it. Sometimes we pushed it. We were gone thirteen hours but we was only paid for six. You see, the firm had to make a time that you should work for your money and it had to be where the work was, on the bed. And the Seasalter and Ham bed where we worked was right out about three miles from Whitstable. In my time we very seldom went to the other bed which was closer in.

'Sometimes you mustered but you never went and you didn't get paid either. If the foreman thought that you couldn't go out there on account of the weather or the tide being wrong with the wind, so you couldn't dredge properly, he would decide not to send you. Another time if you were out there, all of you, and it came on to blow and you was driven in and you'd only done three hours, you only got paid for three hours. If they were short of oysters though, and it was blowing and they still wanted you to go, then all those who would go they would give them their full day's pay even if they could only stop two hours out there because they was obliging them by going for oysters in bad weather when they hadn't got any.

'I think it was 1908. Regatta Day was the last day of August and we'd got orders to go to the beds on 1st September. After we got out there the wind began to freshen and it got right up to a blinkin' gale. Sails began to blow away, because they'd got their summer sails in, you see. They generally got two suits of sails. As they got a bit worn they would have a new set and put the old ones up for the summer when they expected nice weather. So vessels were having their mainsails blow away in all directions. Well, you had to drift with the tide. That's how you caught your oysters by laying to on the wind and going down the beds. Then you had to sail back to the starting point and go down again. Well, when we started to sail back we was half deck under and had to make all our dredges fast, else we'd lose them over the side. All the oysters we caught we had to put down below and we had to sit on the rail because half the boat was under. I remember that when we did start for shore we couldn't come in because the tide was out. We had to stop out there. So, of course, when we thought that the tide should have flowed enough on the flood, we started heading for the shore. We was half deck under all the way in, so the rudder, instead of being upright, was laying over like the boat. We were racing in and just before we got to the bay there's a ridge there, little bank with a buoy on it, and there we laid right over on our side, mainsails almost touching the water because we'd gone into such shallow water, only about three feet or so. Eventually the tide flowed and we got into the bay but then the difficulty was having the little boat, only twelve foot boat, but a good seaworthy boat which took four men in it, we had to bring all these oysters ashore. Of course we could easily have flooded the boat. But we never lost anybody.'

Robert Dale's father was paid 6d. an hour by the Seasalter and Ham company in the 1890s for working the oyster beds. Robert himself earned 4s. a day when he first started. The companies both took considerable precautions to ensure that the men they hired did not attempt to supplement their income by taking the company oysters for themselves. They were frequently subjected to personal searches when they came ashore. Strictly speaking, they were not even allowed to eat any of the oysters they caught out on the grounds while out there. Needless to say, many did. The companies' efforts to prevent stealing were understandable. Oysters were no longer, as they once had been, part of the staple diet of the poor. They were expensive luxuries. Even common oysters fetched over 6s. a hundred on the open market by the 1900s, and Whitstable natives sold for considerably more. As poachers found to their cost, the oysters were also easily identifiable by their shape, taste and colour. The fishermen claimed that they knew the beds so well that they could pinpoint their position in a fog to within a few yards simply by dredging up a few oysters. Poachers, therefore, sometimes found themselves in court simply because they had been found with certain types of oysters in

their possession. Fortunately for them, magistrates, at least in the
nineteenth century, were loath to convict on this evidence alone.
The actual process of dredging was not particularly complicated.
The dredges were simply thrown over the side of the boat which was
then allowed to drift along with the tide. To sail with the wind would
have meant the dredge dragging too quickly over the grounds,
possibly causing damage to the oysters in the process. Pulling the
dredge against the tide resulted in it being lifted off the sea bottom.
The number of dredges in each boat varied, but usually about five or
six were put over from different parts of the boat. The boats themselves, known locally as yawls, were usually manned by a crew of four
on the beds and three on the flats or common ground, and since they
were too large to beach they were moored off the shore and reached
in smaller rowing boats. A dredge consisted of a bag, the under part
made from iron rings, two or three inches in diameter and looped together with a stout wire. Sometimes for working on the beds where
young oysters were laid, a hide base was used. The upper side was
merely strong netting since it was not exposed to so much wear and
tear. The mouth of the bag was fastened on to an iron frame the full
width of the bag but only about four inches deep. The lower part of
the frame was flattened and turned at such an angle as to enable it to
scrape the surface of the sea bed without actually tearing it up. Two
stout iron rods about four feet long were welded to either side of this
frame and connected together into a handle to which the tow rope was
made fast. A wooden rod stretched across the other end of the bag
provided a convenient handhold for the men when they came to
empty the dredge.

Once the dredges had been hauled into the boat their contents
were sorted out or culled. Marketable oysters, usually those four
years or older, were chipped off their cultch with a large knife and the
cultch returned to the sea. Vermin and harmful, smothering seaweed
were piled up separately on one side of the boat. The oysters were
then packed into tubs or boxes or simply collected together in nets
and brought ashore in the small rowing boat after the yawl had been
moored. At one time, when the hoys were the principal means of
transport for taking oysters up to the London market, they were
loaded directly at sea, but by the 1890s most of them went by rail and
further sorting was often carried out ashore before being sent away.
When the number dredged up exceeded the immediate demand both
companies made use of specially constructed storage pits which were
cleaned out regularly and filled with salt water each day by the flood
tide. Dr Bulstrode paid considerable attention to them on his visit in

1896. Both companies' pits impressed him, presenting a 'very cleanly appearance', but he expressed concern over the short distance of the Seasalter company's inlet pipe from the main Whitstable sewer. 'Fortunately', he concluded, 'the pits are not necessary for the operating of the company'. Pollution scares became more common in the 1900s but both companies still maintained large sales nevertheless.

The pattern of work described above, the hiring of flatsmen to work the beds and the system of paying them a daily wage, was comparatively new in Whitstable in the 1900s, at least as far as the Whitstable company was concerned. Prior to 1896 the beds had been worked solely by the Free Fishers and Dredgers of Whitstable. This group occupied a privileged position in the industry, and under their constitution of 1793 membership of the company was restricted to sons of freemen, the eldest son automatically being admitted at sixteen, other sons serving an apprenticeship until they were twenty-one. The profits the men made were equally divided amongst them, with non-working members and widows of ex-members receiving smaller shares. After over a hundred years, however, they were forced to change their constitution into a normal shareholding company with a nominal value of £250,000. Each member of the old company, some 600 in number by that time, received twenty £10 shares, but having experienced nearly thirty poor years when oyster spat was scarce and debts amounting to £60,000 had been accumulated through buying foreign spat to lay on the grounds, many of them soon sold the shares. Control thus passed from the fishermen themselves to a board of directors which consisted of the major shareholders: oyster salesmen, local coal merchants, retired mercantile captains and shipowners. The only privilege which members of the old company retained was that they were hired before other flatsmen when men were needed to work on the beds. Prior to 1896 the men had only been required to work for two hours a day dredging oysters for market, but such a policy did not recommend itself to the new owners. When the daily stint on the grounds increased to six hours the number of men required fell dramatically to a little over 200 by 1914. The whole tone of the fishing in Whitstable also changed. The dredgers no longer worked for themselves. They were paid a flat wage however much the oysters fetched when they were sold. The foremen and the watchmen were no longer guarding their common property, they were company servants paid to protect other men's property. The fishermen who remained at work, and many of them were flatsmen who had never known any other system, regularly complained about the company policies. As W. Coleman explained in 1913, 'The people that worked it before served their whole time and their whole life to it; they were elected every year out from the whole body of members.' The company was now run by men 'not of the same experience'. The change was reflected in the fishermen's political views, as Robert Dale explains.

'I don't suppose anybody voted for Conservatives amongst the fishermen, but they had the Conservatives' free beer in the certain pubs. I remember one man here, he was quite a character, and they were buying free beer to get people to vote for them. This particular fisherman, he was roping them all in to have this free beer. He said, "It doesn't matter who you vote for, come in and have your beer," he said. "You needn't vote for them."

'The fishermen felt they got nothing out of the Conservatives. They didn't even value their employers really because they thought they give them good labour for what they paid them. And when they bought their catch off them on the common ground, they reckoned they wanted too much measure, or they used to beat them down. But in those days there was a lot of shipwrights and they always reckoned they profited by the Conservatives. They spent more money for ships. So we used to have our colours up, red and orange for Conservative and blue for Liberal, and sometimes some of these bigger boys, the shipwrights' apprentices, would try and snatch them off the smaller boys.'

The oyster can still be found in Whitstable but its heyday has long since passed. A sharp frost and a mysterious disease in the winter of 1919–20 killed off a large proportion of the stocks and although trade recovered sufficiently to survive until the 1950s it never again dominated the local economy. The Whitstable Oyster Company lost all its stock in 1962 and since then has bought oysters in from elsewhere for resale. The other company, the Seasalter Shellfish Company, supplies brood oysters. Cultivation itself has ceased. There are no poles marking out the oyster beds off the shore, no watch boats, no picturesque fleet of oyster yawls. The final words are Sonny Stroud's. 'It's like a garden, you know, an oyster bed is. That's the reason it's no good now. It's all open. Anybody can go there now. All finished.'

Chapter 9

Whelk Trappers

1901 they came here from Sheringham in Norfolk . . .

Bob Bishop

The oyster fishermen of Whitstable may have a lengthy and well documented history but its whelk trappers have not. They arrived in the early years of this century from Sheringham in Norfolk, not in great numbers, it is true—only four or five boat loads at first—but sufficient to cause 'great disputes' with the local fishermen. Possibly the migrants' greatest shortcoming, at least in the eyes of the local community, was that they were simply 'foreigners'. But more concrete reasons were soon found to complain of their presence. For one thing, they introduced whelk trapping in pots, a method previously unknown in the area. Whelk catching by dredging or trotting had of course long been carried out in Whitstable. Indeed, whelks were widely recognised as a potential enemy of the oyster, capable of boring through the shell and literally sucking the oyster out, but whelk catching was viewed primarily as providing temporary relief during hard times. As W. P. Coleman remarked before the Departmental Committee on Inshore Fishing in 1914, it was 'intermittent work' carried on only when the fishermen 'cannot do anything else'. Although the whelkers did not, therefore, compete directly with a major

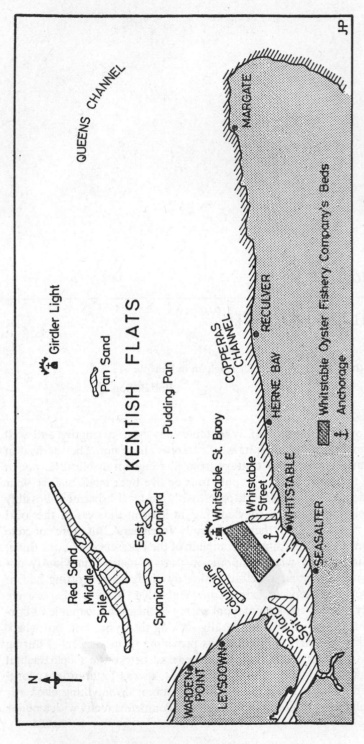

Fig. 3   The Kentish Flats off Whitstable, showing areas mentioned in the text

section of Whitstable's fishing community, and despite the fact that they cleared the oyster beds of whelks more thoroughly than ever before, they were nevertheless heavily criticised.

Trapping, according to the locals, resulted in the decimation of young whelks who formed the basis of future years' catches. Dredging was free from this danger because the size of the mesh could be regulated to allow small whelks to slip through, but, as Coleman explained, '. . . In trapping, you see, you catch all sizes and the consequence is that whelk fishing has declined. They come down to a lower size. A fisherman will take everything he can sell, he has to be protected against himself, but if you confine him to a certain size dredge, and do away with the trapping, he could only catch a certain size and he would not need to come down to that size to injure the fishery.' Judging by the decline in the quantity of 'other shellfish' landed at Whitstable in the early years of this century there could well have been some truth in these accusations. The oyster fishermen persistently called for legislation to limit the minimum size of whelks which could be sold in an attempt to control the trapping which they thought indiscriminate and criminal. Unfortunately the whelkers also laid their pots over precisely the same ground where the flatsmen went dredging for brood and half-ware. They were, not surprisingly, accused of obstructing dredging operations and destroying the beds. When representations on the part of the oyster dredgers to the Sea Fisheries Committee and the Board of Trade elicited expressions of sympathy but no action, the men took retaliatory measures of their own. 'The whelk fishermen', commented the local Sea Fisheries official for 1908 (a relatively poor year for oysters), 'lost a large number of their pots.'

Despite these initial problems, however, the whelk trappers were gradually integrated into the community. Bob Bishop's father was one of the original Sheringham men who married a Whitstable girl and settled there. As a boy, Bob (born 1905) often went out with his father in his boat and, for a few years just after the First World War, he and his younger brother operated a boat themselves and witnessed the gradual ousting of sail by the internal combustion engine. Here he describes vividly, yet in simple terms, how and where the whelkers carried out their business, describes their boats and equipment, the variety of whelks which they caught, the disputes which arose with the dredgers and how the arrival of motors affected the pattern of their work.

'Whitstable whelkers, years ago, never used whelk pots. They didn't know what they were. They used to go what they call trotting.

They used to get fish offal, fix it in bunches, and sink it in the sea and leave it for a short period of time, then they'd go and have these up and the whelks would be stuck to the bait. See, a whelk had got like a tube that sucks everything. It'll clean a crab out, all up the legs as clean as a whistle. So these whelks would actually be sucking the bait. But when these whelkers came, they brought their whelk pots. These had iron frames, cast-iron bottoms, iron ribs and rope twisted round the iron stays but so that there was a gap between the ropes as you went round up the pot. Then they curved over inwards at the top and there was a small hole, and hanging inside that was a small net called a crinny. That was about four meshes deep and it used to hang down inside so that the whelks, when they went into the pot and wanted to climb out again, came up the inside of the pot and got up against this crinny. In the middle of the pot they had what they called a bar. It was two bits of rope with like a button on it, and they used to put the bait in between the two strands of rope and push the button to hold it. That was in the middle of the pot. They used to use fish offal again as bait, and crabs, what we called red bellies. Although you could eat them they weren't really edible crabs. They were a smaller crab. They used to kill these crabs by breaking them, hitting them between the eyes on the edge of the thaught or seat of the boat, and put those in the bar. The whelks used to suck every bit out of them so they'd be hollow and when you went to get hold of them to pull them out the next day they used to collapse. We used to bait up sometimes with red herring. We'd perhaps cut a herring in half and put half in each pot. These whelks, when you pulled them out of their shell and you looked at them, you could tell they'd been baited with herring by the colour. And you could taste it! You could taste the herring. They used to taste horrible, they did really.

'Then there was what we called a strop, a short bit of rope to make the pot fast to the tows or rope. These whelk pots were then put in lines—they were called shanks—about thirty to thirty-two whelk pots in a line with a buoy at one end and a buoy at the other end. We never had big buoys in those days, in fact we had paint cans, gallon or two gallon paint cans. We used to cork them and tar them, and perhaps put a dob of paint or something on them so you'd know your upper or lower shank when you got out to them. Most times you had what they called four shanks of pots, which would be 120. Some had five, which would be 150, 160 whelk pots altogether. Each day you went out and hauled them up and perhaps you'd get hold of what you called the inside buoy one day, and perhaps the next day the wind would be different and you'd get the outside buoy. Anyway you had about eleven fathom of rope between each whelk pot. You pulled them up, emptied the whelks out and put the bait in. While one was hauling the other used to stack them in the boat. After you'd got them all up and baited, then you turned them over a different bit of ground, like. We used to kind of shoot them across the tide, and you had to know which pot was next to throw over the side because you'd got a hell of a lot of rope there, you see.

'Sometimes when it was very rough, the pots used to get moved about on the bottom, and it was surprising how they used to get tangled up. We had to get them up the best way we could, sometimes two or three at a time. Then again, sometimes we'd get foul of the dredging boats. They used to cut them when they were dredging. We'd lose perhaps five, six, eight or even ten pots if they cut some out of the middle of the shank. What we had to do then was grapple for them. We had a long iron, about a foot long, with all these hooks on it, and we dragged it along the bottom until we got hold of the rope in between two pots and then we pulled them up, and had to sort them out. Sometimes the dredging boats used to pull two or three up and they'd bring them ashore themselves and bring them round to the whelkers, and the whelkers had to give them something for bringing them ashore, you see. At times, that was a bit of a racket really because the boats that were dredging had, like the whelkers, poor weeks and that, and they used to make a bob or two the best way they could. The whelkers used to have quite a bit of trouble like that to start with, but in the end they got used to one another and in the latter part of the time the dredgers wouldn't foul the gear if they could help it.

Of course, the whelkers covered so much ground where these dredging boats wanted to go, so that's why they didn't like it. They used to cover a few acres, all these whelk boats did. You see, with four shanks of whelk pots with ten or eleven fathom of rope between each pot, spread out—and that's just one boat—it was a terrific expanse altogether. And of course, when they first got here, the Sheringham men were foreigners and they weren't welcome anyway. Sometimes they even used to foul one another's gear, and there used to be arguments about that. If somebody was catching a lot of whelks and somebody else was catching few whelks, then they used to go and get as near to those that were catching them on a bit of ground. They'd come and shoot where you were going to shoot over the next day, or they'd shoot in front of you so that you had to jump over the top of theirs. Sometimes when you came to haul your gear in one day you'd find there was another piece of rope you were pulling up. Of course, the arguments never got too serious as regards fighting, but they used to tell one another off.

'Most times of course they used to be spread out a bit. They used to go up off Warden Point, up above there in a place they used to call Church in Hole. There's a place up there where you had whelks that were great big things. They used to call them onions, and they had what they used to call Roman writing on them, marks on the shells. The shells were big but the whelks were tough. Some of the customers didn't like them because you couldn't put them on plates and sell them, they were so big and tough. Yet two miles further up to the north, where we used to call up by the Spile Buoy, you used to get lovely little whelks. They used to taste lovely. The best tasting whelks I've ever tasted. But up at the West Spaniard Buoy they were big whelks, and also down at the Queen's, they were big whelks down there as well. I couldn't tell you at all why it was. On what they call the flats, off Swalecliffe like and round there, they used to be lovely little whelks, sweet and nice tasting. The only reason we used to catch those big ones was when you had to get those or nothing at all. As soon as ever they were crawling about in shallower water we used to move in. Another thing about whelks, we used to get what they called a red whelk or Armontail. You never used to get many in a pot but they were lovely to eat. Not a bit tough. Now and again we used to get one in a whelk pot but mostly they caught them by dredging them up in an oyster boat. And left handed whelks. They were very scarce and you'd have a job to notice them, but my father was pretty good. Of course if you went to pull the whelk out of the shell, you could tell then it was left handed because it felt cackhanded to take them out with a turn. You know, usually they had the opening one way but these had the opening the other way.

'With sailing boats they never used to go outside what we called the Red Sand, like we did later with the motor boat, and it was only in hot weather when we used to go out there to get the deeper water for the whelks to crawl. You see, when it's very cold or very hot, they get lazy and never crawl very much so when I worked with my brother in the motor boat we used to take our gear and work in deep water outside the Red Sand. It was very deep there and the tide used to run the buoys under sometimes so we had to be there at low water and work like billy-o so that we could find the gear. It didn't matter how much tow you had on for the buoy, it used to run under in the tide because it was quite sharp. It was pretty hard work out there too. When we were hauling one pot aboard the boat we were also lifting another one off the bottom, if you see what I mean. We weren't out there long of course but it was hard work. When it cooled off a bit and we'd had one or two good showers of rain to cool the water down a bit, then we used to come in close again. But there weren't a lot that used to go out where we did in the Red Sand, the others used to go out this side in the shallow side. Then they used to go out to the bank called the Spaniard, and the Middle. There used to be the Girdler Lightship then on the end of the Spaniard and a buoy called the Gilman Buoy on the end of the Queen's bank and they used to go down as far as them with whelk boats. Down below Herne Bay pier they went to what they call Stone Channel, down off Reculver. My father and uncle once went on a sailing boat called *The Lloyd George*—that was the name of it, because these Sheringham people were Liberals mostly—and they took all their gear down in their boat which was loaded, you can bet. They laid their gear down off Reculver Towers, went ashore, pulled the boat up and got a night's sleep at the pub down there. Next morning, they went out, hauled up the gear and came home. They had all that work for just one day's fishing, but they did it because things were so scarce elsewhere.

'Whelking was often a matter of luck too. Some places, perhaps, one day you could go and your whelk pots would be right full, and you'd turn them over thinking, "Oh, they'll be all right the next day", and perhaps you hardly had any whelks at all. And they used to go off in all weathers that they wouldn't think of going out in today. Well, they were afraid of losing a day's money when things were a bit tight. Sometimes though they wouldn't be able to go to sea for weeks if it was pretty rough. And you never got any help in those days. I've known my father be ashore for six weeks in the winter, but I think that was the longest. In that time a barge came ashore at Tankerton loaded with Quaker Oats, and people were getting that and living on oats. They never had anything else. The dredging boats were the same—all in the same boat more or less, as they say. They couldn't go off. Oh yes, things, at times, in Whitstable, used to be pretty dodgy as regards money and feeding.

'But they had wonderful boats. They were called crab boats because they used to go crabbing with them at Sheringham as well as whelking. Cor, they could put up with some weather they could. They were double ended, sharp fore and aft. They weren't all that big—about eighteen, nineteen foot I should think—but they were small boats because when you were hauling your gear in it was hard work pulling, especially if there was a bit of a tide running. The early boats never had engines. They were all lug sail, what you call a dipping lug and a pair of oars. You pulled the sail up and when you wanted to come on another tack, you had to lower your sail, unhook it off the mast, put it back and round the other side of the mast and hook it on the stern forward, hie on the sail, hook it on and put it up that way. You used to have a ring, a cringle in the lug sail, and you used to hook it on this and pull it up the mast. You could only sail on one tack with the sail up so you didn't have what they call short tacks, otherwise you'd got to keep working really hard to let your sail down, pull it back, and pull it up the other side. We used to make what we called long boards when we were tacking.

'And the oars—well, you never had rowlocks. You just had holes cut in the next to top timber of the boat and you just poked the oar out over the side and pulled it back in through the hole. Actually that was better than rowlocks because if it was rough and you were rolling a bit, the oars wouldn't come out of the hole like they would out of rowlocks. And you had leather fixed round the holes so that the oar wouldn't wear the wood, you see. Used to tack these bits of leather round and wet them so to quieten them down a bit so they didn't keep screaming when you were rowing. As kids we used to go and help paint and tar these boats. They had about a dozen whelk boats, I should think, and one or two were spare ones which they used to change over with while the other one was being tarred. They were mostly tarred up to about the three top planks and then they were painted, blue or white. Blue mostly.

'After the war, of course, they improved on them and got motors and had new boats built at Whitstable down at the end shipyard. A little bigger they were, about twenty-one or twenty-two feet. There were one or two from Sheringham at the latter part of the time with engines in them. They were flatter though and sat a bit on the water. Not so sharp underneath. Didn't draw so much water. Good sea-going boats though. I had a motor boat when I first went out. I was only about sixteen and my engineer, my brother, was eighteen months younger than me. That would be about 1920–23. If things were getting a bit rough, my father used to go and work on the steam boats in the harbour instead of going whelking, getting the stone out. We used to go ourselves, whelking and trawling then. We used to do the two jobs in one to try and make a week's work.

'It was easier work with these motors. You could haul your gear with your engine running slow to keep it over the tide. You see, if there's a lot of tide with a sail boat, when you're hauling your pots you're liable to pull them over on the bottom and you spill the whelks out. Well, we used to haul our gear with a little bit of engine going so that it jumped over the tide. Mind you, the only thing you had was a compass and a watch to go by when you were working. If you were going out a long way you had to wait until you got a nice fine day to shift your gear. Clear, so you could see the land. Then you used to shift your gear and take a bearing on the compass from the gear to the harbour and when you started coming ashore, you used to take the time on the watch, say an hour and a half steaming sou'west. The next day when you went out, if it was dull or misty and you couldn't see far, you used to take your watch out when you left the harbour, set your course, sou'west shall we say to north-east, and you used to steam an hour and a half on those bearings, allowing a little for the tides. That gave you a pretty good idea where the gear was.

'You never had aids or anything to help you. Never had forecasts either in those days. Yet it was strange how they used to forecast the weather and very seldom they were wrong. Lots of old fishermen could look up and tell you what the weather was going to be. Perhaps we'd be off there when I was a school kid and I went with my uncle and my father in the school holidays, the sun would be shining and hardly a ripple on the water. My uncle would say, "Come on. Hurry up. Let's get this haul aboard before it blows." And, sure enough, once we got home it was blowing hard. How he knew I just don't know. My father was just the same.

'My father used to do all his own repairs. He used to make his own masts. As kids we had to help knock the knots off these poles and shave them down and put the block in the top. If she had a leak in her, he put her up on the beach and put new timbers on her. We kids had to hold these copper nails, the head of them, while father was inside putting the rews on and burying over the end of the copper nails. It's funny, but the boat builders in Whitstable couldn't build a whelk or crab boat like they could at Sheringham. There were three of them on one dock being built at the same time once and they were all slightly different. And you could always tell a Sheringham boat because they had galvanised nails which they used to knock through and turn the ends over. But at Whitstable, they had what they call copper bolts and rews and they used to clinch them up. You see, at Sheringham the beach was all open and when they used to land if they'd had rews they would have sprung off, but the galvanised nails if they were turned over, they used to hold. Here they could either pull them up the beach or if it was rough, they would put them in the harbour. At Sheringham it was all open, they never had a harbour. Of course, when the locals here first saw these galvanised nails, they said the Sheringham boat builders didn't know how to build boats. Actually they did and they were good boats at that.

'In the first place the whelkers still used to get their pots from Sheringham. They used to come in a railway truck, loads of them, straight to the harbour. The railway was still running then. Later on a chap named Leney, Harold Leney, a well-known blacksmith he was locally, he used to make them. He used to get the bottoms which were like a cast-iron and he made the ribs and put those in and the rim at the top. Then the whelkers used to have to rope them, put the bars in and fix the crinnies. After that they used to tar them. Boil up the tar so that it was thin, like paint, put them right in altogether, leave them in for two or three minutes, then pull them up and let them drain. That used to preserve them, and it was surprising really how tough and hard they used to get, especially after the tar had got cold in the water. When they first got the ropes, you see, they were only tanned so they used to dip them, tar them. They weren't new ropes. They used to buy them from places like Yarmouth off old nets, second hand. There used to be these bits of net still fastened to the ropes, so they had to be cut off so that you had a clean bit of rope to wrap round the pot.

'Sometimes, if my father had new pots he was going to rope he would do them at home in the winter time. He used to put the pot in between his feet and we kids used to put the rope round loose, just kept wrapping them round the ribs, and he'd keep turning the pot round to tighten them up and put them in position. And of course, the crinnies and the nets, he used to do at home. He had a hook and a short bit of string on the window sill where he could make his nets because he wanted something to lay back on. It wasn't like knitting with ordinary needles. He just had this one needle and he had to have it made fast to something so that he could keep knitting round and round. The knots were like a sheep end. He used to spend quite some time on the nets, because when he came ashore you wanted the whelks in nets to boil them. If you caught a lot of whelks, and I've known them catch fifty and sixty wash, you want fifty or sixty nets, otherwise you were held up as regards getting your work done. My father used to make his own needles out of wood and then he used to buy the rope by the ball, potstuff we used to call it, to make the nets of. The sails were always made at the sailmakers but my father used to do all his repairs, patching and sewing. There was always a lot of work for sail makers and one or two were quite characters. Otherwise my father used to do everything—oh, except I never saw him make oars. There'd be quite a lot of work in them.

'There were only two men in a boat. Now and again they had three, but it was very seldom, and only usually when the motor boats came

1. *A farm bailiff from Chainhurst, near Marden, in 1914, persuaded to don his Sunday best by an enterprising photographer who travelled out from Tunbridge Wells, convinced farm workers that they would be called up for the war and that they ought to leave a memento for their families. With black kid gloves, watch and chain, three piece suit, and bowler he could easily be mistaken for a city gentleman. Dressed in his working clothes he looked completely different.*

2. *A labourer and his family outside their front door at Wingham in about 1907. Apart from a white neckcloth his Sunday best is identical with his weekday clothes, but his children are obviously dressed for the occasion. Note his boots, 'straights', so called because they could be worn on either foot.*

3. *Sheep shearers on Romney Marsh. A man who could shear 40–45 sheep in a day, by hand, was doing well, but some even reached 80. The going rate in the 1900s was 2s. 6d. a score, 2s. 3d. for lambs, and as Jack Prior (born 1892) recalls, 'you had to make a good job of it, otherwise out. Plenty to take your place'. One of the first jobs which boys in the area had was lock boy, employed to pound up the sheep, attend to the gate when they were taken out, mark the sheared sheep with tar, clean up the pieces of wool, and give the men a bean or stone for each animal they sheared so that they could keep tally of their count. The man on the left is Ed Gillett's father. (see chapter 11)*

4 *Opposite. A travelling cider press at Hill Farm, Goudhurst. The stationary steam engine was used to pulp the apples, clearly visible in the barrel on the right.These were then put in a screw clamp and the juice collected in the short barrel. The apples were obviously still edible since the boy on the right is busy eating one. Many hop growers preferred to give their labourers beer to support the trade on which their prosperity rested.*

5. A four horse team ploughing near Wingham with an old Kent plough. The whalebone whip carried by the leading man was never used for driving the horses, only for gently guiding them at the end of the fields. Even then it was rarely necessary, the horses knew just what was expected of them. 'Ploughing', wrote Rider Haggard in his book A Farmer's Year (1898), 'is one of those things that look a great deal easier than they are'. Waggoners often had their own secrets for managing the horses and adjusting the plough which they guarded jealously. 'Nothing is more difficult', continued Rider Haggard, 'than to get a clear explanation of anything they do with their art from men of this stamp'. Ploughing an acre involved several miles of walking.

6. *Hop driers at Chainhurst Farm, 1916. Left to right, the measurer, farm bailiff, two driers, the farmer's son and the farmer.*

7 and 8. *Two very different classes of pickers. Working in the gardens
was socially acceptable for women from the middle and upper classes if
they picked for a charitable cause or for church funds. These ladies
captured for posterity by a photographer near Cranbrook were not
typical of the majority of pickers. Compare their dress and pose with
that of the two hardy characters opposite.*

9. *Folkestone fish market. A photograph full of rich detail; fish crates, a variety of nets, an anchor, even fish heads littering the gutter and laying on the table on the left.*

10 **Opposite.** *Most of the yawls carried a crew of three on the flats, so these four men crews must have been putting off to work their stint on the beds. Robert Dale's crew were forced to tow their yawl from a rowing boat like these when there was insufficient wind.*

11. *Teddy Tart hanging the nets on his kettlenet stand. The poles fixed in the sand in the spring remained in position till the autumn but the nets were taken down whenever rough weather threatened. The size of the bight and extent of the range can be clearly seen. There must have been complete understanding between man and horse for this job.*

12. *The Southerdens, farmers and fishermen at Jury's Gap, drawing for mackerel inside the bight.*

14. *Copton brickfield, just south of Faversham, 1922. Red and fancy bricks were made here until 1924 and were fired with coal. They were generally taken away on trucks drawn by traction engines since the field lacked access to water carriage. Harry Matthews worked here for a season. Compared to stock brickmaking by hand it was 'easy work' with good money but the opportunities for winter work were even less.*

13 Opposite. *Middle Row, Ashford. Although the railway works did much to transform Ashford, the shopping centre still betrayed its market town origins. The whole scene is spotless, and it is difficult to see the details of the window display on the left since the street is reflected on its shining glass. The barber awaits his next customer. Barbers' shops were considered 'the worst form of shop work' for young lads during this period since they were used as meeting places for gamblers and rough labourers, and were thus 'demoralising' influences.*

16. *Partaking of the sea breezes and 'polite' society on the Leas at Folkestone. Umbrellas and sunshades in abundance to protect the dainty complexions from the burning sun. The chairs look particularly uncomfortable and more suited to domestic use.*

15 Opposite. *The Friend in Need in Peter Street, one of Dover's many public houses. This photograph taken in about 1910 shows the publican, Mr. Medhurst, and his family. They also ran a general shop in Tower Hamlets at the same time, mother looking after the pub in the day, her husband returning in the evening when the clientele became a little rougher. They later moved to the Grand Sultan, in Snargate Street, then the main thoroughfare of Dover.*

17. *On the sands at 'bourgeois Broadstairs'* . . . *'a neat, little, placid town clean as a new pin with firm, fine sands'. Apart from one very young pair of knees, hands and faces, no parts of the human anatomy are exposed to the sunlight. The ever-so respectable Mr. Charles Pooter, George and Weedon Grossmith's fictional character in* Diary of a Nobody *(1892) came here for his annual holiday.*

in. They used to work more gear, you see, because they could get to and fro quicker with the engines and could have perhaps five or six shanks of pots instead of four with two men in a boat. Even then, there were some that only had two. Mostly they were family concerns, a father and son in a boat or two brothers. They worked six days a week then. Never used to go Sundays. A lot of the whelkers those days, they used to go to the Salvation Army. Even my father used to go and listen to the Salvation Army band on a Sunday although he'd been in the pub and had a drink, he'd always come out and listen. The boats worked on the tides really, going out on the ebb as a rule and coming in on the flood. Sometimes they were early tides and sometimes late, although we never went out overnight because you couldn't see your buoys or your gear. Two or three o'clock in the morning but not overnight. We'd be out three or four hours depending on where the gear was. Sometimes it would be close, just the other side of the Street, and another time you'd be out in the Spaniard so of course you were longer getting there, you see. In between whelking, years ago, we used to put the pilots aboard the steam boats that were coming in with stone. We called them pilots, but actually they were hufflers, not proper pilots although they knew the way about out there like you'd know the back of your hand. We used to go and meet them out by the Street Buoy, or sometimes we had to go out as far as the Girdler Lightship if it was a strange steamboat that hadn't been here before.

'When you were out in the boat you used to haul the pots up, empty them out straight away on the floor of the boat. Then you baited the pots and stacked them so you knew where they were. Once you'd got all the whelks lying on the floor down aft you shovelled them into a tub, which we called a wash measure, and picked out the farmers and the crabs and threw them over the side so you had just whelks. If the whelks were very small we used to throw those back too. Then you came ashore, pulled them up the quay if you were in the harbour and carried them on yokes—two wash—and then we used to boil them in these big coppers. They're still down there now but of course now they're proper coppers with water laid on and they belong to the council. Ours were all on railway property then, and we used to have to pay the railway company so much a year ground rent. They weren't very symmetrical, these sheds, more like a shanty town really. Not very neat at all some of them weren't, although my father had a good one. Pitch pine it was. Anyway you had to go and get your water and carry it in buckets from a standpipe to fill your copper. Used to get the water boiling and you had three wash of whelks in nets hooked on to a block and pulley over the copper. You pulled them up and dropped them in the copper when the water was boiling. That cooled the water down so you kept them in until they boiled again and you gave them one or two minutes' boiling, pulled them out and put another three wash in. Well, then you put them outside, still in the nets, on racks to cool off before you put them in bags to send them away. Then you used to have somebody come round and pick them all up and take them up to the railway station.

'They mostly went up to London to big firms and to Billingsgate Market. Sometimes you got a good price, another day you got a poor price. Sometimes you used to get a form back to say that they were no good at all. They were a dead loss. You never got nothing for those. They were condemned. Perhaps they'd held them in the market, couldn't sell them one day and held them to the next, then they were no good, especially in hot weather. It was a bit of a gamble really. Then you had several customers that used to buy them by the sackful. I remember one name quite clearly. Frost the name was. He used to have these whelks by the bagful, well, bags full. I suppose he used to sell them and supply his customers. And we used to send them to Ramsgate, Margate, Dover, seaside places, for them to sell on the stalls in the summer. My father used to have regular customers. Sometimes they would want more than others, so if he hadn't got enough he used to go to another whelker and say, "Can you let me have two wash of whelks?" They'd say, "Yes, take a couple." But he wouldn't pay for them. Then, next day perhaps, he'd pay back in whelks instead of money, you see. They used to help one another like that. Well, these customers were your living, you couldn't afford to lose them. If you had a customer and you couldn't supply him, he'd go elsewhere, you see.

'After you'd boiled them up and bagged them, after that might be when you repaired your gear and your whelk pots. Because even the tarred rope used to get a bit rotten and it was surprising how much force the whelks used to put on those to force their way between a bit of rope that was rotten. And then you might have the wash nets, which were about five gallons, you had to net those, or the crinnies which were about four meshes wide and about twenty-two meshes long. I had to do those when I was quite young. My father would say, "Look, before you go out tonight, you do four crinnies."

'When we were out whelking we used to wear thick, navy blue trousers, thick socks and boot stockings. In the first place my father had leather boots, thigh boots, but when rubber came in we had rubber. Then we used to wear flannel undershirts, a thick shirt and thick woollen jerseys and a navy blue, thick cotton jumper which my father used to call slops. That used to keep the wind out and it also kept you clean. Sometimes they were navy blue and sometimes they were brown. My mother used to make them from an overall material like a drill and my father dipped them in a tan tub until they were a tan colour. My mother also made all our shirts and flannel under-shirts, and she used to get the material to make the frocks and my father used to oil them to make them like oil skins. Used to put coats and coats of linseed and boiled oil on and you'd have them hanging on the line with a stick through the arms to hold them flat. He used to do inside and out. Those never had any buttons, because if you're using nets the buttons used to stand a chance of getting caught on the meshes. With whelking it didn't make much difference because you never had nets to get foul of you, but you see with buttons unless you had a weather piece on your oil skins, you'd get the sea and rain driving between the button holes. We used to wait until we got wet through though before we put our oil skins on because we didn't like working in them. The sleeves used to rub your wrists and a lot of fishermen used to get these salt water boils which were pretty painful, you know. My father had one or two but one of my uncles used to have a terrific lot of them. Another thing, these oil skins were a bit big round the neck, so we had special sou'westers which we got from Great Yarmouth. They were more like an American fireman's hat with a big back on them so that they kept the water out of your neck. They were made of the same material as the frocks, but they were stiff brimmed, not all soft like the sou'westers you buy today. Drying clothes was a bit of a problem. The trousers, which were like a navy blue melton—quite good thick ones, you know—when they used to get wet they were fairly heavy. You had to have something spare, otherwise if you kept using the same clothes they used to get white with salt.

'Down Whitstable now there's only about three whelk boats and they are local born people that are using them today. Of course they've got motor boats, big boats they have. And they still catch quite a few whelks. There's not so many at it and they've got more ground to work.'

Chapter 10

Dungeness Drifters

It was a tough life, but it's like everything else. It's what you're
brought up to. And it was a king of a job like compared to the
deep-sea fishermen's.

It would be difficult to imagine a more desolate place than the area
around Dungeness, a vast expanse of shifting shingle, stretching
treeless and unappealing down to the English Channel. Its most
notable claim to fame today is the nuclear power station perched
disastrously close to the receding west beach. Cranes and lorries
which litter the east beach and a concrete road crossing the shingle
to the west bay indicate that man has to struggle to protect this
expensive structure from the sea. Three lighthouses, two of them
disused, a light railway station and adjoining cafe, a lifeboat station,
a decidedly squat public house and a few small houses spreadeagled
along the east bay comprise the rest of man's attempts to settle this
windswept place.

Eighty years ago it was even more bleak and isolated. No road
existed beyond Boulderwall Farm where the solid land gave way to
shingle beach. All goods from the town of Lydd were transferred here
into special wide wheeled waggons which did not sink into the beach.
The inhabitants of the area wore, indeed many still do wear, back-
stays, flat, slip-on, open wooden sandals which distribute their weight

more evenly over their feet and prevent them digging too deeply into the shingle with their heels. The area could have been dramatically altered had the South Eastern Railway developed its ambitious plans in the 1870s for a deep-sea port here. Apart from a rail link with Lydd, opened in 1881 for goods and in 1883 for passengers, nothing ever came of it, but even this single track did much to open up the place. Local fishermen could now send fish more easily to market and the shingle itself began to be dug up and trucked away for industrial uses. Even the vicar from Lydd made use of the line on the Sunday mornings when he had a service at Dungeness, hiring two local boys to propel him down to the point on the hand operated gangers' truck.

The railway, however, was merely a tentacle stretched out across the stony wilderness. It only served the straggling hamlet at the point itself, not the equally isolated communities of Dengemarsh and Galloways, both of which have now disappeared, partly by the erosion of the sea, partly by the forced expulsion of their inhabitants by the armed forces who used the area for training in the Second World War. These settlements were connected with Lydd by narrow cart tracks, but many traders who ventured out to them delivering coal, bread and groceries preferred to plod along the coast from Dungeness on a circular tour from the town. Their inhabitants followed a distinctly limited range of occupations. The entry for all three places—Dungeness, Dengemarsh and Galloways—in a trade directory of 1899 consisted of the following: one shopkeeper, six publicans and beer retailers, ten fishermen, one lifeboat station, one lighthouse and five coastguard stations or coast brigades. The pubs, which were dotted all along the coast, provided meeting places for fishermen in wet weather, accommodation for travellers and of course, beer. They were not grand affairs. The one at Dengemarsh was little more than a few seats in the family's back kitchen.

The publicans themselves often engaged in another trade as well, invariably fishing. Isolated as they were, they had little need to conform to licensing hours when they were introduced. One landlord of the Pilot at Lade is remembered for his habit of keeping a spy-glass trained across the beach for spotting possible representatives of the law. The coastguard stations were an indication of the strategic importance of the area, only twenty miles from the French coast and close to one of the busiest shipping lanes in the world. The area also had a long smuggling tradition. Although staffed by outsiders on short term contracts the men seemed to have fitted in well with the local community.

The primary source of livelihood, however, was fishing. The

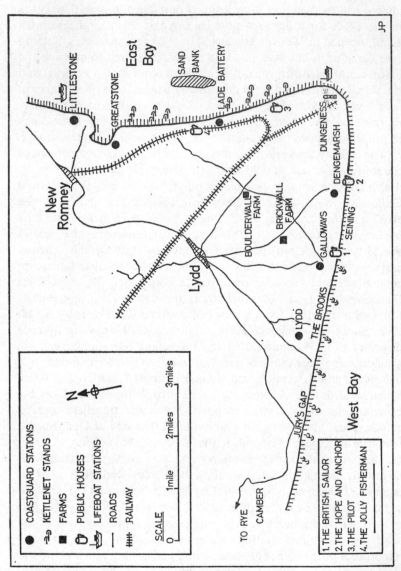

Fig. 4 Dungeness area, c. 1900

surrounding sea was widely recognised as a rich fishing ground and it attracted drifters and trawlers from all around the south coast and, much to the dismay of the local men, from abroad. 'In Rye Bay and Hythe Bay I have seen sometimes 50 sail of French boats right in along the shore close to Dungeness,' commented J. W. Arnold, a Deal fisherman and pilot giving evidence before the Sea Fisheries Commission in 1865. 'They come in so thick that as soon as a fish pokes his head out of the sand he is raked up at once, and it does not matter how small he is . . . You might almost stand on Dungeness Point and stone them, they are as close in as that.' The gradual introduction of large steam trawlers just before the First World War also resulted in bitter outcries from local fishermen who maintained that these damaged the sea bed and harmed the mackerel breeding grounds. Nevertheless fishing continued to provide the majority of the inhabitants with their livelihood. The Board of Trade statistics for the Dungeness station, defined as stretching from Lade No. 2 Battery in the east bay, round the point and down the west coast as far as Camber, rarely show less than 10,000 cwt of fish being landed here each year. The catch consisted almost exclusively of herring, mackerel and sprats, however, and barely topped £5,000 in value, but of other ports in Kent only Folkestone landed comparable quantities of these fish.

Most of the winter fishing was done in the east bay, and the fish were landed at Dungeness and loaded directly on to the rail for Edgar's canning factory at Deal. This firm had an agent there, a Mr Tart, who handled the necessary paper work and communications with the company and paid the fishermen for their hauls in cash. Despite the occasional glut which closed the market temporarily, most fishermen regarded this arrangement as a 'good contract'. The fish was simply carted across the shingle in special wide wheeled trolleys, one of which is still kept as a memento near the Britannia public house at Dungeness, and loaded on the rail. The firm paid the carriage. The fishermen received prompt cash payments based on an agreed rate of so much per long hundred of mackerel and herrings, a traditional measure actually consisting of 120 and 132 fish respectively, and so much per two and half stone box of sprats. Other market outlets provided less certain returns. Fish markets were held at Folkestone and Hastings, and the boats occasionally called there. At Hastings a Dutch auction system prevailed where bidding started high and worked down. Alternatively fish was sometimes sold directly on the beach to buyers from Folkestone or fish salesmen from further inland.

A large proportion of the summer mackerel, which was generally landed in the west bay by fishermen from Dengemarsh and Galloways, was carted up to Lydd and put on the rail for the London market. Although fish was carried at a special low rate by the railway company, and the services of a London salesman were enlisted to look after their interests, supply them with boxes and deal with distribution costs, the local fishermen regarded this method of disposing of their fish with undisguised suspicion. Not only did it involve them in the expense of providing for cartage from the beach to the station but once on the rail they had absolutely no control over their fish and they had no guaranteed return. If the train was delayed for any reason the whole consignment could be lost. Even the middlemen who handled their affairs and sold their fish on the market were regarded as potential swindlers. 'There was nobody from here up there [at Billingsgate], so you don't know whether they done you or whether they didn't. You just got a cheque back. You had to have what they sent you.' The men also preferred cash. Cheques were usually cashed with the grocer or carter. Few fishermen made use of any banking facilities.

The fishermen along this stretch of coastline fell into two distinct groups. One, dealt with in the next chapter, relied on stake nets along the sandy shores in the bays on either side of the point. The other comprised drift net fishermen. Both groups also participated in seining along the shore during the summer months. Steve Prebble, like his father before him, was a drifter. He spent most of his life prior to 1942, when the armed forces evacuated him, at Dengemarsh. His father, a farm boy at Brickwall Farm from the age of nine, branched out into fishing in 1876 when he was eighteen, he and his uncle forming a partnership to buy an old boat. By the time Steve was born, his father was not only operating on his account, he possessed two boats, one for summer fishing, the other for winter.

'I was born in 1893 at Dengemarsh. I walked six miles to school, three mile each way, for eight years. Then I left school in 1907 and went fishing with my father and another person, Jack. The bigger boats as a rule didn't carry a boy, they carried four hands, but occasionally one might have had three men and a boy. There were two men and me on my father's boat. He only went two handed at one time, then they had a coastguard boy before I went because there used to be a coastguard station down there at Dengemarsh. Then when my younger brother left school, well, I was three-quarters a man then, you see, only a year and ten months between us, he come with me and the old chap. The other chap, he'd been with my father about twenty years, he got the sack. He used to get a little bit of money and he'd get up here in the pub at Lydd and wouldn't get back till the next tide, so my father got a bit fed up with him and because he'd got us young 'uns coming along he'd got a bit of an option, so he sacked him.

'Fishing was with drift nets then. We did no trawling. There was no trawling done down there till after the war when we had motors. Before 1914 it was all sailing. We were drifting then, and in the summer time, we also used to go seining along the shore, putting the net out and pulling mackerel ashore.

'You'd start drifting for mackerel about the first week in May and carry on till the end of July. Then you'd have a break of about five weeks, a month to five weeks. Then in the autumn time, about September, you used to go what we called autumn mackereling. The summer mackereling was done in the west bay and the autumn mackereling in the east bay between Dover and Dungeness. You see, in the summer time the mackerel are all coming from the west to the east and in the autumn they were always going east to west, going back again. Mackerel catching would go for about another six weeks. Then the latter part of October, you'd take your mackerel nets out —that's finished—and put your herring nets in. Of course, the herring season was done along the shore mostly with smaller boats than we had for mackerel. Never got further than a mile out pretty often. Sometimes we put our nets out alongside the shore as close as you could get. That's where you can't get now, the anglers won't let you, so you've got to leave them the first hundred yards and very often in the first hundred yards there's more fish than anywhere else. If there were any herrings you'd carry on with the herring nets perhaps up to Christmas, or sometimes you'd start catching sprats in November, it just depended on where they were. Then we carried on with sprats right up till the end of February. Then we had a spell then till about May when we didn't do any fishing. We were getting our nets and boats ready then but we'd got no income unless we got a job for a month, six weeks on the groynes there or at the Brooks. There used to be eight chaps from Lydd working on the groynes practically all the year round, planting faggots on the shore to stop the beach from washing away and suchlike. If they were in any danger we might get the chance of a job there for a few weeks. We didn't make a lot, just enough to keep going.

'There was a lot of hard work those days. I mean to say it wasn't just going out there and coming home again. Sometimes you went away hours before it was time because of the tide. Other times it took you perhaps hours to get home because of the tide. You used to be fishing from the time the water came over the sand till it went back again and you came ashore just before it left it. Or you went as the tide was going down and was gone all the time the sand was there and came back after the water flowed over the sand, you see. It would be about six or seven hours if you went off when the water came over the sand, and it would be, well, you could go to twelve hours if you went the other way, just before it left the sand. The prevailing wind being south west in the winter we used to do all our fishing from the east bay. Sometimes if the wind and tide came round east and we couldn't get round to the east bay there might have been as many as fourteen or fifteen boats at Dengemarsh, but the only thing was then you could get caught if the wind did come round back to the south west in the night. Then there was too much sea to get off and on. The sea in the east bay was sheltered by the point so the east bay really was best when the wind was in the south west. We used to walk across the beach from Dengemarsh to the Pilot. We'd got a hut there with bunks and a stove where we could stay. If we were working two tides, day and night, we stayed there and didn't come home perhaps for four or five days. But if we only did the day tide, we'd go over perhaps at daylight, go off and come ashore just before midday. Then we'd get the fish out just before dark and get home about five o'clock.

'We used to have to put boards under the boats to get them up and down the beach or else they'd have dug right in the shingle and you couldn't move them then. You couldn't get them across the sand at all. Launching off the beach you'd got to know what you were doing. You watch, if you're on the shore, you'll get four or five big waves come in and then four or five little ones. Well, if you went off sometimes in them big 'uns, they'd fill your boat up full of water. So you waited until you got a smooth as they call it and let her down before the next big ones came. If it was a bit rough we'd get the boat down close to the water and then we used to have a rope on anchor out there about a hundred, well fifty yards perhaps, so to pull her out through the surf. One or two men, depending on how many of you there were, would get in the boat and pull while another put the last board underneath and the others pushed. Then you'd got to turn the boat round to sea, because we always went out stern first. Turn her round, head to sea and get the sails up before you let go of the rope. Remember we hadn't got engines. We'd only got sails. When there was a breeze you had a job to get her off the beach. Coming home you couldn't pick your chance. You had to keep sailing and if you happened to be unlucky and come when the big waves were there on what we called the drawback, it might come right aboard.

'Another thing, when you came ashore, you had to wind your boat up the beach with a capstan, a round barrel on a framework with a bar on it and a wire which went round it. We walked round and round with this to haul the boat up. I've heard my father say, when he first went, they had ordinary hemp rope not wire, and by the time they got it round the barrel it made it so big it was nearly touching the uprights on the side. Hastings boats, they're like us they have to wade up the shore, they used to always have a horse to walk round and round. Their boats were a lot bigger than ours. After the war we had a motor winch. Some of the old people round here said it would pull the boats all to pieces, but then you'd no need to wind the boat up any faster with the winch than you had done with the capstan. You could go a little faster but you hadn't got to go too fast else you wouldn't get the boards under. You see, you'd still got to put your boards under the boat and grease them, make them nice and greasy so the boat would slide along them.

'Mackerel catching, you never put your nets over till it was getting dusk. It's no good putting them over in daylight because the water's clear and they'd see your nets. Just getting dusk. Sometimes we had to go off from Dengemarsh about ten or eleven in the morning while the tide was going east to get up in the east bay. You see at Dengemarsh, about half an hour after low tide, the flood tide goes east along the shore. Then you'd anchor perhaps five or six hours and wait for the evening to come. You'd go and get what we used to call a berth out at sea, half a mile, three-quarters of a mile from the next boat. If you got too close to him he'd catch all the fish and they wouldn't come along to you. There used to be the Hastings boats and the Rye boats an' all out there. There was a bit of swearing sometimes! They used to say, "He shot along me last night." See, if the next boat stuck his nets only five or six hundred yards away from you, you wouldn't get no fish. He'd have them all. He sort of robbed you. That used to happen sometimes. There were so many boats then, if you didn't go fairly early and get, like I say, a berth, you would have nowhere to get in.

'Anyway, you always put your nets over at dusk and you drifted whichever way the tide was. One week coming dusk you'd put your nets over at high water. Next week it'd be low water when you put them over and the tide would be going the other way. If the tide was going west you went west with it. If it was coming east, well, you come east with it. But you had to shoot your nets out first across the tides so you always sailed across it with a fair wind. If the wind was in the west you put your nets out one side of the boat, if it was in the east you put them out the other way. It was no good putting your nets out with the tides; you wouldn't get nothing because the fish swum with the tide. Near enough with the tides anyway. Once you'd let all the drift net out from the boat then the tide took it along and took the boat with it. If the tide was going against the wind it still pulled the boat, you'd got enough nets for that. Well, herring nets, you'd have half a mile, and some of the boats had, well, three-quarters of a mile perhaps of mackerel nets. It didn't matter how big the boat was or how hard the wind blowed, if the tide was going against the wind, them nets would have enough hold in the water to tow the boat against it.

'Years ago, when there was a lot of sailing vessels about, same as in the bay, if they got a headwind when the tide was turned and couldn't get round the point, they used to drop their anchors in the bay. Well, if you was down the side the tide was coming from, you had to pull all your nets in, otherwise they'd pull you asunders when you came against their anchor chains. It was a blinkin' nuisance then. You might lose a night's fishing over it. If you couldn't get the nets in fast enough to come across their anchor chain they would part your nets right through. Used to get ever so many nets parted by vessels when they were sailing too. We used to have a flare or torch and we waved it the way we wanted them to go. Sometimes they'd turn round and go back again. Sometimes they would turn. Sometimes they'd go right over you. When the bay was full they'd got a job to turn, you see. That's where we used to come in contact with the Rye smacks. They were trawling. If you were in their way there wasn't many would alter for you. They'd go over you and tear you.

'Sometimes, when you put your nets over, especially for sprats up near the point, as they sunk down you'd see the cork bobbers on your nets going up. They lay flat with your net ordinary, hanging down, but as soon as there was weight in it so they begun to stand up. Sometimes when you'd got a lot of sprats you'd have your whole net laying flat on the water. They would push it right up flat. All you could see was the sprats' noses sticking up. Used to look quite pretty. Another time you'd let down your nets up on the point and you could drift right down past Lydd-on-Sea, Lade, right down to Littlestone before you'd got enough. Sometimes you hadn't got nothing hardly, drifting all that way.

'When you pulled your nets in you didn't pull the nets to the boat, you pulled the boat to the net. Except when you got nearly to the end, then you'd pull the net through the water. In the middle of the boat was the net room as we used to call it. You hauled the nets in and put them back in the boat with the fish still in them, unless you'd got only perhaps a hundred or so, then you picked them out as you went and put them in a box somewheres so you hadn't got all the nets to pull out again. Then, on the beach, you'd got all them nets to pull out to shake the fish out of them, count them up and put them in boxes. You could shake nearly all your sprats out. You'd stand one with the top part of the net, the cork line, and the other with the other part, and you used to have a net on the beach so you could shake them out into this net. Then you hadn't got to clear them off the beach. But it took a long time. You could shake herrings out too—the gills are not too stiff—but you couldn't shake a mackerel out. You had to pick him out and when you had a lot of mackerel, same as autumn time when the mackerel were always fatter, you got some sore fingers. You'd got to keep turning the meshes over. I mean to say it wasn't just going out there, coming home and when you came home you were finished. You'd got a lot doing. Same as winter time, when you were catching sprats it could be night time when you come ashore and if there'd been any rain in the evening or during the day before and the beach was still wet, that beach would freeze like concrete. Then you'd to stand there, couple of hours perhaps, shaking your sprats out of the net with the beach all frozen. It wasn't a very warm job, I might tell you. No. The sprats would be frozen stiff on the beach before you could pick them up.

'Then again, if you'd had a lot of herrings or sprats you daren't haul the nets back in the boat unless you were going straight out to sea again, because the slush out of the fish would rot your nets. So after you'd had a lot of fish you had to get your boat down to the water and wash them. That seems funny perhaps to wash them after they'd been in the sea, but you should have seen the difference. You'd see them come over muddy looking out of the boat and when they came out of the sea again they'd be bright. You see, no air could get at them in the boat, and being cotton nets all in a lump they got hot and slush used to eat into them. They wouldn't hurt if you hauled them right on to the beach and pulled them out the full length of the net to dry them which you used to do sometimes, because they'd plenty of air then. But if you went, say four or five days and you got a lot of fish every day, the mud in the water settled on them. So you'd get the boat down to the sea, just to the edge of the water, still hanging on to the capstan rope, and one man'd get down off the stern and haul them in the water and the other would stand along the shore and haul them ashore. If there was a bit of a sea on it was best, because they had the surf washing up and down them, but sometimes you had to hang on because of the swell. If the water was smooth you had to swish them about. They were always best to wash if they were wet just after they'd been used. If you dried them with the dirt on they didn't wash so quick, they wanted more soaking. But they used to come out like new.

'Practically all of the new nets came from Bridport in Dorset. They'd make the nets according to your specification. There used to be four or five different people come here, travellers. About twice yearly they used to come round. They'd stay in Lydd at the George Hotel overnight and then walk down to Galloways to the pub, get an order and the fishermen there would pay their last bill like they used to do. Then they'd walk across the beach to our place. One traveller, from Gundry's, he always used to stay at our house overnight. He'd take the order from my father and my uncle who lived up in the old house—it's gone to pieces now—and a man named Wills who lived in the pub, all fishermen like, then he'd carry on across to the east bay and finish up down at Greatstone. The postman lived there, the only house there was at Greatstone, and he used to stay there for the night. Where he stayed afterwards I don't know. But he was a temperance man. He never stayed at pubs. Others used to come round too but they never stayed at our place.

'Then of course you'd got to get your nets ready. The mackerel nets were tanned and as the years went on they kept getting blacker. That's how they preserved them in those days. Now they don't want no preserving because they're nylon. The herring nets were left yellowy coloured, the colour of linseed oil because sprats and herrings would be in muddy water and you could catch them in the daytime. But mackerel only stay in clear water and that's why we could only do it at night. For drift nets you've got to have the mesh a certain size because you don't want the fish to go right through or even half way through because when you go to shake him out you'll cut him asunders. You only want their gills to get in. Mackerel nets would have bigger meshes than a herring net would because he's bigger. They used to be about twenty-six to twenty-eight rows to the yard and they were about 120 to 150 meshes deep, while a herring net'd be about thirty-six, thirty-eight, something like that. A sprat net would be about sixty-six rows to the yard. The herring and mackerel nets were always what we called laid together. We tied the ends of each net together—nets were always sixty yards long when you bought them—and then sewed down the meshes at the ends so that it was like one net. Sprat nets were always left separate, only tied top and bottom so when you washed them you could untie them, carry them down to the water, put a rope on them, let them wash up and down a few times and then bring them back. Then, according to the colour of the water, you had to use your judgment on this, you could let your herring and sprat nets down just three feet or you could let them down up to twelve feet. The clearer the water was the farther you had to let them down, but at night time you could always tie them right up close to the top because the fish were always closer to the top of the water, unless it had been very cold in the winter then they wouldn't be up so high. You just put a knot in the line, a special one you could undo quick when you were putting your nets out.

'The bigger the boat was, the more room you'd got to stow the net in. Our boats weren't too big, only about eighteen feet long. Well, we had two boats actually and the other one was only sixteen foot keel, the herring boat. The bigger one had got what we called an elliptic stern, that's a sort of overhang at the back that made the boat about twenty feet long. We had a big shed down at Dengemarsh, corrugated iron—it's gone in the sea now—and in the summer time the herring boat would be in that and in the winter the mackerel boat. Most of our boats were built here at Rye, Phillips at Rye. They were all sorts of boats, all sail of course, lug sail. Hastings boats and Folkestone boats were all the same, lug sails. Well, even the Cornish boats that used to go to Lowestoft and up that way in the summer time, they all had lug sails. They used to carry about nine hands and used to wind up round by Lydd-on-Sea. But they were a bit before my time. A lug sailed boat they always thought sailed faster and if you'd got a boom and a gaff and all that in your way, like you had on a smack, you couldn't get on half so well. What my father had when he started off was one of the first boats built at Rye with a centre keel. They'd never had none before so of course it was going to tear the nets and everything else. But it never did.

'We used to pretty often do seining and drifting in the summer, using the herring boat for seining. If it suited seining in the morning when we came ashore from drifting we went straight away seining. Another time we'd go seining, have our tea and go drifting. It just depended. If there was an enormous lot of mackerel about, you didn't have time to do both and anyway it wouldn't have been worth the trouble, the market would have been full up. Also, if there was a breeze seining wouldn't be no good, because the water would be stirred up and the mackerel wouldn't be in close there. It had to be fairly flat. Lots of Lydd people had a boat for the summer time and a

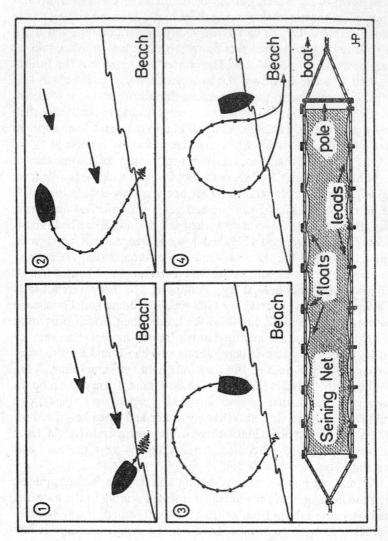

Fig. 5 Seining

seine. They did it for years, well, right up to about 1950, I expect. 'Course, anyone could do that job from the shore. You only wanted a few men in the boat. I don't know if you could go now though or not, there's too many anglers. They own the beach now. We don't. We ain't got anything to do with it.

'You used to have four men rowing the boat. Then there was a rope to the shore, anything from fifty to a hundred yards long depending on how clear the water was, and then two or three more on the shore. The seine net was about 280 yards long. Forty yards each net. Seven of them. Seven fours are twenty-eight. It used to be when I was at school. So that's 280, isn't it? Now on your drift nets you'd just have a piece of net rolled up, an old piece of net which had come off another one, sewed on to weight them down. But on a seine net you'd got corks on the top and a rope on the bottom with leads on it to sink it. They'd row out and put the net out, like in a half circle against the tide, then they'd put an anchor on and stop out there.

'But you could only stop a quarter of an hour or so else the tide would be done before the others who were on the beach waiting had had a turn at it, you see. You had to queue, like, because you could only do seining where there was sand between Galloways and Dengemarsh because there were kettlenets from Galloways and these groynes at Dengemarsh. And once the flood tide was finished you had to finish seining. There was hardly any mackerel then because the water was going down. So we had an unwritten law—you only stayed quarter of an hour. Then you gradually pulled the end of the net round, pulling your anchor in and then you came ashore with the boat, the tide taking the boat and the nets along towards the lighthouse all the time. The boat would be left on the beach where you came ashore. You just pulled it out of the water and started pulling the net in. To begin with you'd got a big circle of net out but you kept pulling it, men on both ends, two on the cork line and two on the lead line, and it kept getting smaller. Of course, as you were pulling it in the tide took it along so you had to keep walking along the beach. You could be half a mile from where the boat went ashore before you'd finished. Me and my brother, before we left school, I suppose I was about twelve and he was about ten, we used to row that boat along so it was ready for the men when they'd finished. Otherwise if us young'uns weren't there, two or three of them had to walk back to get the boat and bring her along.

'As you pulled the net in, the middle part of it would bow out like a bow and the fish used to push against it. If you could see their old noses come up you thought you'd got something, you see, and it gave you a bit of heart. Well, the middle bit which came out last was a lot stouter because you could have anything like five or six thousand mackerel in there and you needed something strong to hold them as you pulled it on to the beach. If you had a lot of mackerel you sometimes had to get round behind it in the water and kneel down to hold it till the water left it, else the weight of the fish would have busted your nets. So all the people what went seining only had old clothes on because they got wet. If it was a nice day or you hadn't got no fish, you didn't get half drowned then. Only got a foot wet perhaps.

'My father and uncle owned all the seining equipment we used. They took a share and a half for the boat and the net, so if there were eight men all told that used to come to nine and a half shares. So you'd got to earn £9 10s. before you got a pound. But a pound in them days was a pound. I mean people up here on the land could work all the week for that. Sometimes if they had a good summer they got as much as £20 a man seining, some of them. We used to have a couple of the coastguards to help us or a couple of chaps across from Lade who walked across the beach just purpose for the summer. They were only shrimping and lug digging there. They hadn't got a boat to row. If it was a nice day they'd automatically know themselves when it come tide time, to be there. But if it had been rough and then gradually got finer, they wouldn't know whether to come. We hadn't got no telephone or anything like that so if we wanted them we'd stick a flag up on a pole. They looked out for it each day. They'd see that and over they came.

'Winter time we used to have a little draw net occasionally to catch a few cod, flounders, or sole to eat ourselves. It was the same sort of principle as a seine net but not half so long and you pulled it along with the tide so you covered the ground. We used to row the boat and pull this weighted net along. See with mackerel, they are swimming along, but cod are only muddling about along the bottom getting their food so you needed to scrape the bottom. It used to give us a change of fish. Some of the cod we used to clean and salt down in the tub for the winter. We wanted a change sometimes.'

Although the families in these coastal communities relied primarily on the sea for their living, they managed to supplement their income in a variety of ways. Men obtained employment repairing the groynes along the beach in the spring and whole families went harvesting on the farms just inland in the autumn. One or two fishermen even invested in small pieces of land. They also achieved a surprisingly high level of self-sufficiency. Goats which could live on the wild vegetation on the beach supplied them with milk, and over fifty of them roamed around the point at one time. Little gardens were scratched together from the soil which accumulated round the roots of gorse and broom, and planted up with vegetables. Their shingle base proved difficult in the summer; water went straight through it. Wild fruits such as blackberries and sloes were collected for preserving or making into wine. The Prebbles also had a pig.

'You could eat everything on a pig—liver, sweetbread, trotters (I like trotters now), even its innards were scraped for sausage skin. All parts of the blinkin' pig. When we killed him we put him in some hot water and then scraped him, like. Then my mother used to have big crocks, great big ones for to put the hams in when it was brought indoors. I remember when she made her brine, she put an egg in it, in the water, then kept putting salt in till the egg floated, then it was right. After it had been in the brine so long, we used to take these hams out, do them up in brown paper and hang them round the house. It was a wooden house, see, you could drive a nail in and hang them round. You'd got pictures! Cut a slice off the gammon when you wanted it. Good meat that was. Wasn't everybody that done it down there, but we used to.'

Even the houses in which they lived were put up for next to nothing.

'A lot of the old places all round here were built of wreck wood where the vessels used to come ashore and break up. Nothing fresh to see an old boat stood up on its end to make a shed, boarded across the front, or an old boat turned bottom upwards for a roof. A gang up here, people called them "The Forty Thieves", used to buy the old wrecks and break them up. A lot of the fence posts round the fields were planks and timbers off the vessels too. My father had a new house built after my two oldest brothers were born, but most of the wood came off a wreck loaded with timber. It was only weatherboard. The sun did more harm to the boards than what the winter did then. See, sun pulls the wood between the joists and it would bend a little. Then when winter came, being on the beach there was nothing in the way and you had the full whack of it down there, the water would come up under the board, through the matchboard inside and wet the paper. It took an enormous lot of paint to paint the weatherboards right round the house. But if it was rigged up properly right round you could see the water going up, blowing over the top of the house.'

Although they made use of whatever means were at their disposal to eke out a living the men who went drifting relied for the bulk of their income on fishing. The same could not be said of another group of men who frequented the sandy shores further along from the point each summer.

Chapter 11

Fishermen without Boats—Kettlenets

. . . not what we used to call fishermen . . . farmers and every-
body else take them.

Local Fisheries Committee Representative (1914)

The coastline immediately around Dungeness is today periodically
dotted with anglers, part-time fishermen usually regarded with a
certain degree of contempt by the old fishing hands. They are, however, comparative newcomers and have merely replaced an earlier
group of part-timers who once fished regularly along the shore. From
Galloways to the west of the point, where a short stretch of sandy
beach first appears as the tide recedes, right down the coast through
Camber and even as far as Hastings at one time, and to the east too,
around Greatstone and Lade, the beach was once punctuated each
summer by rows of stake nets, known locally as kettlenets. These
were owned and operated by a motley collection of individuals who
did not regard themselves, and were not regarded by others, as fishermen. Those at Jury's Gap, explained H. T. Dighton, a representative
of the Sussex Local Fisheries Committee to rather perplexed members
of the Departmental Committee on Inshore Fishing in 1914, consisted of men who were 'not what we used to call fishermen', indeed,
'farmers and everybody else take the kettlenets down there.' The

larger operators who owned several stands regularly employed men in the summer to attend to their nets. Ed Gillett of Lydd (born 1895), the last man alive in the area to operate the nets, remembers his father working for the Southerdens, farmers in the area who owned several nets at Jury's Gap, for £1 a week plus 1s. in the £ cut on the value of the catch.

Unlike modern angling, however, kettlenetting was far from a leisure pursuit. It was viewed exclusively as a commercial undertaking. Nor were the nets merely insignificant, rather quaint legacies from the past which lingered on but fulfilled no useful role in the local economy. In the years leading up to 1914 the kettlenets regularly accounted for 50 per cent or more of the mackerel landed at the Dungeness station each year, and Dungeness was far from unimportant in national terms, rarely slipping outside the top eight or nine mackerel fishing stations in the country. In 1908, for example, drift nets and kettlenets each accounted for about half of the mackerel catch, 3,488 cwt to 3,289 cwt. The collector of fishery statistics commented, 'Large quantities of mackerel were caught during May and the earlier part of June by seines and kettlenets but very few fish were caught by these methods afterwards. Drifting was not successful during May and June and nearly all the fish were caught inshore.' Two years later the kettlenets accounted for over two-thirds of a bumper catch, 9,089 cwt as against the drift nets' 4,458 cwt. What makes the kettlenets of the Romney Marsh coastline even more interesting, however, is the fact that they were unique. Nowhere else in the country practised stake net fishing in precisely this fashion and nowhere else approached the success of the Marsh fishermen in catching mackerel—they were invariably responsible for the majority of the national catch from fixed nets.

The principle behind the kettlenets was simple. They were in fact little more than land traps laid out on the foreshore. A row of poles, fifteen to sixteen feet high, but embedded up to three feet in the sand, was set out at a right angle to the shore line and hung with nets. At the end of this line of nets, or range as it was called, was a circular ring of nets, the bight or pound, which had an opening on the land side only, on either side of the range. Shoals of mackerel tended to cross Rye Bay at certain times of the year, especially in mid-summer, and to swim up the coastline towards Dungeness point. The shoals would encounter the range and turn out to sea, finding themselves apparently trapped in the bight. Although, in theory, they could have turned inshore again to escape, few in fact did so and as the tide fell the net operators, armed with draw nets, simply waded out and

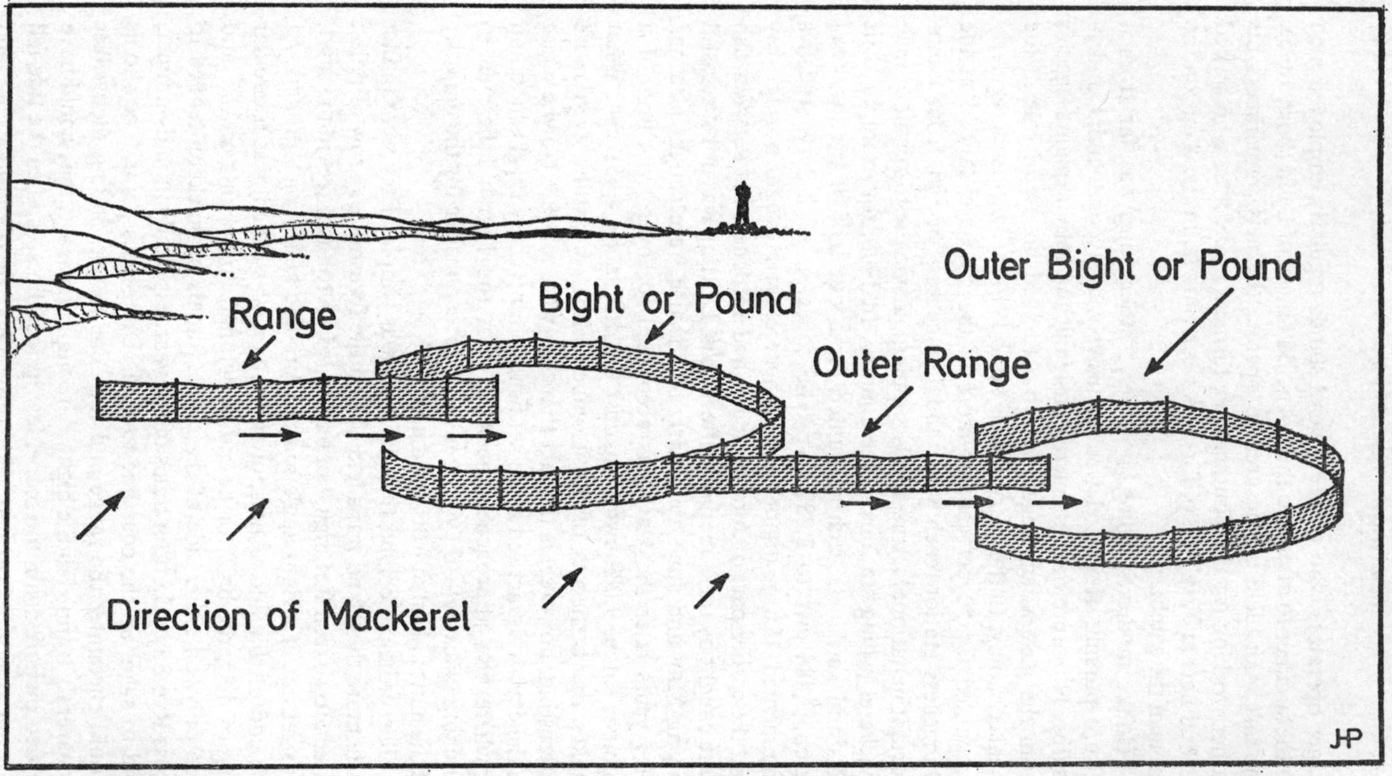

Fig. 6 A kettlenet stand

scooped up any fish interned in the bight. The length of the range depended entirely on the amount of beach uncovered at low tide. Whereas the stand at Galloways consisted of nothing more than a short range and bight, those towards Camber stretched out to sea for several hundred yards and frequently had additional, though smaller, ranges and bights further out to break up larger shoals and catch those fish which stayed out from the shore. The placing of the kettlenets was all-important and only a certain number were allowed along the beach at specified points, certainly no closer than a quarter of a mile apart. Too close together they would have hindered each other's operations and reduced the catch per net to an uneconomical level. Each operator, therefore, was obliged to obtain a licence from the Board of Trade and these were strictly rationed in the early years of this century after the Sussex Local Fisheries Committee, which had jurisdiction over all the coastline west of Dungeness, had lodged complaints about the way the kettlenets were managed.

Although theoretically simple, in practice operating the nets called for considerable skill and effort on the part of the men who worked them if they were to stand any chance of providing a financial return. Of paramount importance were the poles which were staked out in the spring about the time of the equinox to allow the maximum amount of beach to be used, and which then remained in position until the following September. These were usually driven into the sand at eight foot intervals, so the number required depended entirely on the length of the range and size of the bight. Here Ed Gillett recalls how he, and his father before him, used to prepare them.

'We used to get the poles off the hills. You'd order them in the winter to get them by February or as early as you could, because you'd got to get them all ready. You had to shave them—and they're sixteen foot, them poles—the rind off them all had to be shaved and any notch, you had to cut them off and smooth them because of the chaffing of the net. Then you had to sharpen the point, and about fifteen inches or just over a foot up from the point you bored a hole through there and stuck a peg through, about a foot long so it stuck out both sides. Well, then one of you would have the wimble, you know, what you turn to make bonds, and the other would have some hay or straw and you would make a good long bond, oh, from here to the other end of the room. You'd hook that over the peg, see, and keep binding it round and round till you got a nice lump. Then you dug these holes in the beach. You'd have a man with a single spade, he'd open the holes ready and two others would come along quick with their double spade—spades with a chain on them, see—which you kept dipping in, pulling back and chucking out. You'd get down deep as quick as you can, then you put the pole in and that bond helped to hold it. They wouldn't stand if you didn't put them out without a bond on them. They'd got to have that lump on them. You didn't have many minutes to get them in. Used to get about fifty poles a tide. More than that if there was enough in a gang to work two or three tools. They'd put a whole stand down of nets in a tide once they were used to it. You always had so many new poles each year, about half I should think. You could use a lot of the old ones but you always got some broken with one thing and another when it was rough. We had either ash or oak poles. You wanted something that would whip and wouldn't, you know, stand up too stiff. No good putting something in that wouldn't give at all or else they'd soon tear the net because there's a lot of strain on them even with just an ordinary tide with that lot of net on, you see. Oak and ash'd give with the tide. Then we pulled them up at the end of the season, those what weren't any good, well we just brought them home and sawed them up for firewood. But we always saved some old ones.'

The nets which were used were generally repaired and treated during the winter. Gundry's of Bridport seem to have been popular suppliers of new nets but old drift nets were also bought locally. Once acquired these nets were tanned by boiling in a large copper full of cutch or oak bark, and then laid out to dry, occasionally on the Rype in Lydd. They were then hung from the tops of the poles and secured at the bottom with fraps, loops several feet long with knots in the end. These were passed through the bottom of the double line of ropes at each side of the net, pulled tight to get the net hanging straight and then inserted further along the double line of rope on the net to hold them fast. Shrinkage on the net from the water and the weight of the adjoining net were sufficient to ensure that each knot did not slip out. Unlike the poles, the nets were not left up all season but were removed whenever rough weather appeared imminent, otherwise they could have been quickly torn to pieces. A good weather eye was thus another quality needed by the kettlenetters.

Once this equipment was in place on the shore the fishermen were obliged to visit it at each ebbing tide to clear it of fish. Since the poles were fitted at the lowest tides of the year it was rare for the nets to be left high and dry by the tide, and removing the mackerel from their semi-circular prison involved wading out with a draw net and pulling them ashore. Ed Gillett explains how it was done and how the fish caught were packed and prepared for market.

'You'd get in there as soon as you could when the water was up round here, to your shoulders. That's when you went in and got the first lot. Then you could work on them all the tide. When we used to go when it was dark in the autumn time, my father always used to stop before we got to that ring and he'd say, "Hark", and he'd kick his legs up and make a splash in the water. Sometimes he'd say to me, "There ain't nothing," because we didn't hear any of them take the net. See, if you made a noise, a splash, they'd dart for it, you see. They'd get in and kick. If there wasn't any, then of course you never had much to do but if you'd got a lot of fish you just went in and got some of them.

'You had a draw net with two bats on it, corks on the top and lead on the bottom. You'd pull the net out and one of you'd take his corner and go right round the outside of the bight and you'd stand still, there at the end of the range. You'd both work right round till you met one another and then the fish were in there! You couldn't get too many else you wouldn't get out with them. Sometimes they were so thick in there, they were all around you and if you wasn't careful, if you got too many in there you wouldn't get out of the opening without tearing the net.

'We always pulled our nets up on the sands, then picked them up in boxes and shot them into the cart. Some people used to leave the horse out of the cart and hook it on to the net and let the horse pull it in, but you had to be careful or else you burst the net. Others got the cart out in the water and scooped the fish up with a bowl and shot them in the cart that way but we always pulled ours up on the sands. One lot we had, we had lots of fish, and we went out in as much water as we could take, just tiptoed round and kept dragging them in till the water come back on the beach again. 700 stone we got. One tide. That's some fish. And one horse had got to pull all that up over the top over the beach, six boxes at a time, thirty-six stone. We trimmed the beach down to make it easy going up, but by God that worked that horse. You see, we had one horse to do all the fishing. That's all he did, the sea work.

'Then you hired other horses to take the fish away, you see. If you had any quantity of fish you'd run all round to any of the farm people. They'd got perhaps seven or eight horses. Plenty of horses. They'd go down to the coast and either take them to Folkestone or bring them up and put them on the rail for you. We used to get an old pole and stick it in the bank, perhaps another further along and then we tied baskets on them, you see. If there was one pole up you wanted one cart. If there were four or five you wanted five. Any of the women would spy with glasses from the town. Just stand there and watch. When you was spying through the glasses you'd perhaps see an old cart go up over the beach and you'd see someone walk over and throw one pole down, but if he came up and put another one up you'd got to go and get another one sent then. Just after the First War we only used to pay five shillings for a spec. load. You used to say you'd have carts on spec., you see. We'd have them in case we got the fish because you had to be quick pretty often to catch the train. If you pulled your nets in and you hadn't got enough you'd say, "It's all right. You can go." They got 5s. for that, for just coming, looking, seeing if they'd got a chance of a load. If they got a load they had 10s. That was horse and man. It wasn't a lot of money, was it?

'Then again, sometimes carts came from Ashford, from Hythe, all round. You'd see as many as a dozen round one stand, waiting. They used to come down from the country and bring in fruit, cherries, things like that to sell on the way down. They'd generally go further down to the west where the sands showed quicker. Used to buy it off you at the beach. There was only two of you and if you got a lot of fish on the sands where you'd took them up and shot them down, then you wanted a lot of work! They'd be up there pinching them! They'd look all round when you'd pulled them in and if they saw a nice salmon, they'd stick that down their jumper! We also used to have special trains years ago. You'd hear them coming up all night and we've had cartloads there sometimes. We lived along the road there and sometimes we'd say, "There goes so-and-so just going home. They're late." Used to come from Jury's Gap, where Daniel Southerden come from, with two or three horses and a waggon load of boxes. Used to very often have to go down and ask them to hold the train for them for an hour or half an hour if they could.

'We had a yard up here in Lydd where we used to wash the mackerel. There were two fish yards together and we only had one pump for them in one yard and so had to have a hole through the wall with a trough. Next door, they used to come round with their buckets and just dip them in there for to wash the fish. They'd just throw it on. That would be all right. We had one of those prickles, a basket with two handles. They open very wide at the top and don't let the fish through. We'd put them in that, rinse them in the tub. They were done quite clean. Some people used to shoot them straight into the tub then they'd have a skim net and keep baling them out. That's how it used to happen, how they used to have to go on. You had to be very careful with water, because there was no water laid on. You had to get it from the pumps or out of water butts under the downpipe.'

Despite long-remembered enormous catches, working the kettle-nets was a precarious business. 'They are not very profitable,' remarked James Page, a Hastings fisherman before the Sea Fisheries Commission of 1866. 'I do not suppose I have had more than 6d. an hour from them ever since I have had them. I set very little store by them. I would sell my nets for a very small profit.' Weeks, even months could go by when the long trek to the beach proved fruitless, while at other times a sudden blow could result in the nets being torn to shreds on the poles. Even a big catch could pose problems. The nets could be damaged by the large quantity of fish or the carts available might prove insufficient in number to carry away the haul in time, and much of it would be spoiled or lost.

No one relied on the kettlenets, therefore, for a full-time living. Indeed, working them only really occupied a few hours of each day even in the height of the season. Ed Gillett's father was typical of many of the marshmen of his time in being almost impossible to fit into an occupational category. He did 'pretty nigh anything' to eke out a living from the bleak landscape, although apparently he would have been relatively well off but for his inclination to frequent the 'wrong church' (the pub) too often. Apart from working the kettle-nets, hay cutting for Mr Hutchings, a grocer in Lydd who owned a few fields to support his delivery horses, provided Mr Gillett with additional employment in the summer. He also negotiated with local farmers for the right to cut down and keep the grass which grew round the outside of their corn fields since he had to provide hay for the horse he kept for working his nets. His children were employed in leasing for corn and beans to feed this animal and also for wool to sell to Mr White, a local shopkeeper who paid 'a very good price for it'. He also had a trade, that of thatching. Farmers' stacks and house roofs provided him with sporadic summer work, while in winter he would go reed cutting for the following season. He also participated in the annual rounds of sheep shearing, clatting and droving, and joined with other men to tender for the job of sewer brishing each autumn. This involved cleaning out the main drainage ditches, scything down the undergrowth and raking it clear. As his children got older he involved them in clearing out the smaller branch sewers, or petties, at so much a mile. When all else failed he even resorted to following the threshing machine or occasional retailing, buying up smoked herrings and selling them over the marsh or even up in 'the hills', carting potatoes around the coast, or buying sheep from local farmers, slaughtering them in his cart lodge and selling them off to neighbours. This last pursuit was usually engaged in at weekends when Ed acted as sales and errand boy. 'Any meat off Mr Gillett today? Neck and breast 4½d. . . . Loins 5d. . . . Shoulders 6d. . . . Leg 7d.' Even with all these activities winters were frequently hard, and shoes and groceries were bought on tick. Necessity, not choice, was the mother of such an independent and varied lifestyle.

The kettlenets, therefore, were a valuable part of the work routine of the surrounding countryside where seasonal jobs were plentiful but full-time employment was relatively rare. They merely provided one more intermittent and variable source of income for the men who worked them. Although some undoubtedly enjoyed the work, to most men it was merely another job, and not a particularly pleasant one at that, but one where their routine was ruthlessly dictated by the ebb and flow of the tide. It was also a wet job. Most men wore their oldest clothes which they often left at the beach to dry out each time. It is true that the fish they caught sometimes provided them with perks—the occasional salmon or sole rarely found its way on to the open market—but they also caused problems. Weevers, poisonous fish with sharp, dorsal spines, despite being locally regarded as one of the tastiest fish there was once they were skinned, were capable of inflicting considerable pain. To Ed Gillett they were 'a damned nuisance all amongst the mackerel. As soon as you get in there they're like that—their stings up. That's dangerous when you dab your hand down quick. I've had lots of little ones sting me but there's only one time I've ever been stung by a big one. He'd got his old prongs sticking right up and as I pulled the net, he dived and he got me right there, in the calf. When I pulled the net up there he was, but he was dead. Do you know I didn't go another couple of steps and I said to my father, "I can't go no further." He brought me home. That made me queer. I had to go to Dr Proctor and he burnt it out for me and I fainted then.'

Despite, or possibly because of, the large quantities of fish these nets were capable of landing, they were far from popular with local fishermen or the Sussex Local Fisheries Committee. Some of the fishermen's grievances were undoubtedly prompted by nothing more than a natural desire to eliminate competitors. The success of these horse and cart fishermen, who could regularly catch more than they did in a season and who acted to bring down prices by boosting local supplies, must have been almost impossible to stomach. Their complaints—and there were many—were centred on two factors: the possible danger to shipping and the waste involved in trapping. It should not be imagined that these were solely local grievances. They were invariably argued by fishermen wherever stake nets of any description were used on beaches, and oyster dredgers at Whitstable accused the owners of the wooden fish weirs which lay off Graveney of the same crimes.

As permanent features of the coastline throughout the summer months the kettlenet poles were undoubtedly dangerous to inshore fishing boats when they were completely covered by the tide. Drifters shooting their nets too close to the beach at night frequently found that they caught fast and had to be cut away to get clear. Even more serious was the threat the submerged woodwork posed to the boats themselves. Even Ed Gillett readily admits this.

'When it was dark it was very dangerous, you know, with them poles there. It has been known for boats, when they got a bit lost, to go right over the poles and for them to get stuck right through the boat. Some of them had to swim for it. They didn't come off. But old Bill Croucher, he come on one *and* he come off. He took his old tan frock off and he said to his mate, "Here you are, put that over the hole and sit on it." He had to sit on it all the way to Dungeness.' The buoys or dans, a flag on a pole or simply a floating object, which the kettlenetters were obliged to place beyond the end of their bight were frequently of little use at night, because they were tarred black to preserve them.

Impelled apparently by the laudable desire to preserve fish stocks, fishermen and local authorities also regularly lambasted these shore fishermen for their violation of certain basic tenets of fishing. In the wooden fish weirs at Graveney, according to A. O. Collard in his book *The Oysters and Dredgers of Whitstable*, published in 1902, 'Large quantities of fish used to be wasted by want of attention in collecting them when caught and the weirs got into bad repute on that account.' The same criticism could not be levelled at the kettlenets which were emptied regularly. Indeed many of them were temporarily lifted to allow the fish to escape if the catch was too large for the men to land in one tide or there were too few carts available to carry them away. Local fishermen, however, did successfully pursue this line of criticism. Fish 'in tons' was 'washed up right along the foreshore from Rye Harbour to Dungeness' in the late 1900s, according to Mr Dighton in his evidence before the 1914 investigatory committee. This motivated the local fishermen from Rye, Hastings and even Brighton to get up a petition to try and stop the kettlenets. An inquiry was held, but nothing ever came of it except that the Board of Trade were made aware of the 'mischief' which the kettlenets caused and ceased to consider applications for licences for new stands. The Local Fisheries Committee were also at pains to demonstrate that the kettlenets employed a much smaller mesh than that found in most mackerel drift nets and that they regularly caused 'a very great destruction of small fish'. The range nets, pointed out Edward Page, the Chief Fisheries Officer in his evidence in 1914, varied 'from 30 to 32 knots a yard and the pound averages 37. I have seen some 38, 39, 40. They have not got what you call a standard mesh. It varies according to the shrinkage of the net. Sometimes you will find nets over 40, but the average is about 38 or 39 . . . We do not use for catching mackerel a drift net of more than 30 to the yard. We have no bye law but that is the medium size they use.' Mr Page rightly realised, however, that the validity of this particular criticism could be questioned and he did not press it. The purpose of a drift net was to trap mackerel individually in the mesh as they tried to pass through, while kettlenets served merely to divert and imprison the shoals. Of greater concern, therefore, was the size of the mesh used in the draw nets. Kettlenetters were repeatedly accused of employing too small a mesh for drawing, thus effectively eliminating any chance that under-sized fish may have had of escaping from the trap. The result, the authorities maintained, was that boxes originally intended to hold 60 mackerel were being sent off to market with over 200 in them, most so small that they could barely stay fresh for twelve hours.

Looking back, it is difficult to distinguish reasonable from unjust criticism. Without doubt increasing competition from offshore steam trawlers, often of foreign origin, prompted many of the inshore fishermen, faced with falling catches per trip, to find an easy scapegoat. Even the apparently unbiased Local Fisheries Committee could be relied on to support their case since half of the members were professional fishermen themselves. In the end, however, it was not action brought by rival fishermen, the Board of Trade or the Sussex Local Fisheries Committee which led to the disappearance of the kettlenets. The mackerel shoals simply ceased to frequent the shoreline in the same numbers. Most operators gave up in the 1930s, Ed Gillett in 1953. Nothing remains today to betray that they ever actually existed except a few old photographs and the recollections of older inhabitants of the area.

Part III
_____
Town Dwellers

Chapter 12

Town Life and Work

God made the country, and man made the town.

William Cowper, *The Task*

By 1901, over two-thirds of Kent's population, 667,170 people, lived in towns, and the proportion was increasing. The county's population grew by 15.7 per cent in the 1890s and 8.8 per cent in the 1900s, but the urban districts showed increases of 22 per cent and 10 per cent during the same period. Although rural districts as a whole also showed a small increase most of it was accounted for by a few areas on the outskirts of towns where housing developments were encroaching outside the administrative boundaries. Between 1891 and 1901 the population fell in 214 rural parishes, over two-thirds of the county's total, despite the fact that the birth rate exceeded the death rate in all of them. People were clearly leaving and becoming town dwellers. In contrast, only two urban districts, Tenterden and New Romney, witnessed a fall in population during the same period. Neither of them were typical of the majority of Kentish towns of the period and both recovered some of their losses in the next ten years.

Urban growth was far from even in the county. The older mature towns barely increased in size during the period. The city of Canterbury in the 1890s increased its population by a mere 8 per cent, from

23,062 to 24,899, and even experienced a small decline in the next decade to 24,626. Maidstone grew even less between 1891 and 1901, by a mere 4.3 per cent to 33,516. Large-scale emigration also affected several towns in the 1900s. Faversham's population fell by 670 between 1901 and 1911, Sittingbourne's by 563. Gillingham, on the other hand, nearly doubled in size from 28,040 in 1891 to 52,252 twenty years later. The seaside towns of Margate, Folkestone, Herne Bay, Broadstairs and Ramsgate also increased appreciably in size.

County and Municipal Boroughs, Urban and Rural Districts in Kent with populations in excess of 20,000 in 1901 and 1911

Authority	Population	
	1901	1911
Gillingham M.B.	42,745	52,252
Dover M.B.	42,672	43,645
Dartford R.D.	37,532	39,909
Chatham M.B.	37,057	42,250
Maidstone M.B.	33,516	35,475
Tunbridge Wells M.B.	33,373	35,697
Folkestone M.B.	30,650	33,502
Rochester (City of) M.B.	30,590	31,384
Ramsgate M.B.	27,733	29,603
Bromley M.B.	27,396	33,646
Gravesend M.B.	27,196	28,115
Beckenham U.D.	26,288	31,692
Erith U.D.	25,296	27,750
Canterbury (City of) C.B.	24,899	24,626
Malling R.D.	24,724	24,233
Margate M.B.	23,118	27,085
Sevenoaks R.D.	22,687	24,029
Penge U.D.	22,465	22,330
Bromley R.D.	18,808	21,958
Dartford U.D.	18,644	23,609

The most remarkable urban developments, however, occurred in north-west Kent, as the villages and small market towns there were enveloped by London and turned into one enormous dormitory from which workers were 'sucked into the City at daybreak and scattered again as darkness falls'. For example, Erith's population rocketed by over 88 per cent to 25,296 in 1901. Bromley grew from 21,684 in 1891 to 33,646 twenty years later; Beckenham from 20,707 to 31,692. The ornate, miniaturised villas hastily erected by speculative builders were envied by some, ridiculed by others. The inhabitants of these new towns were C. F. G. Masterman's 'Suburbans', people whose lives were characterised by three peculiar qualities—'Security, Sedentary occupations and Respectability'. Their homes were 'little red houses in little silent streets in number defying imagination'. H. G. Wells, always an astute critic of his own society, was brought up in this area and often used it, thinly disguised, for locations in his novels. He paints a grim picture of 'Bromstead' and 'Beckington' in the opening chapters of *The New Machiavelli*: 'The outskirts of Bromstead were a maze of exploitation, roads that led nowhere, that ended in tarred fences studded with nails . . . in trespass boards that used vehement language. Broken glass, tin cans, and ashes and paper abounded.' The area, he claimed, lacked identity: 'All effect of locality or community had gone from these places long before I was born; hardly anyone knew anyone; there was no general meeting-place any more.' Of Penge he wrote: 'I have forgotten the detailed local characteristics—if there were any of much of that region altogether.'

There can be no doubt, however, about the social status a residence in these new suburbs bestowed on people. Rose Trinder (born 1896) grew up in New Cross, the daughter of a painter and decorator. As she recalls, even within the immediate locality a person's address spoke volumes about his standing in society.

'We all had our districts, and the very fact that you lived at New Cross meant you were someone better than people who lived in Deptford. I mean, the Deptford people would in their way think themselves someone who was better than those that came from the other side of the river. Anyone the other side of the river were rough people. You imagined so. Now I've heard of people who lived at Islington who were quite respectable and lived in nice houses, but at the time, the general impression was in our district, well, there were more working class people and likely to be more pub crawlers, dancing on the pavements when the public houses shut, and that sort of thing. Well, in New Cross, you were that little bit much higher and you wouldn't do that sort of thing in the street. And if you went a little bit further along to Lewisham, or Bromley—I had an aunt once who lived in Bromley, Kent—you were, oh!, really sociably some-body, you know. You never did vulgar things like sing in the street or anything. Oh, no! Good Heavens no! You were made to know your districts in London. The very fact, I don't know if it was something in your speech, or what it was, or whether it was just the district you lived in, but the districts kept themselves socially apart.

'I know my aunt that lived at Bromley, Kent, she had originally lived at Streatham in a very nice house. Her husband happened to sell papers and magazines and printing material, that sort of thing, and she always had a daily maid. We were very much concerned. We weren't allowed to go if the maid was in. We were allowed to go the day the maid was out. To keep the class, you see. She wouldn't have it known that she knew us people that lived in Deptford or New Cross. And her name was Sarah Ann, but she wouldn't be called Sarah Ann. She was Maud. Oh no, you were very select, and no one ever called unless you sent the card saying you were going to call and that sort of thing. It was very much so.'

Rigid class associations were not restricted to London or its suburbs. Every town in Kent acquired a certain image. Canterbury, for example, was invariably referred to as a respectable and dignified city by people from elsewhere. Even though some of the locals ungraciously described it as 'all parsons and pubs' they still recognised the overriding importance of the cathedral and the hotels which catered for visitors and pilgrims. The Medway towns had a less attractive image. An old saying described Chatham as a place where 'every third house is a beer house and every third man is a soldier'. Ashford's railway works projected a working class image to outsiders. Tunbridge Wells and Folkestone's aristocratic clientele bestowed a genteel reputation on them.

Within each town, however, there were, and still are to a large extent, rigidly defined, yet unmarked boundaries delineating distinct and separate social zones. Some of these were easily discernible to an outsider; others were not. Frequently the social tone of a neighbourhood could change within a dozen or so yards.

Canterbury was much more than a cathedral city, populated by well-to-do, respectable citizens. These existed in great numbers, it is true, especially in the imposing villas which lined the New and Old Dover Roads, and London Road. Dirty washing could be seen leaving by handcarts one week, destined for housebound wives in the poorer parts of the city, and returning the next scrubbed and ironed. Lads could be seen plodding up to their back doors each morning to perform menial tasks in the gardens or kitchen before trudging off to school. Above and below this detached group there was a multitude of others. The social elite of the city were undoubtedly those involved with the cathedral itself. They dominated the city socially in much the same way as the building dominated it physically. Insights into cathedral life, however, are difficult to come by. The lady quoted below worked for a short while in the early part of the First World War in a canteen just outside the cathedral. Although herself from a wealthy doctor's family and brought up in a society in which she was acutely aware of the infinite gradations on the social scale, she found the cathedral environment beyond her range of experience.

'I worked in a voluntary canteen with a minor canon's wife and an ex-canon's daughter who lived in the precinct so I got a lot of the back chat. Ye Gods, it was dreadful! The snobbery! It was out of this world! I mean, when you spoke to the Archbishop, you hardly expected him to reply. Nobody was humble minded. It was dreadful. They were chosen by God and that was that. Very few of them had friends in the town. At least that's my recollection.

'I remember an awful hoo-ha, because the Dean's wife gave somebody else precedence at a dinner party. Oh! And in the cathedral, if you went into service, you'd got all the canon stalls at the back, and the non-residentiary canons would occupy them on official occasions. When they were not occupying them, each of the residentiary canons and officers would be allotted one or two of the stalls for their families, so they could have their families sitting with them. Well, in front of them there was a tier down and more seats. Those were for what they called the parishioners, the local, well-known people who attended the cathedral regularly. In front of that was another tier for the cathedral servants. Well, anyhow, at five and twenty minutes past six, the head vesturer, a very good looking, big man, used to walk down and everybody had their eyes glued on him, looking round at the pews, looking to see which was occupied and which was not occupied. Everyone would try to catch his eye, and he'd go like this to somebody as if to say, go up higher brother, because he filled all the best seats with people he'd picked out from the rest. It was the most awful piece of snobbery. Don't you think it was?'

A stone's throw from the cathedral walls was Northgate. Close to the barracks and full of pubs, this area of town was even shunned by working class residents from elsewhere in the city. It was renowned for its fighting and rough quarters. Even the police patrolled in twos. Yet even here there were distinctions, the respectable streets and the dark corners.

People were slotted into the appropriate rung on the social ladder by a variety of factors: their jobs, income, cleanliness, material welfare, whether they had lace curtains up, whether they had a table cloth or a newspaper on their dining table, whether they frequented the pub or not, and most important of all, where they lived. St Radigund's folk invariably regarded themselves as socially superior to the totters, diddikais, and rag and bone men who lived just around the corner in the now demolished Knotts Lane, even though the latter were probably better off financially. Golden Square, another area which has also disappeared, was similarly held in low esteem by locals.

The physical layout of the town, therefore, reflected the social divisions within it. Each town consisted in reality of a cluster of separate little communities each operating its own set of rules and living apart from the rest of society. A glance at other towns reveals the same phenomenon. Faversham's Northgates were the districts around Tanners Street, Abbey Street and the Brents; its Old Dover Roads were Newton Road and the Mall Avenue, a tree-lined approach road to the town heralded in a guide of 1908 as 'very picturesque . . . the villas on the left hand side coming down the road furnish a pleasant and desirable spot for residents on account of their high and healthy situation'. Folkestone divided cleanly into two, the imposing villas and hotels to the west and the working-class quarters to the east. The social zoning of the Thanet seaside resorts and of Dover are also clearly portrayed in the chapters in the rest of this section. The days when all the residents of a town lived cheek by jowl in the centre had already gone. The layout of towns now reflected the divisions within society.

The occupations which those town dwellers pursued varied to some extent between towns. There were significant colonies of railway workers at Dover and Ashford. The holiday trade provided a valuable source of income in many coastal towns. The dockyards at Sheerness and Chatham, cement works at Northfleet, paper making along the Darent and Medway valleys—all these provided important local sources of employment. As *Kelly's Directory* of 1915 comments, however, 'Kent is not remarkable at present for any great manufactures,' and 'the occupations of the people of Kent are very much diversified.'

A considerable number of men were employed in small-scale, scattered industries: tanneries, food processing, and engineering. Even more were involved in building trades, transport, and the provision of food, drink and lodging, the three largest occupational groups after agriculture. Possibly the most noticeable group was the armed forces. There were approximately 20,000 service men in the county at the time, often concentrated into a few localities. Nearly 3,000 officers and men were stationed at Shorncliffe near Folkestone in 1901, 2,287 at Dover, 3,661 at Gillingham, 1,543 at Chatham, and over 900 at Canterbury.

Whereas over 75 per cent of men over the age of ten were returned as occupied in the census returns, barely one in three women were listed as being in work. In 1911, for example, there were 435,303 females over the age of ten but 309,603 either lived on private means or were housewives, schoolgirls, or children retained at home to help with the family upbringing. Of the 125,700 returned as occupied, 98,522 were unmarried. Whether these figures present a true picture of the extent of women's work is debatable. As we have already seen, it was common for married women to take part in seasonal work in agriculture, especially hop picking. Many others undoubtedly earned a few shillings taking in washing or going charring on a part-time basis. The range of employment for women was distinctly limited. Over 69,000 were classed as involved in some form of domestic service, the largest occupational group in the county, exceeding even agriculture. Among these domestic servants were house servants, hotel workers, laundresses, charwomen, hospital cleaners, caretakers, and those in washing and bathing services. The overwhelming majority, 51,400 or 40.8 per cent of the total female workforce, were employed as indoor domestic servants in private houses. A further 3,475 worked in hotels. There were 47,630 unmarried indoor servants alone, and the majority of them were teenagers. Service possessed several indisputable advantages as far as many parents of these girls were concerned. It took them away from home and gave them full board and lodging, taught them the discipline of housework and was socially respectable. Two ladies, one from Wouldham on the Medway, the other from Faversham, explain.

'Service, that's all there was. There wasn't all this employment in factories. There was one factory, that was Sharpe's Kreemy Toffee in Maidstone, but there were very few girls went there because I think the parents thought that, well, it was degrading in a factory. You was better off in service really. They didn't have to keep you, did they? Didn't have the inconvenience of having you at home. Really I think they was glad enough to see you working.'

'Neither of my parents wanted me to go down the powder mill where, if you couldn't get a job, that's where you had to go. That was down West Street. When the girls went down, we used to see them going, they had pig tails since their hair was long and they had to be tied with a shoe lace. They didn't have to wear any steel buttons, nothing steel at all, because you was dealing with powder, black powder. Explosives. I couldn't for a moment see myself doing that job and that's why I went into service which was better for me. When you go to service and live with another gentleman's family, you see a lot, you learn a lot, which to me is a finishing education to every working man's daughter.'

Even more respectable was dressmaking which accounted for another 13,716 of the female workforce in 1911, and the provision of food, tobacco, drink and lodging which included a further 12,760. Both these groups often required recruits to undergo lengthy apprenticeships with little or no pay because they were viewed as

socially acceptable occupations for women. The social status of shop
assistants was generally taken to be 'distinctly above that of ordinary
dressmakers', according to an assistant commissioner reporting to the
Royal Commission on Labour in 1893. She continued: 'They regard
it as respectable and accept a small salary in the hope that it will not
be for long. Marriage is their ultimate and not remote hope.' This
lady worked for a time in Lefevre's wool shop in St Peter's Street in
Canterbury.

'I went as an apprentice, 1s. a week. Then after a year I became an
improver at 2s. a week. A fortune! Of course you had to provide your
own uniform, a black dress, out of the money, and in those days you
all wore mittens in the winter because everyone had chilblains. There
was no heating in the stores like there is now. No, I won't say it was
a good job. It was respectable, shall we say.'

Schoolteaching was even more respectable. Female teachers out-
numbered males by over two to one in 1911—5,979 to 2,511—and the
majority of them, 5,440, were spinsters, often very young ones,
recruited as pupil teachers and trained in schools by serving teachers.
Once again their pay was low. Social acceptability was the main perk
of the job. Mrs Jane Banks (born 1893) passed an exam to attend the
newly opened County School in Bromley where she was persuaded to
enter the teaching profession. She explains her initiation here.

'I went to a county school. Well, there the head teacher would say
what she thought some children ought to be, but you had a certain
amount of say as to what you would like to be. So I became a pupil
teacher. You sat for what was called a Preliminary Certificate of
Education and if you passed that you went as a pupil teacher in a
school. I went back to the school where I had been in as a primary
school and I became a pupil teacher there. I was seventeen. I worked
four days a week in the school and every Tuesday went back to the
county school to keep up my book work, otherwise I would have let
that go and would have lost half of it before I sat for my final teaching
exam.

'You weren't in control of a class. You were following teachers
around to learn the procedure. But you had to work very hard as a
pupil teacher. You were fully occupied the whole time. There was no
slacking. You had to look after the stock room and cut up the
necessary needlework for children, and you had to take classes
occasionally.

'I got 10s. a month which I had to go to the municipal buildings
to collect. All the other teachers had their cheques sent to them but
as I was so young I had to go and fetch it. 10s. a month! You see,

little girls who went into service, they used to get 10s. a month but they also got a roof over their head and they got their food given them. But when you were a pupil teacher, of course, your 10s. had to do everything. In the second year you got 13s. 4d. a month.'

Over 80 per cent of fully employed women were engaged in one of the occupations listed above. The rest were scattered in small numbers through a variety of trades, with occasional concentrations occurring, as in paper making.

Unlike the country child who had few opportunities for part-time work while still at school and who was generally allotted domestic chores to do, the town child from an early age was expected to contribute to the family income. Fourteen was the official school leaving age but many were able to take advantage of local schemes which allowed for earlier exemption, half-time from twelve, and full time from thirteen, provided a certain number of attendances had been recorded in previous years or the child had reached a certain standard. Economic citizenship for some of them started even earlier. There were 3,126 children under fourteen in full-time work in 1901, the majority of them boys. The work which children of this age could undertake worried the authorities immensely. Almost all of the boys even up to the age of sixteen were forced to take up 'blind alley' jobs which lasted only as long as the employer could get away with paying them low wages. Once they demanded a man's wage they were simply replaced by another boy. These openings were especially common in the service trades—retailing and distribution—which required a large, relatively unskilled labour force. Over 30 per cent of boys under fourteen in Kent were classed as involved in the conveyance of messages. Most of them had no chance of promotion. The danger of a large alienated body of young unemployed and unemployable men was one of the major issues in the Edwardian period, not simply because of the human tragedy involved. 'The tale of the boy's life is a series of unrelated incidents,' wrote one social investigator in 1912, 'it needs to be unified by progressive organisation in the interests no less of national character than national economy.'

Frank Honey (born 1902) survived his early years well to become successful in his own sphere. Here he describes the jobs which he took on while still at school in Canterbury in the 1900s.

'I was never forced to go out to work. I was expected to. Let's put it that way. In those days everybody had to. I was one of a big family and every money was welcome to my mother.

'My father would never let me be a newsboy. That was un-dignified. I couldn't be a newsboy but if I could work in a house where I wasn't seen, that was all right. My father was the foundry foreman at H. M. Biggleston's and I worked for one of the family whilst still at school. I used to go as a house boy to his house on the road to Bridge and I had to be there at six o'clock in the morning and I stayed till eight. Then I walked down to St Peter's to school. I worked there for about two years when the family closed their house down and I got another houseboy's job with some wine merchants. They had a house at South Canterbury which is near the hospital. I didn't like that place at all. It was hard work. They had boys going to King's School and they used to have these heavy brogue shoes and I had to clean them with a skin blacking. That was one thing I didn't like there. Anyway I gave that job up.

'While I was working for Biggleston's I also used to work for a veterinary surgeon by the name of Mr Crowhurst. When he made his evening calls in the outlying farms around the Canterbury area I used to accompany him in his horse-drawn carriage and open the farm gates for him and hold the horse while he went to attend to his animal patients. In addition to this, in the school holidays I used to go with another boy to his little farm which was at the top of a road which I believe now is Hall Lane, and we used to go weeding there. We used to get 6d. a day for that and a jug of milk.

'Oh, and I also had another job at the same time. One of the carriers used to come in from one of the villages, Wootton, and I used to deliver his parcels for him when he came on Saturday afternoon because he used to park his cart in Iron Bar Lane where we lived. I used to take the parcels out to various parts of Canterbury. I got about 3d. from him for doing that.

'When I gave my second houseboy's job up I went doing other odd jobs around Canterbury, including the veterinary surgeon's job, bottle washing, running his errands and still going out with him in the evenings to the farms. In addition to that I was with other boys too up at the stations carrying parcels for a halfpenny or a penny as the case may be, to various parts of Canterbury.

'Then sometime after I left this second job I went with another boy who used to live in Notley Street and his father used to do shoe repairs and he had to take these shoes back one night to a house in the New Dover Road. I believe the name of the people was Kingsford. I think he was captain in the army. They had a very big house there and a racehorse, and the daughter even had a shetland pony. We went into this house and the lady of the house invited us in, and she said to this other boy, "Do you want a job?" He said, "No, I don't want a job." But I said, "I do!" So I got a houseboy's job there and that was the best job I've ever had in my life as a boy. I had again to be there by six o'clock in the morning. My first job was to groom two big black retrievers they had and then I had to let them out into the garden. Then I used to have to chop the wood and clean the shoes, the knives and the forks. There was no stainless steel cutlery in those days. We used to use brick dust. But the beauty of that job as far as I was concerned was that I had a jolly good breakfast. Prior to that I might have taken a piece of bread and butter to school with me when I went out but I used to get eggs and bacon there, something I never got at home. I could also work there on Saturday mornings and if I worked that I got an extra 6d. on top of the 2s. Of course, I only got about a penny or two of that. Because in those days, we only got about a halfpenny a week pocket money.

'Of course, in addition to all the part-time jobs, we all had our chores at home as well. There was always dad's boots and shoes to be cleaned and the knives and forks. And we had to scrub the big table and chairs once or twice a week. Chop the wood, fetch the coal, we had to do all these sorts of jobs. We had to fill the boiler on the kitchener. That was another of our jobs. I've scrubbed floors when I was eight or nine years of age. It wasn't all pleasure, I can tell you! But we didn't regard it as a particular hardship.

'I left school at thirteen and a half. Providing you had reached a certain standard in school you were allowed to leave before you were fourteen. There was no careers advice. I went full time at a gents' outfitter's shop where I had been messenger boy and shop boy for a time. I was only about fourteen years of age, only been there about six months, when I was put in charge of the shop! Then my father decided that I should have a trade and I was apprenticed to an electrician, and my first week's wage with a war bonus because the war had just started then was 4s. a week for 56 hours. After I'd been there a year the chap who owned the chain of shops which I'd worked for came and saw me and he said, "Look, would you like to come and work for me again? If you care to come back here to work, I'll give you 30s. a week and I'll put you into the wholesale business!" Of course, I wasn't allowed to do it because my father thought a trade was more important. But I don't regret it. I ended up pretty comfortably off in a job.'

These, then, are a few of the characteristics of urban life and work in the period. There are obviously many aspects which have not been touched upon: the town's relationship with the surrounding countryside, its entertainments, the extension of local authority services, the life of the middle and upper class. To unravel the complexities of town life would require more space than is available here. Even the three chapters which follow merely scratch the surface, but it is hoped they will provide insights into the life and work of certain sections of Kentish society upwards of seventy years ago.

Chapter 13

North-Kent Brickies

The present speculative age for the manufacture of bricks occasions considerable bustle at places where new brickyards have been established.

The Maidstone Journal and Kentish Advertiser, 14 June 1825

Rapid urban growth in the latter half of the nineteenth century, especially in the 1890s, greatly increased the demand for building bricks. Small brickfields, situated close to towns wherever there was suitable clay, continued to proliferate and to cater for much of the demand. Although these fields held one great advantage over their competitors from further afield and were able to keep down transport costs, which formed a large proportion of the total cost of bricks, many of them were short-lived. Water carriage offered cheap movement of heavy bulk cargo and, increasingly during the last thirty years of the century, an extensive brickmaking industry developed along the north Kent coast from Faversham to the Medway which was able to tap the large London demand by sending its products up the river by barge. Many of the brickmaking firms were also barge owners.

Two additional advantages recommended this stretch of coast to brickmaking firms. Many of the necessary ingredients could be found locally: sand, chalk and, most important of all, suitable brick earth or pug. Furthermore, London was able to supply them with all the firing for their bricks. The return load for their barges was 'rough stuff', an appropriate name for the city's rubbish: vegetable matter, paper, glass, ashes, clinker. Once this had been left to decompose on the sides of the creeks, it was sifted, usually by old men and boys, and the soil or fine ash was mixed in with the clay, while the breeze, anything combustible, was used for firing the bricks when they had been stacked in cowls, or brick 'mountains'. Since no coal or fuel had to be bought for the process, costs were kept down. The unsightly mounds of rubbish on the creeks and the pits left by the brickmakers' search for clay must have produced a desolate appearance over the whole area.

The number of men employed in the industry in Kent reached a maximum of 5,119 in 1901, having risen rapidly from 3,335 in 1891. These census figures may not indicate the full extent of the trade, however. They were collected just as the brickmaking season was starting, in late March or early April, and there may well have been fields which had not yet opened up for the summer. There can be little doubt, though, about the adequacy of the statistics for portraying the rise and decline of the industry, for by 1911 there were only 3,198 men listed as brickmakers. There were several reasons for this dramatic fall. First, a highly developed brickmaking centre sprang up at Fletton and Peterborough in the late 1890s which gradually undermined the importance of local supplies of hand-made bricks. Secondly, the supplies of clay were being exhausted. Brickies were having to travel further afield to find suitable supplies and the clay then had to be pumped in liquid form to the brickmaking sheds, or berths, which remained firmly wedded to the coastal area to facilitate transport of the final product. This was not only inconvenient, it was time-consuming and expensive and increased capital requirements. Thirdly, and most significant of all, however, was the national house-building slump which set in from the turn of the century. After 1903 activity fell persistently until by 1913 the level of house construction was lower than at any time since the late 1850s and early 1860s. The decline was accentuated by the war. By 1918 house-building had virtually ceased.

This change in fortune had disastrous effects for the men employed in the industry. Many of them left to find alternative employment. Hundreds were driven to emigrate, usually to Canada, attracted by posters offering a new life. Horace Adley (1886–1976) was one of the brickies who stayed. He married in 1909 and settled on the Brents, the area just outside Faversham where the majority of the town's brickies lived in a motley collection of houses and wooden bungalows. 'Finding a house? I had the pick of fifty on the Brents. Everybody was flowing to Canada. The brickyards were all shutting down. They'd used the earth up. I had the pick of fifty. There wasn't a pane of glass hardly in the house. All the floor was stones and bottles and that when we looked at it. Mr Wheeler, the landlord, he had it all done out and put up a kitchener in and done it all up.'

The age structure of the workforce also changed in the Edwardian period. Young men were no longer attracted to brickmaking. The accompanying table shows a marked increase in the proportion of older men. Men over 45 years comprised over 23 per cent of the 1901

Brick, Plain Tile and Terra Cotta Makers in Kent 1901 and 1911

	1901		1911	
Age group	Number employed	% of total workforce (approx.)	Number employed	% of total workforce (approx.)
10–15	212	4.2	96	3.0
15–20	898	17.6	462	14.4
20–25	772	15.1	296	9.2
25–35	1,137	22.2	730	23.0
35–45	921	18.0	646	20.2
45–55	618	12.1	499	15.6
55–65	376	7.3	293	9.1
65–75	156	3.0	151	4.7
75+	29	0.5	25	0.8
Total	5,119	100.0	3,198	100.0

labour force, but over 30 per cent in 1911. Whereas 37 per cent were under 25 years in 1901, there were only 26 per cent in 1911. Brick-making, always a tough job, now no longer offered the prospects of quick advancement and better money. The best jobs were already taken by the older men and, in the tradition of the industry, they tended to favour their sons for other jobs. Although the industry lingers on today, it has never approached its former prosperity and hand-brickmaking is now a thing of the past.

Brickies were never exclusively town dwellers. Many of them lived in industrial villages dotted along the coast—Murston near Sitting-bourne, Conyer, Oare—and they were not averse to turning their hand to agricultural work during the winter when it was available. Many of the brickfields, however, were situated close to towns, and the brickies tended to form separate communities on the outskirts. They looked to the town for their entertainments and their facilities.

With few exceptions, all the bricks made along the north Kent coast before 1914 were made by hand. Men worked in gangs of six in berths or sheds located alongside two or three washbacks, large square storage tanks for the clay. Once moulded the bricks were stacked in hacks to dry for a few weeks and protected from the wet by a cloth and wooden boards, known locally as loos or lews, along the side. When sufficiently dry they were built into cowls for burning, by men called crowders. Once firing was completed the bricks were stacked by sorters into separate piles depending on their quality and grade before being packed, over 40,000 at a time, in the barges. The whole process, with the exception of the actual moulding itself, took place out of doors. Frank Pack (born 1897) tried his hand at it near Sittingbourne when he was fourteen but it 'didn't appeal to me in any way whatever'. He can remember clearly, however, just how the brickmaking gang operated.

'It was very interesting to see how bricks were hand-made at that time. In the first place, the clay was in what they called a washback, a big deep brick square, built above ground level. It was poured in there as a liquid and left to set. Then they put about two feet of fine ash, ordinary coal ashes, and a bit of commons, that's common earth, with it, and a little chalk. Then there was a man, the temperer, that dug that out with a spade and put it into the pug mill which was on the outside of the berth. It was just like a little pit and in this was two big knives going round mixing this clay up with the ash, and the commons, then pushing it out into berth just like sausage meat coming through a sausage machine.

'And then inside the berth there was a moulder, flattie, and barrow loader. Well, the flattie had a curved, two handled knife arrangement and he chopped a lump of this off and rolled it along the bench towards the moulder, and by the time it got to him it was more or less like a pyramid, this lump of clay. Then the moulder comes along with this iron mould which he's already passed through dry sand and bangs this mould on top of it, rolls it over, that's turns it upside down, strikes it off with a board, back over and strikes it again. Then he left that board on top of the mould, rolls it on to the bench, lifts the mould off, and then there's the other fellow along side of him who picked up the brick and put it on to a barrow, a flat-topped barrow with only one wheel. We would call it these days a fishmonger's barrow with a flat top. They lay these bricks on it singly. Then in came a boy with an empty barrow, stood it alongside, took the full one and ran along a little, about six inch wide plate laid on the ground up to the hack. The hack is what they called the rows of bricks that were stacked up outdoors in the sun with air going between each brick so that they dried. The off-bearer was the man what took the bricks off the barrow and put them in the hacks.'

The men were all paid on piece work by the firm but the responsibility for hiring and paying them rested with the moulder, the most senior man in the gang. At the turn of the century a gang was paid approximately 3s. 4d. per thousand bricks. Generally, the off-bearer, temperer and moulder took shares of about 10d. each since they had the most arduous and difficult jobs and sometimes interchanged them to give each other a break. The remaining money was divided between the other three members, the flattie receiving 4½d., the pushie 3½d. and the barrow loader 2½d. Nearly all of them became expert at mental arithmetic. Harry Matthews (born 1890) spent much of his youth in the brickfields, helping out.

'I never done much schooling. I wasn't struck on it a lot. I reckon I learnt more away from school than what I did when I was up there. In the brickfields, directly I knowed how many the gang had drawed I could reckon up how much we had coming, and I wasn't more than eleven or twelve then. When I was pushing out, 50,000 bricks at 3½d. a thousand, that meant 14s. 7d. Then flatting it was 4½d. If you had fifty, that would come to 18s. 9d. I knowed all that before I left school. I could work all that out. And when I used to go over the old tot shop where they used to buy rag and bones and all that tackle I could generally reckon up the cash what he'd got to pay me for things, like.'

Barrow loaders were invariably the most junior members of the gang. Under the legislation controlling the employment of children in factories, boys were allowed from the age of twelve to attend school on a half-time basis, and many of them were employed as part-time barrow loaders. Harry Matthews began his working life as one of these, although prior to that he admits to spending a lot of time as a young boy 'knocking around the old brickfields'. Here he describes his job and the other work done by youths in the industry.

'A half-day barrow loader I was. They wouldn't let you work all day until you was twelve. If you could pass exams at twelve then they'd let you work all day. Two of us used to do the day's work, barrow loading. One week I started work about quarter to six and I used to have to go till dinner time, then the other boy took over in the afternoon and I was supposed to have school in the afternoon. I used to go round the creek, round the sea wall and lay round out there out the way. Then we changed over the next week and I went afternoons. We was all paid piece work then and we used to get 2½d. a thousand between us. That meant for 50,000 bricks we used to draw 10s. 5d. That was 5s. 2½d. each, wasn't it? The moulder generally used to make it 5s. 3d. But you didn't get the same every week. If you didn't make bricks you never got the money. It was a job to struggle along to get a bit of cash at all.

'Next season I went there all day barrow loading. I took the job on. The bloke I worked with, his name was Woodfine. Well, that was supposed to be his name. He came from Greenstreet way, I think. He used to lodge just along here. He was more or less single, you know, on his own. And he was a bit of a lad, old Wally was! Where he lodged, the woman had her husband and two sons on the berth next to us and every day she used to cook the hot dinner and bring it down to them to the shed at twelve o'clock, and she used to bring old Wally's dinner as well. Old Wally, he was a bit of a lad for a half pint, you know, and if he'd been out the night before he only used to eat about half of it. I used to sit there and keep guard, and he always used to give me half his hot dinner, Wally would. We used to have three breaks during the day. We stopped from eight to eight-thirty for breakfast when we'd been to work for two hours. The temperer used to go down the engine house and get half a bushel of tea. They used to make our tea for us down there and we used to have it in big drums. No milk, but it was good. I used to like it anyway. Then we had another single chap, Fred Cripps. He come from Westgate Road way, I think. He used to say, "There's a little rice pudding in my basket. Do you want to save that for your *bever*?" Then dinner time I had old Wally's dinner too. I used to have grub off anybody.

'Next summer was pushing out. That used to be 4½d. a thousand. But there was only us two lads, like, and the flattie. Some of them had wooden legs and were crippled. They were mostly invalids and couldn't walk but they could do flatting. I know we must have had some been fifty or sixty year old that used to do that just to earn a bob or two in them days. You'd got to be middlin' old and married before you could get any higher than flattie. And it would follow on from father to son. That's how brickmaking was in them days. It would be father and son working together.'

Frank Pack's brief excursion into the brickfields involved him in two of the jobs usually done by boys, pushing out, or as he calls it, rolling ahead, and sifting the rough stuff. Neither appealed to him.

"Course I went to the brickfields for a job more or less in the office. That's what I actually went there for but then they said they'd give me a job "rolling ahead" as they called it. I didn't know what that was until I got there. Some of them call it "pusher out". I had to meet this boy who was pushing the barrow out halfway to the hacks because as the hacks got further away from the berth that used to hold up the moulder so they put on another boy to help this boy. I took the full barrow from the first boy and pushed it on a little further and of course brought back an empty one and met him.

'Well, the first day I got on very well. I didn't have any accidents. I was all right. The second day, the boy that was bringing them up to me was running along this iron plate and I wanted to be clever so of course I run up to the off-bearer, and then I got a couple of minute's rest sometimes. I come to grief properly. I run into the side of the hack with barrow and all the bricks on the barrow, they all went squoggy and flat. So of course, they were no good and so I had to pick them up and put them on the barrow and take them back to the berth. I expected to get my ears boxed when I got there but I didn't. But anyway I didn't like it so that I finished up, I told them I wasn't coming in no more.

'So they found me another job. The foreman sent me down into what they called the rough stuff. There was this ashes and breeze and we had to screen it to get the fine stuff out of it, and the lumps that would burn from the stones and one thing and another. We had more like a sieve, wires coming from a frame, which we put at an angle and we had to shovel and throw this stuff up in the screen. As it ran down the fine stuff ran through the wires and of course the big stuff kept outside, and that's how you separated it. There was an old man with this old beard, a rather dirty old fellow he appeared to be, and he was with me. I threw the stuff up in the screen and got it out, and he was there with a shovel and took the coarse stuff away and put it in another lump somewhere. We got paid so much a yard for that. The smell was terrible. That was too dirty for me. I went to the office and packed that up. I don't think they expected me to stay on that job much.'

Although boys and old men usually performed these more menial tasks in the brickfields, they were sometimes done by women. There were never many listed in the census returns, and the annual reports of the Inspectors of Factories and Workshops during the 1900s considered that their involvement was declining due to 'the recognition by the women of the degrading character of the work for them' and the 'rapid growth of the fruit and market gardening industries in the county' which offered alternative and less arduous employment. They still graced the brickfields with their presence, however, right up to the Second World War, especially around Sittingbourne. Recognised by the authorities as a 'rough class of girls', the brickies too viewed them with a certain amount of surprise and detachment. Harry Matthews remembers here some of those he saw in his childhood in Faversham and the ones he met while working over at Sittingbourne in the early 1920s.

'I knowed a woman she could do anything in a brickfield. An old woman. I expect she weighed about twenty stone. She could flat as well as what us chaps could. And she could make bricks, this woman could! There was her, the old man and three sons. That was five out of six. They had a berth just out here on the Brents. And she used to come out in the afternoon and have a little spell with any of them. Give them half-hour spell. She'd go flatting or something and they'd have half-hour's rest. They used to take all the money. All but what they barrow loader had, like, went to this one house.

'Mostly they used to do barrow loading, women did. Nothing else but barrow loading. My wife, when she was about eleven, twelve, thirteen about here, she reckoned she used to go barrow loading. I can remember seeing a woman named Wilcox. She lived over Oare, where my father was tempering, putting the stuff in the mill for to make bricks, she was barrow loading there. But up Sittingbourne everybody had a girl barrow loader. I had a girl barrow loader, Cissie Hudson, her name was. But that was in about 1923, 1924. They was pretty much all round about twenty, I should think. That's all the work they could get in them days. And it wasn't bad pay for a girl, not barrow loading.

'They used to stand sifting that rough stuff too down there, because they used to go to work in the winter time down there, you know these gals did. Ha, you'd see them standing there sifting this rough stuff, going home for dinner—they had one of the sheds where they used to go into for to have a bit of breakfast—and the rest of the time they was up to their waist in this rough stuff, throwing that out into a barrow. Then the old platter boys, they used to be platter girls too, they would be picking out these bits of rubbish what wouldn't burn. And there were some ladies too! Cor! Oh dear, oh dear! But if you went up there Saturday night you wouldn't know them, how they used to be dressed up. You didn't think they sifted rough stuff. Cor! How they used to be made up. And there was a lot of them what was roaming about there.'

Whether men or women, the members of the brickmaking gangs had to work hard and continuously. They had every incentive to do so because it was universally the case that 'If you didn't get no work, you didn't get no money.' The mechanical tasks were particularly unpleasant during the early spring mornings, as Harry recalls.

'You'd start mould again, about Easter when we used to start mould again, as we used to say. When we first started your hands used to be sprained because you was lifting some weight when you was a brickmaker, a moulder, like I was. Your hands used to swell up. Cor, it used to be horrible for a week or two until you got used to it. And about that time you get the frost in the morning and there used to be such cold winds. It didn't half used to lay you up. But that was how it was. Sometimes you had another chap what you changed with to get a change.'

A good brickie could make 900 bricks an hour if all went well, or about 50,000 in a week and one million in a season. Working at such a high speed—the bricks were leaving the moulder's hands every four seconds and the pushie trundled a barrow containing about thirty of them over to the hacks every two minutes—required considerable energy and an ability to blot out the monotony of the task. Not surprisingly, brickies are remembered for their heavy drinking. Here is Harry again.

'In the brickfield, you know, they done nothing else much more than drink beer. They used to have some beer going! I must have been only about eight or nine when I used to go to and fro to all the pubs to fetch beer. I used to wait outside the Willow Tap and sometimes I used to be waiting for him to open at six o'clock. I used to have to paddle through the brickfield past Davington School out to Oare. A pint in a bottle. Well, generally I used to get three, a pint of ale and beer and two pints of beer for the three men what was working in the shed. When I got over there I had to go to the Windmill, get three more pints. That would be about seven o'clock. I used to go right along the berths—there was about seven berths in Cremer's over Oare—and one would sing "Bring us back a pint." It used to be twopence a pint in them days. I'd bring them all one back. Then back home. But my father did drink beer! He was a beer drinker. He was a temperer over there and I've heard one fellow tell me what drove the engine over there, that my father would nip over the Windmill and have a pint and come back again while they was making a couple of barrow loads.

'And they never used to pay for it till the end of the week. Used to have to stick it all up. If they didn't get it down the Willow, perhaps they got a bit short, they used to go to the Windmill. It was always Shepherd Neames's beer both of them. They used to go and square up Saturday, then start putting it on the slate again.'

A good start to the season was crucial to the brickies. Many would have had debts to pay off after eking out the winter as best they could with odd jobs. Bad weather and holidays like Good Friday and Easter Monday were both classed as unwanted nuisances enforcing them to be idle. To level out their weekly earnings the men sometimes came to arrangements with the owners to have a draw, that is, to take money on account for bricks which had not yet been made. During the rest of the summer they had to square up, and if they still found themselves in debt by the last week they might find themselves working for nothing to pay it off. Alternatively, during good weeks they could draw less than they were entitled to, putting some money by for the end of the season so that they could be sure of a handsome final pay packet.

Brickmaking ceased each September. Only the moulders were guaranteed jobs digging pug, although they always took on some of the younger men or boys to help them and paid them out of the sum they were allowed by the firm. Harry Matthews describes the winter routine for those men who were laid off and for the moulders who continued their piecework existence and outdoor work in the cold, inhospitable winter months.

'When I was very young my father used to go up to Woolwich then in the winter time. They used to go up to Woolwich gas-house, Greenwich gas-house and get a job in there for the winter. But you'd got to be in the know and in line for to get them jobs. Sheerness too, they always wanted men over there. You could get a job in them in the winter when the gas was wanted more. Most times night work it was. I used to hear my father talk about going up there. Perhaps they wouldn't have enough to come home every week, so they generally used to work it so that they come home once a fortnight. Come home and get a bit of fresh clothes and spend the rest of the time in cheap lodgings up there. That died out before I was any age at all though. Certainly by the First War. I heard my father say that them blokes what worked there regular didn't really like you. I used to hear him telling me mother how they used to threaten them if they done anything which they didn't think was just right. Terrible job.

'Later years when they got stood off, say September, second week, well the first thing what I know my father used to do, he used to get a bit of taters in, digging up taters. One season he went to Swalecliffe, in between Whitstable and Herne Bay. We had about a week there. Slept down in an old stable, got lousy and come home. Didn't stop there for very long. Then hopping perhaps. We'd go hopping for a week or a fortnight. My mother, she always used to have the wurzel pulling. That used to happen just about after hopping. My mother used to have that job. Used to get about ten bob a cant, I think. Then my father he had one or two places that he used to nip round and scheme three or four bob now and then two or three times a week. He'd also go along the creek of a morning, about six o'clock, and the creek would be full of barges with corn or coal and perhaps if you was lucky you'd get a job on one of them that would last a couple of days.

'But pretty near all brickies would scheme something. My father used to have so many. He used to be the potty man, the cellarman up the Sun in West Street. He used to get a bit out of that every week. Sometimes just before Christmas me and him might get a week's work up the big houses. There, Christmas time, they used to have all these people and they'd have a week's shooting for Christmas. I had an uncle, he was gamekeeper over there at Syndale Park and he always used to work me and me father in for beating. You used to get three or four bob for your day's beating, going through the woods, knocking and poking about, and they used to give you about half of a bottom of a loaf and big bit of cheese and a pint. When you'd done, like, they perhaps used to give you a rabbit.

'Some of the lads would go to sea. There used to be in the region of fifteen or sixteen boats here and they would go over to France, all sorts of places. The Beryl, the Aubrey, the Goldfinch. They was quite big, what you called coasting barges. They'd already got three hands and they would perhaps take a boy and give him five bob a week and his grub. It wasn't a bad corner. There was quite a number of kiddies I knowed. They done all the chores, washing up, cooking and that for them. They would cross the fourth hand off in the summer when the weather was good and he used to come ashore and work.

'Another stunt that you got on in the winter time round the farms was thrashing. The corn thrashing. They'd stop the night out there. It was a regular job for some of the lads following the thrasher unless it rained. Then they used to dig in between the hop hills in them days. Half a crown a day, three bob, that was all you reckoned to earn. But not everyone could do it. Only had what they called hop digging forks, a three-pronged affair.

'If you hadn't got no work and you wanted anything, you had to put your appearance in over the workhouse Friday afternoon and state your case. Then if they was going to give you anything, they'd give you perhaps half a quid's worth of tickets. You could go to the store and get a bit of grocery, flour and bread which they used to bake over there. They was about the length of two ordinary loaves put together. Parish bread they used to call it. You couldn't buy no cigarettes or bacca off the paper what they give you. You could only go to certain shops and on these tickets would be so much for cheese, or whatever. If you never could get no work and you went over there and got too much of a stage they used to give you a ton of granite to break. You had to crack it up to put on the roads and if you broke a ton of granite they used to pay you fifteen bob for it.

'A lot of old brickies, old 'uns mind you, finished up over there. That was their home then over there. We always called it the Spike, you know. I don't know why. That was the name it got. When they got too old they had no pension or nothing in them days and they used to have to go over there and make ha'penny bundles of wood. They used to get all the old hop poles from the farmers, cut them up and then you'd see perhaps five or six of these old men in the lodge over there making bundles of wood and tying them up. Then two would bring them round all these little shops in town in a truck and sell them.

'The moulders, they would go pug digging, digging the earth. I can remember when the pug came from straight off them houses right through to Ham Road, but when they was run out all round this way they used to have to go further afield. The last place what we had when I was over Oare was over Bysing Wood. I had seventeen winters there digging pug.

'We'd perhaps have about September kicking about down the field looking after the bricks what you had got made which had to be picked up and put in the cowl. If the weather was like this, you know sort of damp, then you couldn't get them dry and you had to know whether a brick was dry or not before it was burned. If you could break one in half you could tell whether it was what we used to call a little bit green, so we'd have to leave them down there to dry out first. Then of course we would chuck the sand up in a heap and clean up a bit. Then we'd go up pug digging about October, and we'd have perhaps till February pug digging.

'There was generally four or five of you together, and each moulder used to want a couple of tidy sized lads for wheeling the barrows. "Don't forget us this winter, moulder. Don't forget us this winter." They used to come along with us. They was generally flatties. We used to pay them.

'We used to dig pug by what they called the thousand. That was 64 feet along the top and then every foot you went back that counted a thousand. We'll say I got pug over there eighteen foot deep, well that was eighteen thousand to come. And then I think about every seven and half yards we went back we used to get another penny put on the rate. If you could do anything within the region of about 8–9000 a day, you wasn't doing too bad. We used to load it in barrows and these lads used to push them up to twenty-five yards, and there was this blessed great mill which used to wash it. Chuck the dirt in and water, mix it all up more like soup than anything else and then it was pumped from there down to the brickfield to run into washbacks. Then it was left to settle again and then when it come to using it the water had all gradually been drained off and the chalk was mixed in with it.'

Another winter job which started after New Year was sifting the rough stuff in readiness for the next season. Men and boys could often be seen at other times of the year, however, rummaging amongst the rubbish for coal or firing for their houses or trinkets which they could sell to the local rag and bone men. The rubbish provided some of them with valuable and much-needed cash, although their activities were frowned upon by the police and school authorities alike. In this final section Harry Matthews relates some of the experiences he had on the breeze and recalls some of the useful items which he found there, veritable treasure to a youngster.

'Pretty nigh every morning when we got to school, first thing the master used to say, "Come out the boys that have been on the breeze lumps." There'd perhaps be about four or five from Oare and some from this way and we used to go out and stand in front of him and he used to send us home to have a wash and clean up, because we smelt so where we'd been on the breeze, what they called the rough stuff. Whether you'd been on it or not when he said that you went up because that meant we never used to go back till after dinner. Pretty nigh every morning out we used to troop. I always used to be on there.

'I admit that I was most times on the breeze lump. I've been out here before it was daylight and I can remember raking the snow off once for to get some breeze to have indoors for a fire. I've been out there and got that before breakfast of a morning, the firing what come out of the breeze what they used to burn the bricks with, see. That was another thing. A policeman caught two of us getting this coke and we had to go up over the market in the court house. But we got off with it.

'I could go and earn money picking up bones, totting on the rough stuff. Every day I could go and earn anything like say 9d. to 18d., a couple of bob, picking up rubbish what you could sell. I used to pick out Bovril bottles. I used to get 3d. a dozen for them. Sauce bottles, any sauce bottles I could get 3d. a dozen for. Only you'd got to get a dozen. I used to get them and hide them up or take them home and store them until I'd got a couple or three dozen. Them jam jars, when they unloaded the rough stuff over Oare, you'd find a jam jar half-full of jam nearly every shovelful. Well, you'd four one-pound jars for a penny. You used to have two-pound jars too in them days. You'd get three of them for a penny, and if you had three-pound jars, they used to give you ha'penny each for them. I was never without a few coppers. I could buy or sell anything I could, I reckon. Even as a boy.

'There used to be perhaps three or four sieves down there and the old boys, other old boys like me, what they used to find, I used to buy it off them. Men's pipes in them days, they just had a little silver ferrule on them. I expect you've seen a man's pipe with a little ferrule about halfway up the stem. They used to be silver, most of them in them days. I used to give the lads a penny each for them, but I knowed where I could get 3d. for them. You could get a packet of Woodbines five cigarettes for a penny then and in these shops on the Brents you could buy them one for a farthing. But anything they found, like silver, a bit of a brooch, I always used to know within a little what it was worth. 'Course I always used to make sure I was going to double it. Used to take these ferrules to a bloke named Jones, just by the Ship Hotel in West Street. A jeweller there. He used to buy old silver. Sometimes they used to find silver spoons. I used to say to the lads I'll give you 10d. for it, perhaps a bob, if it was a decent one like and hadn't been worn a lot. I knowed I could get half a crown for it. I'd always got a tanner or a shilling in me pocket. I don't know why but I had.'

This has been but a brief glimpse of the work and lifestyle of the old brickworkers. Crowders, sorters, horsemen, odd men, bargees—these have all been omitted not because they are less interesting than the men who comprised the actual gangs themselves but because space does not permit their inclusion. One thing is true of all brickies, however. Those that survived can now look around and point to almost any building in the area and still see the results of their work. Few other workmen can do likewise seventy years on.

Chapter 14

A Childhood in Dover

The childhood shows the man
As morning shows the day.

John Milton, *Paradise Regained*

Historians should be, and are becoming, more interested in the study of children. Children have always borne the full force of society's attempts to put over and preserve its values and attitudes. They have been bombarded with parental advice and discipline, religion and education in an attempt to mould them into adults fit to take their place in the world. The events of childhood are indelibly imprinted in almost everybody's memory and can often be readily and vividly recalled by people as they get older. By allowing elderly folk to pin-point the events which had most significance for them in their youth, the patient historian can compile a fairly accurate picture of a society which is usually different from his own, freeing him from the shackles of his own upbringing. As the following account clearly demonstrates, efforts to tap the memories of childhood can be highly successful. There is no trace of nostalgia or rose-tinted spectacles here. It is a solid assessment of his childhood life by a person well qualified to give it.

Childhood memories can also provide a mass of information about areas of life not covered by traditional documentary sources: family life, entertainments, shopping, street communities, house interiors, class attitudes and diet. Although the diet of the wealthy may be studied through recipe books and surviving household accounts or printed menus, no comparable records exist for what C. F. G. Masterman described as 'the great multitude'. Indeed, as he astutely commented as long ago as 1909, 'We know little or nothing today of the great multitude of the people who inhabit these islands. They produce no authors. They edit no newspapers. They find no vocal expression for their sentiments and desires.' Glimpses of their lives can be obtained only through oral recollections.

Dover, which is both the stage and the backcloth for this particular act of childhood, is usually portrayed as a relatively prosperous but not highly industrialised town, with a castle, a military presence, some seaside resort facilities and above all a bustling cross-channel traffic. It had another and less welcome claim to fame in the Edwardian period. In 1905 the Board of Trade carried out an extensive survey of the cost of living and Dover was discovered to have the highest retail prices of any town in the country, higher even than London. Groceries there were 7 per cent dearer than in the capital, coal a staggering 17 per cent. Only meat was fractionally cheaper. Although comparatively low rents pulled down the overall cost of living index to just below that of London, the low level of wages in Dover meant that for the majority of the working classes it remained an expensive place to live. Of the trades for which details were collected, only stone masons received above average wages, and these were predominantly migrants attracted to the town to work on the harbour extensions. Little wonder, therefore, that another gentleman who visited the town in his youth thought it remarkable for the number of soup kitchens and charity organisations or that these features largely in the following account.

Steve Tremeere was born in 1897 and died early in 1977. His childhood tale, despite its many amusing anecdotes is, above all, one of hardship and grinding poverty. He tells it with such verve and gusto, however, that the bare skeleton of figures provided by the Board of Trade are fleshed, clothed and come to life.

'Mother had what they called a breakdown. She was taken queer and what they done was take her straight over to the asylum and she was there till she died at the age of fifty-four. Well, father had been just an ordinary fisherman. He'd been brought up in the workhouse and he'd come out at thirteen and was apprentice to a trawlerman at Yarmouth. Well, he had to leave the sea and he went as a labourer. I was eighteen months old, there was my sister four years older than me and my brother Reggie in between the two. Aunt Maria, she wanted to take the girl, and Annie wanted to take Reggie. But father said no. "I'll bring them up all on my own," he said. With the aid of an old woman he looked after us. The wickedest old whelp that was ever born, she was. She was wicked even to her own kids. I'm telling you she put the broom shaft across my back many a time. But father was between the devil and the sea and had to have somebody to look after us while he was at work, and I admit I wanted keeping an eye on. My sister was a bit more refined and took after my mother. He was a bloody good father. When he was half cut he'd always come straight home to us. I could go in a pub and say to him, "Come on." Out he'd come. The years he had us and it wasn't very easy for him. If there's a throne up in Heaven where they say you're going if you're good, I reckon he deserves the top one. We'd have been separated, lost, wouldn't have known where we were if he hadn't kept us.

'Well, any rate, I went to school when I was three and half. We wore petticoats then and we was left in another room, and we all played together. Wasn't like supervised by a teacher. Sometimes older girls looked after you. Sometimes my sister came down there for an hour and looked after us. Well, then I went round to St Mary's School, that was in Queen Street, when we was six. You went there up to eleven then you went to the big school. Our teacher was an old spinster, a proper martinette for discipline but she had a heart of gold. In her desk there was always an apple or orange or something which she cut up in little bits for us. Well, then we went up to the other school. You had exams then and you had to get so many before you could go up into the next class. If you didn't get that you stopped down there. I know some boys that stopped in number one till they left school at fourteen. We had one teacher who could take everything, every subject the whole of the year. Within a fortnight he knew every boy, and within one month he had you all weighed up. Them what could get on with their work used to go up the back of the class. All them what were backward he had down in front of him. Always forty, forty-five boys in one class.

'Well, when you got up to ex-six, you could go up again. There was an upper school and a lower school. The upper school was tradesmen's boys and they had little hats with a badge on it and they paid 6d. a week for the privilege of it. We wasn't allowed to mix with them. We had our play time and they had their play time. But the last year when we went up we had to sit next to them. They always had great big collars on, you know. It was a great temptation when it was

just pen and ink, that collar was. Oh dear, oh dear, yes. We used to
have some capers like that. We was the harem-scarems. Didn't matter
about clothes. No school uniform then. As long as your hands and
face was clean, that was it. You could go to school and you'd see
some boys with a pair of trousers on and you wouldn't know what
was the original cloth, it was patched so much. That's honest to
goodness. The only thing they looked at was your face and your neck
and your hands. If he caught you, you went out to the wash-house. It
was cold water. And you washed yourself too! If you didn't wash
he'd send a couple of older boys to wash you. They always had good
swimmers at St Mary's. Used to march us down to the sea baths.
They was on the sea front then. That was the only good wash some
of us had when we got in the baths. They won the schools' cup year
after year after year. But it didn't matter about your clothes. Not a
bit. Some of us had jumpers out here somewhere—the old man's. And
you could get a pair of boots for 1s. 11d. then. Hobnails. They had to
last you.

'The old man used to do all the cooking and all the washing for
us kids after he came from work. He used to go at half past five in
the morning. We was ready for school at half past five! We used to
get our own breakfast, bit of bread and milk—condensed milk. Or
perhaps a bit of bread and jam. Then you could go to the shop and
you could get a farthingsworth of tea, a farthingsworth of sugar, and
ha'porth of milk. As long as you'd got the hot water you'd got a cup
of tea to warm you up before you went. There wasn't no weekly
shopping like we do now. You'd dive down in your pocket in the
morning and see how much the roll call was. Dinner time, he never
came home for dinner, we used to have to get our own. We'd come in
and have a bit of bread and something, that's all. Then my father
came home at night. He might bring in some fresh herrings or something like that. Bloaters. Sprats. Something like that. They'd go on
the grid iron. The hot dinner we had was on a Sunday and then he'd
make a great big steak and kidney pudding or something like that.
Great big pot. I used to have to go along to old Wood's in the
Market Street for two pennorth of pieces. Only two pennorth but it
was meat though and you could eat it. Oh yes. And that would go in
with onions and one thing and another. He'd strain off the cabbage
water and say, "Come here, you." One cup of cabbage water every
week. Medicine. Yes. Cabbage water. Sometimes I drink it now. It's
good for you, for your blood and everything.

'The food then, it was good and it was cheap. If you had the
money, mind you. But you didn't want overmuch money because if

you only had a penny, you could get something with that penny. As for bread, you never bought a new loaf of bread. You took a pillow slip or bag down to the bakehouse next morning for two pennorth of stale. That was only yesterday's. You got a whole loaf and half a loaf. Nobody ever bought a new loaf. The only thing you bought new was on Saturday nights and Sunday mornings when the muffin man come round here. A big basket, great big blanket on it, white blanket, and it was full, red hot they were as you took them out. You took them out and buttered—marged—them straight away. They were lovely. He'd come round with the old hot rolls on a Sunday. Six for 3d. No, seven for 3d. All red hot. That was the only times of enjoyment. Otherwise we was having stale bread all the time.

'Butter you never had. Marge, 4d a pound up the Maypole. You had to go to the Maypole because if you didn't go and get half a pound of marge you didn't get a clapper. That was a bit of cardboard with a bit of paper in it, and as you moved it round it went crack. We had to watch all these shops where they gave something away, us kids. Where they were giving a little bit of bunce, that's where we used to go. If they hadn't got the clapper we didn't want the marge. Go down to Pearks's then. What did Pearks's used to give away? I don't know if it wasn't a little tin whistle. They all used to give something away.

'Two pennorth of pieces of bacon. That was all the cut pieces, all the bacon slips. Take the basin with you for two pennorth of cracked eggs. You got half a dozen cracked eggs perhaps, all depended how many he'd got there. There's eggs and bacon! Oh, living like little lords. We thought we was in the Hilton Hotel. Then if you had a stew, you had two pennorth of pieces for stewing, a pennorth of pot herbs, that was carrots, onions and turnips. All went in. And a pennorth of potatoes. They averaged about seven pound to the gallon. So about two pound of potatoes. Well, that was 4d. and you had a lovely stew. Used to get fry, three pennorth of fry. Mind you, you could eat it when it was fried. The old man would bash it about there with a rolling pin or broom handle, flatten it out, and it would go in the frying pan. Do you know how he used to make the gravy? Well, father would get a big white metal spoon. He used to fill that up with brown sugar and be used to poke it in the fire and it all used to burn and go black. Then in the frying pan went the little bit of water and a bit of flour, mixed up, then in with that. And it was lovely bloody gravy, I'm telling you. That was another dinner.

'Then on Saturday morning, the covered market was full up with pigs one side, right from one end to the other. At the end was all the pork loins. So we goes down. Two pennorth of pork loins. Big armful. Bring them home. The old man would chop them all up and they went in a big iron saucepan. We never had a gas stove or anything like that. We used to have a big stove with an oven. Well, when it was boiled it used to go on the trivet and it boiled all Saturday and all Sunday. Then Sunday evening father would get the basins and fill them all up. When they set in the morning, they all come out, oh, lovely brawn. Give you a huge chunk and a lump of bread on top and say, "There's your breakfast. Eat it." And you was full up. It was good. It was nourishing and it kept us going.

'But the winter months were bad. Well, they was in my family. Had nobody to cook for us. We used to take charity soup. If we was lucky we'd get a ticket for a bowl of soup and a roll. If we wasn't, father used to leave us a penny. Used to take a washing bowl jug and run round to the soup kitchen in Market Street, and when all the tickets had been given in they used to chuck another couple of gallons of water in and give it another boil up and we used to buy a pennorth. That was our dinner many a time, with bread in it.

'Christmas time would always be a giblet pie or something like that. When we got very hard up we'd go down to the poultry keepers and ask them for chicken heads. Get a pile of them, poke them in some boiling water, scalded them. Then all you had to do was to pick the feathers off them and all the skulls went back with some soup powder in it and made a nice stock for supper. That's true. That's how we used to eat. You might not think it, but it is, the honest truth. But the butchers, if you went down at night time, late at night, they'd give the meat cheap. All they had was an old ice block and you see they couldn't save much. You'd get a lump chucked at you for about a tanner. Half a leg of mutton perhaps for eighteen pence, if you had eighteen pence. Eighteen pence was a bloody lot, you know, then. The only tinned food then was tinned milk. We never had no fresh milk except we used to get skimmed milk when the milk man came round. He used to come round with a big yoke and two cans. "Skimmed milk-o, skimmed milk-o." Penny a pint, see. Rush out with a halfpenny for a jug. Half a pint of milk. Well, when he came round you could go and get a ha'porth of rice. The old man would put it in a bag and boil that rice, then put it into a dish and on went the skimmed milk and in the oven it went. That was rice pudding. Have a fill up. Your little belly used to come out and it used to go in. That's how it was. Didn't do us any harm. Made bloody good men of us, I think.

'Fresh fruit? Used to help ourselves out of the orchards. All up the big houses up the castle. They had long gardens, and they'd all got apple trees and pear trees. Used to get our fruit all right, don't you worry. The shops, they all had the fruit outside. Always had a coat with no pockets in it. You put your hand in and it was free, in your pocket like, but you was picking something. You got up to some capers. Used to go up on the banks and then have a sort out what we'd got. Have a share. One had a pineapple perhaps if he was lucky. Used to get caught out sometimes. You'd pinch an orange and think you'd got a nice orange and you found you'd got a Seville orange when you bit in it. We didn't thieve it. There was one motto we always learnt at school, "God helps those who help theirselves." So we used to help ourselves thinking he would help us. I don't know whether he did or not. He didn't say nothing.

'When I was a boy, when I was at school, my ambition first was to get a pair of pram wheels. When I got a pair of pram wheels I wanted a Tate sugar box. I got one of them, got the bolts and made a barrow. I used to pick up four bags from the old girls in the street on a Friday night and their tanners, and I used to walk from there right up to the Coombe Valley Road, to the gas house there, for four bags of coke. They'd tie them up and they'd poke them on and off you went. I got a farthing for each bag. So that made me a penny. Then I used to go to the Cause is Altered pub with my little barrow and I used to have to take all the bottles of stout to the old girls in the Gorley Almshouses, their weekly orders. I would take them all round. Sometimes I got a farthing from one, but generally I used to come back with a bag of cakes. One would give you a fleed cake and another would give you a currant cake instead of a halfpenny, because they hadn't got it either, you know. If you didn't earn it you never got it. There was no pocket money given you then. Not for the likes of us anyway. You could run from here to bloody Timbuctoo for a penny if you had chance too.

'Hard to believe, isn't it, but poor or not, beggars an' all, we all went to Sunday School. It was a sprat to catch a mackerel. You had a card, a stamped card. If you went to school on Sunday, the teacher would stamp it with a star. You had to have so many stars before you qualified to go to the school treat in the summer. Father used to give us whatever he could muster then, generally 6d. We'd all go down there in Chitty's and Mannering's carts what they used to cart the flour about in with great big canvas cloths. They used to fill the carts up with us kids and take us all the way up the town to where the mill is, along the bank there. All at the back was all fields and that'd be where we had the treat. Muffins and bits of bread and lumps of seed cake and one thing and another. Then there would be little sports as your ages went up. You got a little memento. And there were little stalls where you could spend your tanner. Farthing worth of dosh, toffee. It used to be wrapped up in paper, newspaper. You could never get it off that once she'd wrapped it in that. Farthing's worth of Scotch peas.

'I don't think anybody along our street went to church though. Well, there was one or two of the old tits used to go there with their bonnets on and their prayer book in their hand. Go down St Mary's church there. Come home, off went their bonnet, on went their aprons and they was down the boozer getting a pennorth of porter. Why did they go? So they could get these charity coal tickets and charity soup tickets. They didn't go for the religion, don't you worry. If you went to church you got a charity coal ticket. That was a hundredweight of coal come round. A man'd come round with a cart, ringing his bell, "Charity coal!" "I've got one, mister." Out came the ticket and you had a hundredweight of coal. Or when the soup kitchen was open they got soup and a roll for nothing.

'If you wanted a doctor you had to go round to one of these big shops, to one of these church people and get this form to fill in. Take that down to the doctor's. Then he pleased himself whether he come or not. No welfare state then. No. Oh dear, no. If you hadn't got a ticket and you hadn't got a half a crown he wouldn't come in the house and look at you. The most dangerous things was diptheria and scarlet fever when we was kids. Everybody had a dose of senna pods or brimstone and treacle every week. Kept you healthy—regular. For colds we used to have to go down to the chemist for two pennorth of Friar's Balsam, pennorth of aniseed and a pennorth of sweet nitre. Father would get a spoonful of sugar and put three drops on it. Two drops for us kids, three for him. Your cold was cured. You can't get it now. In the winter he'd get Russian tallow and he used to rub it on our chests, and another thing we used to have in the winter when the weather was cold since our clothes weren't thick, he'd rub us with Russian tallow and wrap sheets of brown paper round us. There was children, some was starved. You could see the poor little buggers, they come out with rickets. Irons on their legs. Or you might be playing with this girl, same age, and when she got about twelve, you could see it going, consumption. That was very rife amongst them. Any rate, most kids they wasn't so big as these now because they never had free milk or anything like that. Half of them never had dinners. But we always got one good one at the weekend.

'Well now, the houses. Our house was in Chapel Street, Chapel Place. That went from Queen Street through down to Market Street, where the Roman remains are now. Well, we were living on top of that. We didn't know our houses were built on them. Our house was a living room here at the front with a little scullery out the back. All brick floor. Table and chairs. No sideboards or anything like that. On the mantelpiece was a great big clock and a couple of little vases, old ones, and very cheap. We went up one flight of stairs we came to the first bedroom. That had no bedroom door, it just had a net on it. Never had no stair carpet. Ordinary bedroom. You got a big bed, washing stand there with a bowl and bucket on it. A chest of drawers in the corner and that was full. Then you went upstairs to our room. You'd got a big bed in there and a chair, and that was all there was in there. There was a little window at the front of that and that was the box of our theatre.

'On a Saturday night that window was our look out. They'd think we was asleep but we'd get up there and watch all the old women down there, all chinwagging. If there was a fight out there we could watch it in the grand circle without anybody interfering with us. We often got up there in the middle of the night and had a look. Then we could look out at the back and watch them all there too. There was a big lodging house out the back of us, Irish navvies in it, all sorts, while they was building the breakwater. Irish navvies and their women. You ought to have heard the language of them! No wonder we learnt it when we was little. Drink. Fight among theirselves. Then you'd see old women popping down there every half-hour, sometimes less than that. Pennorth of porter. In the pub at the bottom or else the one over the other side of the road, the Cause is Altered. They drunk more beer indoors than what the old man drunk outside, then they used to shout at him because he'd been drinking!

'But most of the people in the street, I'll tell you what, there was nobody ever locked their doors then. We didn't have much to pinch and nobody ever seemed to want to go in. Nobody seemed to go into each other's houses. They'd go outside chinwagging. The kids, we used to go in other people's houses like when we played together. I've gone in some houses and they ain't had a chair. They've had beer barrel crates and orange boxes for bloody tables. Didn't take them long to do a midnight flit when they went. There was always somebody doing a midnight flit out of the street. We had curtains up but sometimes they had potato sacks, anything up. Some of them had nothing up. The only thing about thieving was the outsiders. If they see'd anything on the line they'd have the trousers or shirt or anything like that. But there wasn't many trousers on the line. If you saw a pair of clean sheets on the line you know somebody was going

down the pawn shop Monday morning with them. That was a regular
thing.

'Up round the corner, where it says Adrian Street and Durham
Hill, the police on their beat had to go two at a time. It was a bit wild.
Wilder than what we were. They were the same as us only a little bit
rougher. Dockers, poachers, and anybody that had any fiddling.
Used to be the Durham Hillers and the Clarendonites as boys. We
was with the Durham Hillers then. They'd shout at us. All come up
Adrian Street, up the sixty-four steps. There was bricks, chalk,
everything till one lot retreated. But there was none of the gangs
like they are now, kicking and booting. We were all good pals afterwards.

'Up the King Alfred, up the hill, when the army and navy was
here, they used to have army pickets out and navy patrols. If we saw
the patrol or the picket we used to open the door of the pub and yell,
and they used to come out the windows, front door, out any way.
Because when they picked a bloke up they didn't walk him, you know,
they frogmarched him. They'd have them for anything; in a pub,
buttons not fastened up to the top of their chin, or if they was a bit
unsteady down the street. Many a time I've seen a sailor come flying
round a corner and there have been four or five old women there,
"Get in there, Jack." They've all stood there and the patrol's come
round the corner. Chinwagging away. When they'd gone they'd say,
"There you are. Away you go." Never used to give them away.

'Then they'd have fights. They was always fighting each other,
the soldiers and the sailors. Snargate Street was a battlefield at times.
Everybody, including the police, would be in there then. And they
was the good old days, you know! Then there was a theatre in Snargate Street. We used to get people from the theatre up in London.
Harry Lloyd and all them used to come there. There was boxes—
they was about £1 each there—a circle and an upper back circle.
Then there was the pit, and the stalls in front. Then there was the
gallery up three flights. That's where we used to go. That was 2d.
then. We used to filter through with the sailors. There was a little old
box just the same as up the railway station where they give you a
ticket. We got underneath there so they couldn't see us, up the stairs
and get in amongst the sailors, and while they go in there pushing the
old bloke back what took their tickets, we was out from behind their
legs and away. Little monkey nuts being dropped on bloke's heads
below.

'Then there was the Phoenix in the market, what they call the flea
pit. Went in the door at the bottom, the bar was there and that used

to be flowing with beer and one thing and another. People went in there drunk. It was a cheap place and all the boxes were nearly on the stage. They used to have all the plays on there. Well, when *Uncle Tom's Cabin* came there we used to get up there three or four times. The poor old slaves would be coming across the stage, the snow was coming down and there was a bloke with a whip. Then you'd hear the cat-calls and the boos. Big old Sam, he was about six foot four, ex-guardsman. He used to have this big coat with medals on, any disturbance he used to go in and say, "Now what do you want? Your money back or a rough house?" I've seen him get hold of a sailor or soldier what have been arguing, bump their heads together and march them out the door and kick them in the market. Oh, he was a big powerful bloke. I didn't come up to his knees. That was what they called the flea pit, and down the bottom in the pit there was generally beer all round where they used to take their beer in. Drink all over the place.

'Pubs. There seemed to be 365 pubs in this town then, one for every day of the year. There was. It was well known for that. I can tell you thousands, well dozens, what have gone. They even had pubs for the privates and the matelots. Matelots, they always called a sailor. And they were always open at five in the morning. Four down there on the market mornings. You could go in the Duchess of Kent and get a cup of coffee and a fleed cake. And lodging houses. There was four up at the back of us. At the Eight Bells there was one. One round the back of the church. Two up the top of Adrian Street, oh, and one down in Five Post Lane. All the old regular habitants used to come round. The tiger hunters, they used to come round. They used to get old frayed mats and they used to trim them all round, sew the rope round again and make net mats of them. They mostly come round with the grinders, the scissor man who had a great big wheel on a barrow. Tiger hunters, well, they had a vocation they learnt in the stir, prison. Them what mended umbrellas were mush-fakers. See, a mush was an umbrella and they used to fake them, put stuff over them, didn't they. Mend them. Oh, there were lots of sayings. There were some queer characters about then, I can't remember all of them. And some wicked ones too, I can tell you, Father wouldn't leave his trousers out the back otherwise they'd be gone in the morning. Some-one would be wearing them down the street before he could.

'All the beggars used to come round singing. They all got a farthing. Even the poorest always used to take them out a halfpenny or penny. What was that song they used to sing? . . ."Throw out the lifeline, throw out the lifeline, someone is sinking today." They kept on at it till they got some money. Then the Italians start coming over. Hokey-pokey and lovebirds. The old dames used to pay a penny and this lovebird would pick out an envelope with their fortune on. Then there was the Russian bear men. There was always some monkeys up the lodging house at the back of us. All sorts. You could go in and you'd see them at the big fire, the big stove, all cooking up. They had what they called a padding kens stew. They didn't call them lodging houses, they called them padding kens.

'I'll tell you the most pathetic thing I ever saw when I was a kid. I'd be up Union Row, well it's Coombe Valley Road now, where the workhouse was then, and us boys would be up there Saturday morning getting the coke on the barrow, perhaps eight or half-past. You'd see an old girl and an old bloke come up here with a little handkerchief with the little things what they had got left, the old girl on his arm, crying her bloody eyes out. We'd watch them till they got up to the Union. You'd see her hanging back as they got up near the big doors. Didn't want to go in there. At last they had to go in there. The matron would get hold of her and take her away, and the master would take the poor old bloke the other way. That's the last they saw of them. Wicked that was, parting them at old age when they'd been together as long as that. I wouldn't be parted like that.

'Every night you'd see the tramps come up the workhouse. Every night at six. They couldn't get in before six, you know. Not the next day, the day afterwards, you'd see them all come trooping out again. When they went in there for a night they had to do a day's work the next day in the garden or something. There was one old chap what was in there, old Tom, he used to come out about once a month. He used to come and see the old man. He'd been an old shipmate with him. He hadn't got nobody and he'd been forced to go in there. He used to have a little handkerchief with little bits of Dutch cheese in what he saved from his rations. The old man always used to give him half an ounce of tobacco. He generally used to come dinner time and us kids there we always made old Tom a pot of tea. We called him uncle. When the old man come home he'd have tea with us and the old man would give him a couple of pints and a shilling. Away would go old Tom again. Be another month before you see him. One time, the old man said, "Has old Tom been up?" I said, "No, Uncle Tom ain't been up." "Oh," he said, "I'll have to find out why." Well, he found out old Tom had passed away. Never said nothing. Nobody ever said anything to him. They used to go out in an ordinary plain box, like an ordinary wooden cabbage box to a pauper's grave.

'See how they looked after poor people then! I'm certain we're better off. If I thought I had to go through what the old people went through then, I wouldn't bloody well live. I wouldn't. I'd do my bloody self in before I'd have that. I've seen some wicked things. You could go along the street and see them sitting in the street, old people. You could see they was dying. Nobody took any notice of them. The police came along with a stretcher, and that was on two wheels. Pick them up and chucked them on the stretcher and wheel them off.

'There was always a prostitute in the street. There was two in our street. Good as gold. Never interfered with anybody. In fact, us kids used to like running errands for them because you was sure there was a bloody halfpenny from them. Usually you only got a farthing. Prostitutes always had more money than anybody else. Some of them, if they'd had a good time, they'd go and get things out of pawn for people and chuck it at them.

'As for helping anybody, everybody helped everybody else. You'd get two or three old women sitting there, they'd say, "So-and-so's in the club again, ain't she? I wonder how the bugger'll get on." Well, when that was coming off you'd see somebody go in and take the sheets off their bed and wash them for them. Another one would go in with a pot and pan or big washing bowl. There was no hospital or clinic. Nothing like that. All of a sudden all the kids would be shoved outside and down would come another kid. The mother would have one, the daughter would have one, and there was plenty brought up and they never knew the difference. They thought they was brother and sister. Most of the girls that I knew that got in the family way they were got in by businessmen as servants. But all us kids knew what was happening. It didn't happen in my house but I used to hear it in other houses because I was always in somebody else's house. The old man used to come home three parts cut on a Sunday from the pub and he'd say to the old woman, "Let's have a lay down. All you kids out." A few months after, she'd say, "You've done it again ain't you? You've filled the cupboard up again." Well, we knew what happened. I hope this ain't too crude, is it? Well, that's how it was.

'Uncles. The men with the three brass balls. Every Monday morning you could see the exodus. "Mother says the same as last week." Sometimes it was the old man's waistcoat with his medals. They wasn't allowed to lend you any money on the medals really so they had to be on a waistcoat before they'd give you anything on them. You'd hear a rumpus on Saturday night. "Where's my suit?" It hadn't been got out. They'd all christen each other with different names what they hadn't been born with. Many a time I got myself a halfpenny mid-week, popping down to Market Street with a parcel or to get one back. Over one side was Hart's great big Jewish clothing shop. On the top was a whatsisname with an arrow through it, "As Swift as a Hart, and True as a Dart." And on the other side was the pawnbroker's, Hart's the pawnbroker's. Same establishment.

'Never had a holiday in my life, apart from hopping and I only went once when I was little kid. Went with a woman what lived in the street and her boys, but I didn't like it. I think it was because it was away from the town. It was all foreign. I cried my eyes out the first night. I couldn't put up with it. So dull and dreary and no noise, and then in the morning all the birds started clacking. I got sent home after a fortnight. I was supposed to have been there a month. I've liked it since. We've been since every year for thirty year till this last two or three years.

'School holidays. The first was Ash Wednesday. We used to look forward to that. All used to troop out of school, cross Queen Street, through the market, up to St Mary's church, for a service. You'd never seen so many backsides wiggling about, so much itching to get away while the old parson was speaking. Then Easter holiday—a week. On Empire Day, the whole of the school went down to the sea front. We lined up one side of it and the other side, from the clock tower up to the dockyard, was all the regiments in their greys, blues, greens and yellows. They used to fire rounds and they used to rattle round the town. Then the bands would all play, Scottish Brigade, Dubliners, Munster Fusiliers, the Royal Irish Rifles. And you had the fleet at the back all decked up. The Empire and the King and Queen's birthdays. Always had a holiday for that.

'August, we used to get eight weeks and it generally used to be lovely weather. We were all out on the beach, anywhere. Sunday nights, lovely days in the summer, the old man would put his best cheesecutter hat on and in the summer time he had a white jersey on and he'd take us right up river. Take us all round Kearsney, call in the Donkey he'd have a pint and we'd have our ginger beer. Then he'd walk back and get as far as the next pub, he'd have another pint and we'd have a ginger beer. By the time he got home he was blown out and so was we. If he didn't go out Sunday afternoon, he'd sit on the doorstep and knock a nail in the doorpost and he'd sit there knitting nets. Cabbage nets. Sprout nets. Having been a fisherman he could make nets. And you'd get a big ball of string for a halfpenny then. But I used to be all round the dustbins. There was any amount of string laying about them. I used to bring it home, take it all to pieces.

Sit there at night time, especially if it was cold and rainy and take it all to pieces and make it into big balls. He used to sit there and knit them. Cabbage net would be two inch or inch and half mesh, and sprout meshes would be a bit smaller. Women used to cook in them, in their big pots. He used to get 2d. or 3d. for them.

'August Bank Holiday, up in the club and athletic grounds, the Kent police held their sports every year. Oh, it was a good do up there. There used to be tug of war, bicycle racing all round the perimeter, stalls and barrow boys. Some of them tug of wars had great big policemen, men from the gas works, and soldiers in them. There were all sorts of things. It was nothing to get in.

'Used to go up to the citadel for the church parade some Sunday mornings. Lovely especially if they had a drum head one. All the soldiers in the square. Everybody used to go there or if not there, on to the sea front to see the Gordon boys. They were from up Townwall Street. They were all orphans. They used to come out Sunday mornings and had their church parade at St James's church, all in their little kilts and Scottish uniform on. They had their little pipers and they used to go right up the sea front, turn round and pipe their way back again. People used to flock down to see them more than they did the soldiers. Old Mr Blackman was in charge of them. Oh, a hard life they had. They had discipline on them, them boys did. They was tough little monkeys, any rate.

'On the sea front there, what is Marine Parade, that reached from one end to the other, all the rich people lived in there. They all had four or five servants. Then at the back you had Liverpool Street, that was just the same. On this corner of Liverpool Street you had the Grand Hotel and the other end you had the Burlington Hotel. Then facing the sea you went up to the castle into Victoria Mansions. They had their mews at the back where they kept all the horses and the coachman over the top. Off the Connaught Road there was Harold Street, Leybourne Road Terrace, right up to Castle Mount, Park Avenue, they was all good class houses. All posh. We never went near them. Used to go round the sea front on a Sunday afternoon, though, see them all out on their verandas watching out and then zip round down in the back and touch up the cook for some cake and bits of bread and one thing and another. Then rush back into the timber yard, make a little house in there and sit eating it. That was regular that was. And us kids used to get down outside the gate of the Western pier where all the ferry boats used to come and what the porters didn't carry we used to carry as far as the hotels. We'd grab a bag or two and go flying off to one of the hotels. Finish up with one of them Belgian coins with a hole in it, worth about a farthing. Anything to get hold of anything.

'Then there was the old bath chair men. They used go to some of the big houses down the front. You know, big wheels and wicker basket and a little wheel in front and a handle at the back. They used to help these invalids get out, turn them round, pull them about. Old retired colonels with their gout and such like. Take them along to the sea front, stand there till they wanted to come home. I knew one old chin, he was an old soldier and I always knowed he was going out doing this because he had his cleanest shirt on. It was a bit frayed but it had a little bit of a tie of some sort. And his boots would be polished up. We used to follow him. Helped him up Castle Hill many a time when he's been pushing one of these old dames about. They used to be out there sometimes when it was raining. *They* was all right in their great big waterproof right up to their chin with the handle just sticking out. The poor old blokes what had to pull them about, they earned their money.

'Then there was the college, Dover College. We was always scrapping with them. They was better boys than us, they was well fed and they used to give us boys a thrashing. And the Boys' Life Brigade. They were tradesmen's boys and one thing and another. We never worried about that. They had a little round hat on and a little chin strap. All us kids used to follow them out on a Tuesday and Thursday night when they paraded, singing,

> We are the Boys' Brigade,
> Smothered in marmalade,
> A twopenny halfpenny pillbox
> And half a yard of braid.

Then there would be fights between them and us. Tormenting little buggers we were, I admit.

'Mind you, I'll tell you, we wouldn't have no bullying. No. If a couple of boys started on a little 'un, you'd soon have four or five more start on them. No, we wouldn't have it. And old people was always respected. If you was saucing one and somebody come along and heard you, it wouldn't matter if you was their boy or not, they'd clip your bloody ear and say, "Oi, don't talk like that." Oh yes, they kept us in check then. Same as at school, they used to hit you with a stick. I wish I had as many pounds as I've had sixes and twelves across my backside. Well, I deserved them. I admit it. But you couldn't go home and tell your father that, because he didn't take no notice. He'd say, "I'll give you some more if you come and sit here." Generally I'd be prepared. I'd have something in my trousers, a bit of cardboard or something. I know one bloke he put a tin in his trousers. A biscuit tin. When he hit him, it went bang. If it had been cardboard he wouldn't have heard it. Bloody tin went bang like a bell. That soon came out. Got it on his bare backside then. We used to put alum and one thing and another on our hands when we was going to get it. Resin. Harden them up . . . Is this all going down? Oh, there won't half be some sayings. I can't remember half the things I think about when you're away.

'We kids always respected a policeman too. Mind you, we used to get a clip round the ear off them. But you had to be really bad before they took you in. If a bloke was drunk, if they could get him to go home, or get one of his pals to take him home, they'd say, "Go on. Push off." But if he got obstreperous they'd throw him on a barrow, that stretcher they had, strap him down and way he went. And all the prostitutes had their photos taken and put up in the pub. They was barred from all the pubs. They had to do their business other places.

'Anyway, I reckon it was an enjoyable life. I reckon I've seen more excitement then than what the kids do now. Shan't say we was happy. None of us was happy, but we was contented though. Didn't have the opportunity these youngsters have got. You didn't seem to be able to get out of it, did you? Every time you went to church there was always that hymn:

> The rich man in his castle,
> The poor man at his gate,
> God made them high or lowly
> And ordered their estate.

Well, we knew where our estate was without having it drummed into us enough times. It's only a few got out and got away from it. If your father was in the mill or the timber yard you could get in there, but outside kids never had a chance. It was all mowed, cut and dried in this town.

'If you could see the change in the last fifty years as I've seen—well! Whether it's for the best I don't know. I doubt it at times.'

Chapter 15

The Holiday Trade

Whate'er from dirty THAMES to MARGATE goes:
  However *foul* immediately turns *fair*!
Whatever *filth* offends the London nose
  Acquires a fragrance soon from *Margate air*.

Peter Pindar, *Praise of Margate* (1800)

The holiday trade was one of Kent's most flourishing and highly developed industries by the 1900s. Almost every coastal town from Sheerness on the north Kent coast right round to New Romney and Littlestone on the south vied with each other for a share in the expanding market. Investors ranged from local councils and large entrepreneurs who sunk huge sums of money into piers, promenades, hotels, theatres, entertainment facilities and even new towns, down to the humble landladies who purchased extra sheets and crockery and let out their spare rooms in the summer season.

Most resorts originated as refuges for the privileged upper and middle classes who sought not only rest and recuperation but the opportunity for a high life and good time in the company of people from similar social backgrounds. Some, like Margate, had a long history dating back into the eighteenth century when it was fashionable and convenient for wealthy Londoners to make use of the regular hoy service to the town down the Thames. Herne Bay, too, planned on a grand scale in the 1830s, hoped that its position would recommend itself to water-borne visitors from the capital who by this date were able to make use of the faster and more reliable steam packets. The resort was, however, lucky to survive its first thirty years before eventually being assured a future when the railway reached it in the early 1860s. Even in the 1890s it exhibited 'visible tokens of failure', according to one guide book for the rival Thanet resorts. In contrast to these resorts on the north coast, Folkestone owed its success entirely to the South Eastern Railway which developed it as a cross-channel port from 1843 and encouraged the development of the resort. By the 1900s it was indisputably the most fashionable seaside town in the county, and the wealthy and famous clustered into its magnificent hotels, the Metropole, the Queen's and the Grand, and enjoyed each other's company along the Leas.

Efforts to attract the well-to-do continued well into the twentieth century. Only a tiny fraction of the working classes could afford the time or the money for an extended visit to the seaside. Most of them crammed everything they could into a day trip. Margate, despite being a resort popular with day trippers by the 1890s, still appealed to the middle classes for its long-stay visitors. A guide book for 1897 advertised 'A week at Margate, seeing all the remarkable sights, visiting every principal place of interest in the Isle of Thanet, paying all your expenses and taking home change out of a £5 note.' Despite an emphasis throughout on the relative cheapness of this holiday—travel was invariably by the cheapest means possible and at least one afternoon in the proposed schedule was put aside for sleeping, 'to save unnecessary expense'—it is clear that a substantial income would have been a prerequisite for any visitor planning to stay at this 'gay and giddy' resort. For the working classes £5 represented a lot of money. Many domestic servants barely received that for a year's work. For the agricultural labourer it was equivalent to seven weeks' full-time labour. Nor was the £5 the amount required for a family holiday. It was for one person.

The majority of the wage-earning class, therefore, only visited the seaside at weekends, or on Bank Holidays (introduced in 1871), relying on special rail and steamboat excursions, organised work outings, or perhaps most common of all, at least for the children of Kentish people, Sunday school outings. They generally headed for those resorts within easy reach of their home or those which made some effort to cater for them. Whitstable, with its shrimp teas and simple attractions, was a favourite with many Sunday schools in north-east

Kent. Many families also seemed to have walked there from Canterbury or surrounding villages for a day out. The majority of the day
trippers, however, tended to converge on Margate. By the 1890s the
London, Chatham and Dover Railway was offering regular cheap
excursions from London throughout the summer at fares calculated
to attract the day tripper. The return fare on Sundays and Mondays
to any of the Thanet resorts was a mere 4s., and weekend tickets
could be obtained for 8s. return. These day trippers were not always
made welcome when they reached their destination, however. Local
residents had often moved away to the seaside specifically to escape
from large crowds of people. Hotel and guest house keepers complained they received no benefit from the day trippers and they
tended to drive away more respectable clients. Restaurant owners
were against them because many brought their own food with them.
Shopkeepers moaned that they spent too long on the beach and too
little in their shops. Monied visitors drifted away to other resorts less
contaminated by these rowdy undesirables trying to sample for a
single day the pleasures which they were able to afford for a week, a
fortnight or even the whole summer.

　　The literature produced by the traders and local councils in every
Kentish resort continued, therefore, to emphasise the select nature
of their town, often commenting cruelly and unjustly on neighbouring rivals. Each tried to project its own individual image to distinguish it from the others. A guide to Thanet for 1893 summarises the
resorts there as follows: 'Royal and respectable Ramsgate . . . restful
and recuperating . . . the bourgeois Broadstairs . . . the popular
Margate . . . the far advanced aristocratic Westgate on Sea . . . the
rapidly rising artistic Birchington on Sea.' Margate traders advertised
products and services in guide books which were well out of the
reach of the majority of day trippers. Jewellers displayed a wide
range of expensive adornments. Chemists praised their own effica-
cious cures. The Seabreeze Cycle and Motor Works offered specially
constructed bicycles, 'Cycle lessons given by Experienced Instruc-
tors', and 'Motor Cars and Motors built on the Seabreeze Special
Designs or to Order'. The Clifton Baths supplied warm baths from
1s. each and ozone baths from 3s. It also promised deliveries of hot
and cold sea water to all parts of the town, let baths out on hire and
advertised 'Softened water specially for drinking' at 4d. for two
gallons. Margate Golf Club was open to visitors for 10s. 6d. for a
fortnight and there were special first class concessions on the railway
for its members. 'Of this highly favoured watering-place', concludes a
guide for 1897, 'it may be with propriety observed that it contains

within itself everything to gratify the senses and much to improve the body and mind; and it can be safely asserted that no other sea-bathing place has such attractions.'

When day trippers threatened to drive away monied visitors during the summer months, in response the advantages of winter were unashamedly extolled. Some resorts like Folkestone, where it was fashionable to stay whatever the weather to be seen in polite society, had no difficulty in attracting the all-year-round visitor, but others had to manufacture elaborate and compelling reasons for frequenting their towns. It was claimed that the bracing sea air was particularly good for invalids in the winter. A sojourn at Ramsgate, according to one authority, was preferable to a visit to the south of France, and, what was more, it was freed from the social pretensions of that place or English resorts like Brighton: 'At Ramsgate, a visitor can do just as he pleases, and dress as he likes. There is, thank Heaven, no morning or afternoon parade, no driving up and down a fashionable monotonous mile, and repeating the nods and becks and stereotyped smiles of the London season. Life is not dull at Ramsgate . . . It is all life from morning to night . . . Ramsgate Brightonized would be Ramsgate spoilt. A "fashionable watering-place" it can never become. A delightful, health-giving, go-as-you-please seaside place it will ever remain.'

For those visitors able to afford overnight stays in any resort there were several forms of accommodation available. The most expensive rooms were in the hotels but for those insufficiently well endowed there were innumerable lodging houses which offered varying degrees of comfort for varying prices. In some instances they provided all meals for an inclusive charge, in others they gave only bed and breakfast, but the most common system in operation was that of cooking and attendance where the landlady cooked food bought by the guests and cleaned the rooms each day, acting in effect like a general servant. For those who preferred to rely on their own servants houses were available for letting to families for several weeks at a time, or even for the whole summer if required. The very wealthy were already beginning to buy second homes in some of the resorts. There were special boats and trains at weekends for working husbands to visit their wives and families who spent most of the summer at the seaside.

Nearly all these visitors seemed to take for granted the facilities which they used. Similarly, studies of the development of holidays concentrate on the visitors, the customers, rather than on the workers who catered for them, despite the fact that in other industries most attention has been paid to the workers and very little to the consumers of the goods. For a large number of local residents in these holiday towns, the summer was far from a season of relaxation and leisure. It was a frantic and hectic period when they had to earn sufficient to see them through the long, bleak winter.

It is virtually impossible to calculate the number of people who relied on the holiday trade for their livelihood in this period. Over 2,000 female boarding house keepers are listed regularly in the census returns, but since these figures were collected in the spring they undoubtedly understate the numbers involved in the height of the season. Many landladies simply took visitors in when they could during the short summer season, often relying on members of their family for labour. Guest houses and hotels took on short term staff. Shops hired extra assistants. Children on holiday from school obtained employment displaying posters, distributing leaflets among the crowds, pushing invalids in wheel chairs, or carrying luggage from the railway stations. Bathing establishments, theatres, restaurants— all these required seasonal workers many of whom were outsiders attracted to the area by the prospect of a whole summer at the seaside. Many discovered to their cost that they had little or no time to spare from work to enjoy the attractions of the resorts. One gentleman remembers being enticed to Margate by an advert in a local paper for a boy to help in a guest house. His daily routine, which began at 5.30 a.m. allowed for no time off. He received no pay, only his board and lodging, and he *never* left the premises the whole summer. Conditions for these seasonal workers undoubtedly varied considerably, those in higher class establishments probably receiving better wages and more time off. Whatever their position, however, the seaside meant only one thing to them—work. Yet it was work which offered them no security and no prospects but rewarded them with the sack at the end of the season, unless the establishment they worked in had a substantial winter clientele.

Three of the following recollections deal with these seaside workers and attempt to show how and why they involved themselves with catering for the relatively ungrateful armies of occupation which annually invaded their towns, occupied the best rooms in their houses, crowed on to their beaches and pushed up prices in the shops. The other evokes the appeal of one of the Thanet resorts through the eyes of a lady who visited it as a young girl in the 1900s.

A visitor to Thanet in the 1900s

Dr Ina Beasley was the daughter of a sales representative for a silk spinning firm in the City of London. As a young girl she regularly went for family holidays to Brighton, Eastbourne, Scotland and most especially Margate, or more precisely, Westgate. Here she describes some of the preparations involved in the holidaymaking of the era and some of the clear-cut distinctions between the resorts which were widely recognised at the time, and which still linger on today.

'Everybody went for holidays. Mother would have thought it very peculiar if she hadn't gone for a holiday. Her father and mother had always gone for a holiday, so it was all part of the family custom. Grandpa said it was better than medicine which of course is true. He was very keen on Brighton. Oh yes, you had to go for a holiday.

'Why Margate? Because it wasn't all that distance from London and my father had an idea that the air was very pure. He liked good, cold, brisk air and he liked fishing. Also because it wasn't a very difficult journey. We could come by train, and there used to be great excitement when you got to Whitstable and you had to be the right side of the carriage to get the first glimpse of the sea, or the other thing was to come down by boat. That was very exciting. The *Royal Sovereign* all the way down from Tower Bridge to Margate Pier. In those days they had luggage in advance, so what would happen would be that a large trunk would be packed and sent off two or three days beforehand and there'd be nothing to carry. Somebody would call for this enormous trunk at the house. You'd put a card in the window "Pickfords Wanted" or whatever, and then the van man saw your card, called and took your luggage. It was as easy as that. Life was a lot easier in those days.

'It wasn't always the same lodgings but I'm sure we stayed twice at Garlinge. It may have been more, because my first memories of Margate are of this walk across the corn fields. As far as Westgate used to be corn. It's a housing estate now. I don't think we ever came down for a day trip but a lot of women of my mother's ilk did. The pattern was, she would take a day trip early in the season, have a look round and fix all the lodgings for us to come to. What the lodgings were like it's very difficult to say. They must have been clean or we wouldn't have gone. I don't think they were very grand but we didn't expect them to be and we weren't in the house very much. Mother bought the food and the landlady cooked it. I can't remember eating at a restaurant down here. Life wasn't geared that way, you went home to meals because you weren't very far away. We had the sitting room and our meals were served in there. I suppose it's possible there were other people in the house but we were never with them. We often wondered though what happened to the family of the landlady because they weren't enormous houses. They must have been a bit squashed, I think. During the season they probably expected to be uncomfortable. Usually they were probably the wives of artisans, labourers of some sort who possibly had a better house because they were able to take in lodgers than they would have done if they'd been living off his pay completely. As people I wasn't concerned with them. My life was centred on the friends I had outside and on playing on the beach mostly.

'My mother didn't particularly care for beach pursuits and she always kept on her shoes and stockings. She wouldn't have dreamed of paddling or bathing. Other people's mothers weren't all like that but that was my mother, she didn't like it. So we would go down to the beach with my father and she would go and do the shopping. We took no interest in that side of affairs. We spent all our time in the mornings on the beach. I remember it being a very friendly place. Lots of cricket on the sands with all sorts of people joining in. Bathing parties, where we would all bathe together—and we would bathe whatever the weather as far as I can remember—blue with cold sometimes. Then there was always food after you'd bathed. We knew it as a "chittering bite". Cakes, that sort of thing. I don't know what the theory behind it was. We were often shivering though. It's a cold place to bathe, Margate. But we loved it. It was very much a beach holiday and we often had other people who came with us from our own circle of home, relations and friends. It wasn't at all lonely. Although you came down with your family you didn't just keep with your family. There were always lots of people about.

'It was also almost entirely within the Westbrook area. Margate harbour was vulgar. No two ways about it. We were brought up with an idea of what nice girls don't do—it may have been useful, I suppose—but Westgate was rather higher in the social scale and Margate rather lower. There were the whelk stalls and . . . how self-conscious one gets these days . . . the sort of people who went there you see were rather hard-drinking, loud-voiced types of people. It was just in one of those strange ways considered that this end was more respectable. Cliftonville was, as far as I remember, rather mixed. A lot of Jewish people and theatrical people. Well, it's very easy to understand that that would be an easy journey from London on Saturday night after a show. Westgate would be the family part where all the . . . do we talk about middle classes these days? . . . you know what I mean, where people like that used to come.

'We used to go down in the mornings to the beach, but not in the afternoons. We dressed fairly respectably even on the beach, certainly not going about looking like a tramp. We always had nice cotton frocks however cold it was, and generally a pair of canvas shoes that could get rotted in the salt of the sand. But in the evenings and the afternoons we dressed up a bit. You know, cleaned up tidy, put a pair of stockings on. Not gloves, but a nicer dress. It was just part of the set-up, as it were. You made yourself look pleasant if you were going for a walk along the promenade to listen to the band. You looked at the other people. We looked at the boys and the boys looked at us as we were getting a bit older so we made ourselves look nice. Of course, we all had long hair and the difficulty for girls was that you couldn't keep it tidy in the wind. We hadn't got over that one. Occasionally we used to go on excursions or out in a small boat with my father who was fond of that sort of thing. Then there used to be a big round pavilion just before you get to the Nayland Rock—it's blown out to sea now—but it was quite a feature of this part of Margate before 1914 because there was always a band there in the mornings. I think there may have been an orchestra in the afternoons and there were very good concert parties. At least I thought they were very good. That was quite a feature of the entertainment as we got older.

'We were carefully restricted as regards spending money. We couldn't have innumerable donkey rides when we were young. We had to be a bit thrifty on things like that. We were brought up to make our own entertainments and at home too. We were never expected to sit still and do nothing. If it was wet we stayed indoors and we always had a pack of cards put in the trunk. We were always provided with games. And people walked a lot in those days, you know. To be taken for a five mile walk on a Sunday morning when I was about eight years old was nothing. Quite common. We used to buy rock. Nasty, sticky stuff. Very pink. And ice creams of course. One was allowed a few ice creams but we weren't supposed to eat them in the street because that wasn't what nice girls did. We probably had to sit down and eat our cornets. You weren't allowed to eat them outside.

'I think practically anybody on the sands would be a visitor. Most local people never went on the sand or near the sea. A doctor in the Canterbury Road, his wife used to bring her girls down to bathe and that's how we got friendly with them and we used to go and stay with them after a bit. But they were quite unusual, I think. You meet a lot of people in Margate now who say they never go near the sea. Anybody who was on the beach, in those days at any rate, probably was a

visitor. Of course there was a big notice up that said you mustn't undress on the shore. The exact wording was "Bathing is forbidden
from the foreshore after 8 a.m." As a child it took a bit of explaining.
I couldn't quite see what it meant. I don't think you were even
allowed to come down in a bathrobe. You had to go into a bathing
machine, tent or hut. I don't know what the difference was, I'm sure.
I think you hired the tent by the week and the bathing huts you just
fed your 6d. or whatever it was. You could hire a costume too if
you'd come without one.

'To put on weight and to get a good colour was a sure sign that
you'd had a good holiday. I don't think people wanted to be brown
all over. That wouldn't have been considered quite nice to expose
your flesh to the sun, but lots of people sat with their faces in the sun.
It was, however, perhaps a little vulgar to get too red but that
depended on what sort of skin you had. But there was nothing dis-
reputable about being sunburned, not in our circle anyway. Possibly
we were part of the feminine movement in a sense though. We
weren't frail little violets or anything of the sort.

'It doesn't sound very exciting does it? But you know, we loved it.
Simple tastes.'

A Margate landlady

The gruelling nature of the landlady's work has rarely been appreciated. Indeed she is often cruelly portrayed in jokes and on postcards
as a grasping, intolerant woman eternally trying to ruin everyone's
holiday while wringing every penny out of her guests. Her job was far
from easy or pleasant. Not only did she have to labour seven days a
week, twelve to fourteen hours a day, but she had to share her own
home with strangers, some of whom showed little consideration for
their host. Forced to live in the basement, her work was literally on
top of her, and she and her family generally found themselves sleeping in the smaller, less airy rooms which guests would not take and
fitting their meals in to suit their visitors. Little wonder that her
patience occasionally ran out and she grumbled and groused about
the habits and high spirits of her inmates. She suffered these hard-
ships, indeed many still do, for a few shillings a week to see her
through the winter. If she could obtain unpaid labour she naturally
took it, and to be brought up in a house which was turned over to
visitors in the summer involved labouring from an early age. Mrs
Florence Parker spent much of her childhood helping her grandmother before leaving to find employment and good money in a fancy

goods shop along the front at Margate. Here are some of her recollections.

'I was born in 1 Neptune Square, Margate, in 1896. I lived with
my grandma until I got married. My mother left me for this poor old
soul to bring up. It wouldn't have been so bad if her husband hadn't
been laying ill, but my grandfather was an invalid. I was born in the
February and he died in the April. I used to create about my mother
because I think she should have helped her mother. But she didn't.
So the old girl had a very hard life. There was no pension scheme then
for old people or widows. I don't think she got anything until she was
nearly seventy. She wouldn't go on parish relief. Oh, dear, dear, dear
no. Sometimes she was very grateful when they used to give her a
philanthropic ticket—I can never say it properly—and they used to
be a shilling. Her landlord used to pay so much a year into this fund
so he had so many tickets to give to people he knew and he used to
give her some. You could go to the butcher's or the grocer's and get a
shillingsworth of stuff with it. But she never had a penny from parish
relief. As poor as she was she wouldn't think of that. That would be
terrible.

'She had to do something so in the summer she did letting. My
aunt stopped at home and helped in the busy time but she couldn't
give her any money. She always reckoned her letting was her firing
and gas and lights. Things like that. And she always used to try to
pay the rent up in the summer and then she hadn't got anything
to worry about in the winter. She must have worked hard to get it to
pay it all up in the summer. I know once she went and worked for the
landlord, washing for them and cleaning the shop floors and that for
him because he had a shop. She worked hard, our old girl did. Gran
always used to say if she got a letting in early June, well she was all
right. She'd got the wherewithall to buy the extras she wanted to start
with, all the stuff for cleaning, papering and painting. And if she got
perhaps a week or fortnight towards the end of September, well that
was just a bit of bunce for her, a bob or two for herself. That went
perhaps to buy new sheets. She always used to go to a women's meeting and they used to have a club she always paid something in so
she'd got the money to buy so much sheeting to make new sheeting.
She bought the unbleached calico and made them up herself. She'd
make them, then the old girl would soak them in cold water, give
them a couple of washes and then they were quite white ready to put
the visitors in. The visitors always had to have the best. You had to
have what was left. If there happened to be a torn sheet you had to
have that mended and you had to have that.

'There were seven rooms we had there. That was a fairly big house really. There were four bedrooms and then a big attic which my aunt, nan and I had to share. Then we had a basement kitchen but that was all shut off in the winter. We had all the comfort in the winter and we always had the best rooms then. That's the only way we could do it really. Some of the houses used to get somebody in to help if they could afford it, and the big houses up at Cliftonville, they always had maids, chamber maids and that sort of thing. Some of the very big ones had waiters. But we never had any staff, only ourselves.

'Sometimes you had to do cooking and attendance. They'd bring their own food in and you'd cook it and dish it all up. Then you only charged them so much a week for the room. If you got twenty-five bob a week you were lucky. If you'd got an extra big family perhaps you would work thirty bob a week out of it. If you did bed and breakfast they wouldn't pay you more than a couple of bob a night. I don't think she ever charged them for breakages or anything like that. I suppose some people did. I think people like myself thought, well, they are only working people. We weren't out to fleece them, but of course a lot of people did. They'd charge for all sorts of silly things. They used to charge them for cruet, the salt, pepper and mustard and all those sorts of things. We did used to create though because nan didn't charge enough. Not for the work she had to do, but then everybody was the same then. You didn't charge much because you wanted to keep the same people if they were nice people. We had some for years and years, the same people. I mean sometimes she'd take them for a guinea a week and do all the cooking and everything, the early part of the season.

'Cooking and attendance they bought their own food. Well you couldn't do much on twenty-five bob a week for them, could you? Especially if you were keeping four of them in one room for that money. You couldn't afford to do it. It was blinkin' hard work. Daily routine would be up in the morning, they'd all want cups of tea. Round you'd go with a blimmin' tray of tea to every room. Then they had to have their meals in their room. We had a sitting room but only one lot had that because that went with the bigger bedroom because they were bigger families, so the others, they had to have their meals in their room. Well, then you'd have to get their tray ready and if they went out before breakfast you'd to go up there, empty the slops, make the bed and lay the breakfast. Then you had to cook the breakfast and have that ready by the time they came in. You'd have to do that to all the rooms, see. Then you had to wait for them to go out and then go and collect all the trays. Then you had the basement to do and all those stairs. You'd go out with your brush and dust pan, broom and duster, top of the house down, each room and the stair-case.

'If you were late somebody else had got to start doing all the veg. Some places they used to provide the vegetables but we never did. We always said you bring your own and then you know what you've got and you know what you're paying. So you had to keep everybody's vegetables separate. You had to know whose vegetables were whose, and you couldn't cook everybody's greens together because they didn't always all want greens or somebody had got different potatoes. You had to do all that separate. You can imagine the saucepans you had. And we had to remember whose meat was who. You had to mark all that. Oh dear, it used to be a game. We'd try to get the dinners as near as possible to each other so we could get all the washing up done. Sometimes they'd say could they have a meat pudding but that was barred. I mean that took a long time. You had to boil it for four or five hours, you couldn't spare the time or the stove with other people's dinners to do. Nan didn't mind doing pastry, pies, and that but she thought puddings was a bit much. They always wanted their money's worth whatever they paid. And they got it.

'Then some of them would say, "Can we have a cup of tea after dinner?" If the old girl was in a good mood she might say yes, but if she didn't feel energetic or like the people she'd say, "I'm sorry. I haven't got the time." Then we'd get all the dinner things done, washed up, then we'd got to go round clearing all up and tidying up again, laying the tea. And perhaps the old girl would say, "Well, I think I'd better start my washing." You kept having washing all the time to do. After tea it was clear away again, go round and empty all the slops, turn down the beds. Then some would have cheek enough to want suppers. They wouldn't be satisfied with just bread and cheese, they'd want anything else but. You had to cook that. If they wanted fish and chips though they had to bring that in on their own. It was three months' *hard* work, but it got us through the summer and the winter really.

'Cheerful sort of people we used to have in those days. Nan always had her little book. You know, who came, when they came, and what they paid. If there was somebody came and you didn't like them, you put a cross against their name. No more. You had some of them so often she used to look in her book and say, "So and so hasn't been this year. I wonder if they've died." She used to have some very good people. January, February they used to start writing and say will you be able to take me so and so? Nan'd write back if she could and she'd tell them the dates she'd got. She didn't have to advertise. We had a ticket up if we'd got the rooms but otherwise you got people recommended. You had to watch what sort of people you had, although you didn't have much trouble with them when you have family people. When we used to get the flaming girls on their own, that's when we had trouble. We had two girls once, they had what we called the front room, bay window and we couldn't understand the noise we could hear. A couple of chaps were trying to get in and those girls were hanging out the windows after them. Nan used to lock the door round eleven at night. If they were going to be late they had to tell her. She used to say eleven was quite late enough for anybody to be in the street. All the pubs were all turned out and all the entertainments were over. "They should be home," she used to say. "We've got to get up and do all the work in the morning so they should be home at night."

'Sometimes you'd go up and you'd find the knives and forks and that sort of thing were gone so you always had a table with a drawer somewhere and you put them in there. They'd pinch your towels sometimes. They'd take the blasted towels out on the sand, go swimming with them and then forget them. Then they'd say, "Oh, can we have another towel? We must have lost it." But they never gave her any for replacement. Occasionally you'd have them walk in and book a room, she didn't take a deposit and off they'd go after they'd had a couple of nights. Just walked in and walked out. You lost that lot.

'We had one very big room at the back of the house and she took this party in and she used to say,

"I believe they're Jews. I wish I hadn't taken them."

She didn't actually object to the Jews, but she objected to their ways because if you were cooking for them you had to take it up as you cooked it in the meat tins. She got ratty over that. I think there was a man and a woman and two or three children and when my aunt took the food up one day she came down and said,

"Do you know, there's about a dozen up there! They're all waiting for dinner."

They were all having a bit off each and using the tins and everything else. Nan had only laid for so many. She wasn't half cross. She said she wouldn't have them any more, put a black mark on to their name. So they never came any more. I always remember her creating about that.

'Oh dear, dear. Wet days. We've had them indoors and they've been playing cards and all the kids running round and round. Kids wanted paper and pencils. You'd find them those if the mothers hadn't had any. There wasn't any toys for them because I was the youngest one. I mean we didn't have any little kids to give their toys to them. Then you'd got to go in about half-past twelve, quarter to one, "Will you start clearing up please because I must come and lay the dinner?" Oh dear.

'I had to stop at home with gran to help her when I was old enough to leave school, and not until quite a long time after did I go to work. Used to work thundering hard too for one lot of people. I was a shop assistant in a general fancy goods shop next door to what used to be the Cinque Ports pub. There was only that shop and another one, the West End Hotel and the Cinque Ports, and the others were all beautiful big houses along the front. They gradually went. There isn't one there now. I used to go in at eight to half past every morning and sometimes come home at twelve at night because if she wanted to go out she wanted me to mind the kids. The old girl, nan, used to get awful worried because of course I'd got to pass so many pubs, you see, to come home. But I got £2 a week if I was lucky. That was a lot of money. The bloke next door wanted somebody and he said to me what wages was I having. I said £2 a week. Oh, he nearly touched the ceiling. He went right in and asked her if it was right.

'It was only a seasonal trade. You wouldn't like to work along there in the winter really. You couldn't walk along there sometimes. You'd get to the bottom of the High Street and you'd be drowned. Water came right up. There was no work for anybody in the winter. But in the summer they used to open seven days sometimes, when they got permission to open Sundays. You could only have so many Sundays. If they wanted me to go in Sunday, looby used to go. No more money, but they used to give me a meal. Weekends, when we had the men trippers, they didn't used to go back till ten, half past, so we kept open. See, when they come along sozzled you used to get more money out of them. You didn't charge them more but you could flog them more, you see. You could push some of them off with marvellous stuff. But we, the staff, didn't get any extra. Then Monday was ladies' day during the summer. All the old women used to come. You should've seen the sights they used to look when they used to come out for their days. Wednesdays was Sunday school treat day and you'd have the kids coming in straight away, buying stuff and "Will you mind it for me?" You had to mark their names all on it and put it away. Otherwise they'd spend all their money and then they wouldn't have anything to take home. Then Saturdays was the men. We always knew which days we'd got to get the stock all up ready for.

'You couldn't clear off and leave anybody in the shop because you'd find something missing. It used to be terrible really, the stuff that would be pinched. We had a marvellous yacht one day in the shop and we used to have a stall outside as well for postcards and that sort of thing. The governor was out there with one of the girls and he came in and he said, "Who sold the yacht?" I said, "I haven't." None of us had sold it. They'd walked out that shop yet the governor was out there and they didn't see it go and nobody in the shop saw it go. Now how did a thing like that get out? The only thing I can think of was two of them went and backed it out between them.

'Do you know I never went bathing! I never went in the water. Lots of Margate people never went in the water. I mean in the summer time you'd be too busy and in the winter you couldn't get near the beach. I even got a bit scared of going near the water. It frightened me to death. And I never had a holiday until after the war. I don't remember the old girl having a night away from home. Those things weren't thought of.'

A guest house and cafe worker

Cissie Roblin was sixteen when she answered an advert in her local Gillingham paper for a domestic help in a Margate guest house for the 1911 season. Although her memories include references to happy times on the front there, they deal mainly with her work which she found 'very hard going'. One season proved enough for her and the following year she ventured down to Folkestone to work in a restaurant, an experience she found much more to her liking.

'I answered an advert for Margate. I thought, oh, it'll be nice down there. My friend and I, we both went, and we got jobs next door to each other. We just went for the season in those houses immediately opposite the Winter Gardens there.

'The owner herself had been a governess to a very wealthy person on the continent. I suppose she finished up and had this idea of having a guest house. She used to tell me some very interesting things. She was very educated. And we had some very, you know, very cosy people. Comfortably off. One turn there we had an author in the top room. She wanted quiet just for writing. Her paper basket used to full of memo paper. But you could never get who she really was. Then we used to have people come there with the nurses, with their children. We used to try and get off with any boys. I was only young.

One time we had a family of Jews and there were about ten of them. One of them's name was Cissie, like mine.

'She said to me, "Would you accept a letter for me?"

"Well," I said, "what's the idea?"

"If my father knew I was betting, he'd kill me."

'So I used to receive the letters. He was a horrible old man. He used to follow the girls out in the evening for their walk or concert. He'd go snooping around to see who they were with. He brought one girl home and smacked her in front of us and she was quite a big girl. Another lady we had, we used to call her Flo, her sister was an actress. She'd got all sorts of rings and diamonds.

'I said one day, "Wouldn't it be funny if we had somebody from Gillingham."

'She said, "They aren't rich enough there."

'Blow me down, next week, along come our wine merchant from Gillingham, a man named Croft. He'd been going to her for years.

'He said, "I believe you're a Gillingham girl."

'I said yes.

"You don't know who I am, do you?"

'I said, "I have a faint idea. You're Mr Croft."

'He was a real, you know, real gentleman.

'So he said, "Are you enjoying it here?"

"When we're off duty it's very nice," but I said, "it's very hard going."

'I was strong, I know, but you can have too much of a thing. You can be driven too hard.

'We used to get one night a week off. Not Sunday, a whole Sunday or anything like that. My friend and I used to go down the front to see the concert parties. Used to think it was the cat's whiskers to go down and see them. She used to work it on Sundays so's we'd have an hour break, that's all, perhaps as soon as you got the teas up for the evening. That's all. Everything had to be washed up at night, the whole issue so that you could make a fresh start in the morning. She put out the trays, the food they wanted. The visitors rarely went out to dine. You took up what they wanted and the crockery and that. But she would insist on them being on time. If it was one o'clock lunch they had to be there or she'd raise merry hell. "You can't run a place like this haphazardly," she used to say. Sometimes several of them would be out to tea and you'd say, "Oh thank God." But when they went out you'd got to go and do all their rooms. I always remember because she used to say, "Make a bucket of water and put paraffin oil in it." It was supposed to promote a little bit of polish and move the dust more easily. I couldn't see the sense of it. It's a memory I wanted to forget.

'We got paid very little but of course you had all your food. That's what they used to say, well, you get your food as well. Sure, they should give you food. You couldn't work without it, could you? I don't know if you'd find it interesting but she had a friend that lived in the Fort Hotel. She used to go down there and she'd come back with all chicken giblets. We used to live on giblet pies, giblet this, and giblet that, because she got it all for nothing. I said to mum when I got home, "You know, you don't half waste a lot. All we had down there was the giblets." It was so repetitive. It got you down in the end. But it was very good fun and I used to get fairly good tips from people. Some half a crown, some five shillings. In the case of the Jews I got ten bob, I think. When I first went there I used to have my little bedroom which was outside the house. A thing this woman had had built on. It was habitable. It wasn't a dog's house sort of thing.

'One morning I couldn't get up.

'She said, "Come along," she said, "time's getting on."

"Oh," I said, "I just can't get up. I do feel ill."

'I hurt. I don't know whether it was running up right down from the basement to the top of the house with the food the people all wanted carrying up to them. You think—there was no lift or anything. I think it was too much for me. I was no age, only about sixteen, seventeen. Anyway we didn't have the doctor in.

'She said, "Well, you lie in for a couple of days."

'Anyhow, I must have suited her because the next year she wrote to see if I could go again. I didn't.

'I went to Folkestone next year, as a waitress. I went to a cafe down there, Cave's Cafe. They went right along the south coast. There used to be one at Chatham. Quite a good class restaurant. I really don't know if there's any more left. That was before the First War. Cor, I earned some money there. You had a fair wage but you made it in tips. The money I made! I mean it was fabulous then. I mean 10s. would be an enormous lot, wouldn't it? You'd get that in a day. But that was very hard work. You only did it in shifts, and you were on the go the whole time. Never had a let up. If you went on at one o'clock you stayed there till ten at night. In the morning you'd go early and come off at one. I don't think a person could do it the whole day. But you didn't have too long so that's how it was it was better at Folkestone. The enjoyment was there. And you had your food at the restaurant. That's the first place I had a peach melba. Cor, they were lovely. And I was satisfied with the money.

'At Folkestone we used to get a lot of French and Germans over before the war. The downstairs of the cafe was like a lounge-cum-smoking room. We used to call it the coffee room. I was nearly afraid to ask what they wanted. You'd have a fat old German come in and he'd say his language. We used to have to help one another out. "What's so and so?" Then they'd go in the bodega, the wine place there, and in those days they had whole cheeses on the counter. Oh, they were crafty. They used to go in there for a drink and they'd cut lumps of this cheese out and made it their lunch. Whether they had a late dinner or anything I don't know. But they were very generous in tips. They very rarely left without leaving something.

'Then they used to have a lovely German band. It was beautiful. As soon as the war was imminent the conductor, he scuppered off to America. We had all the first showings of the plays before they went up London to the West End. Of course I revelled in that. I did have some wonderful times there.'

Inside the Folkestone hotels

Albert Packman was a country boy, born at Hernhill near Faversham in 1892. Rural life held no attractions for him. His one ambition was to be a page boy, to be dressed in a smart suit with lots of buttons. His first expedition away from home as a house boy to a family in Sussex was far from what he had expected and he soon found himself back on the farm where his father was bailiff, working hard in the hop gardens. There he decided that his best hope for escape was to write to his cousin in Folkestone asking him to find him a job in one of the hotels. Much to his delight, his cousin proved to be his saviour and he eventually obtained work first in a hotel at Sandgate and then in the Grand Hotel on the Leas at Folkestone which had only been open since 1903. A natural storyteller, he relates here his experiences from the time he first wrote to his cousin to the time he left Folkestone to take up employment as a footman at Marlow in Buckinghamshire. Like Mrs Roblin, he too had time to savour the delights of this swagger resort for himself.

'I wrote to my cousin in Folkestone. Dad used to send down cartloads of fruit and vegetables to him from the farm and he used to go round delivering. He had his orders from the hotels in Folkestone and the cross-Channel steamers. Tremendous big place he had. It really belonged to my dad's boss. He bought it and put him down there in charge. It was a smashing job, he had the run of all Folkestone and Sandgate. So I wrote to him. I said, "Can you find me a job?" I knew they had these page boys in the hotels down there and I still wanted my pea button suit. He said he'd have a try. He was sure he could.

'I was doing the hop gardens. I'd got a tin bowl in front of me, I suppose eighteen inches wide and foot deep full of soot round my neck. I had to go round, handfuls, throwing this soot over the rows of hops. Just the roots ready for next year. I was doing this job and I was like a nigger. The wind was blowing it all over me. I was in a state. Mum comes running up with a telegram. She said it's a telegram from Folkestone to come at once, your clothes to follow, not to worry about bringing any clothes. Down went that tin, quick as anything. I was home before mum had time to turn round. I got home and washed up as clean as possible and I was all ready and dressed in my best clothes. Didn't have high-lows. I had boots. Only better children had high-lows. I had to walk to Canterbury which was six miles to get a train.

'She said, "Well, we'd better go and tell your father."

'So I said, "That won't matter. You can tell him when he come home. I don't want to wait. I want to get down."

'I was sick and tired of living on the farm. I wanted to get away.

'So anyway, I got down to Folkestone and my cousin, he met me there in the van and took me back. He'd put on the telegram that he had found me somewhere but he hadn't, but he said he soon would. The next morning I went out with him along the Leas there. A big hotel there, they wanted a page boy. I went in there, and of course, I'd got my best suit on which wasn't a suit to measure or anything like that. It fitted where it touched. So smart.

"Well," she said, "you want to be a page boy. What have you been doing before?"

'I said on the farm.

'She said, "Oh, yes, I see. Well, mmm. Well, you know a lot of other boys have been after the job. I'll have to leave it and let you know."

'Of course we didn't hear. So we went after, I suppose, about half a dozen places, all the same, they looked me up and down and I didn't look the type. I was broad shouldered. I was fat and plump and the suit fitted where it touched and all the rest of it.

'My cousin said, "You'll never get a job in those clothes. I'll go and get you a suit and some different shoes."

'So he bought me a suit, ready made, but a suit that fit me, and a pair of socks—not hand knitted like we used to have—and a pair of shoes. He made me quite smart.

'I said, "Don't write and tell dad you bought me these clothes. I'll pay you back as soon as I get a job. I'll pay you back so much a week."

"Don't you worry about that," he said.

'He came in one morning and he said, "I think I've got the job for you. It's a kitchen porter in a hotel."

'So I said, "Well, it'll be something to start on, won't it. I can work up from that."

'It was at Sandgate, the Royal Kent Hotel at Sandgate. It's gone now. It's been flooded by the sea and washed down. It was right on the front. So we went down there.

"Five shillings a week is all I can pay you," she said.

'Five shillings a week all for myself! Nothing to buy, no food, just my clothes. I was fourteen and a half. So five shillings a week, good Lord, I was a millionaire before I started. So, right, I started there the next day. My cousin took me down there in the van with my box.

'I was upstairs in a room with all the others. There was a hall porter, head waiter, waiters, cook, chamber maids, I think there was about twenty servants all told. I thought it was smashing. We'd get down there teatime in the servants' hall, the lot of us there. I'd never known anything like it. Brought up in a little tiny three house place where you never met anybody, just the school people and those from the houses down there. To go there and mix with all these people at that table! Of course, they nearly brought tears to my eyes several times with my comical language. They used to keep repeating what I said, see, in another manner, and when I heard them saying it it sounded so funny. Anyway within eight or nine months they broke me of most of that lingo and got me speaking normally.

'As a rule they had about thirty people staying there and I had all the crockery to wash up for all these people. Three or four course, maybe more. The saucepans and all the plates and dishes. I had a double sink and big draining board and all the rest of it. The first night I thought I'm not going to wear my best clothes for washing up so I put my boots on. Anyway I got in there and I had to go up three steps from the scullery into the kitchen and I had to collect all this dirty stuff. I come out of there with all these plates up my chin, I wanted to show I could do it all right. You can just imagine it, can't you. Three steps to go down. I forgot all about them. You never heard such a clatter in all your life. I went down and the plates shot through all on the stone floor, the flagstones in the scullery. I thought, "This is it. My five bob's gone. I've lost my job and everything." The missus, it was a woman that owned it, she came running out there.

"Oh," I said, "I'm awfully sorry. I really am sorry. I won't do it again. It was these boots. I shall get some lighter shoes to wear. I'll pay for them at so much a week. I won't do it again, honestly."

'She said, "Oh, don't worry about that, but do try and be more careful, that's all."

'I thought that's not so bad. I got through that.

'I soon got the knack of washing up in no time at all but it used to worry me because they would finish the cooking with the saucepans around the kitchen and they would just shine them along the stone floor, slide them about to throw them up to me. Anyway I got them all washed up and after that I was free then. I could go out for an hour, go to bed, go and sit with all the others and chat, do what I liked. First one or two nights I'd just go out for half an hour and look. I'd never been in a place where there was shops and lights.

'About the third night the hall porter said, "'Course, you know you get every other night off free completely after tea and every other afternoon for two hours. It's your night tonight," he said. "Where are you going to go?"

'"Don't know," I said. "Don't know what to do."

'"Well," he said, "look. You just go down—it's only about four or five hundred yards down the road in the High Street here, Sandgate, it's a sort of music hall called the Bricks. You can get in there for 2d. upstairs in the gallery. You'll enjoy that."

'And I did too.

'"When you come out," he said, "go over the road opposite. There's a fish and chip shop."

'I'd never heard of fish and chips. I knew cooking fish, having it at home with potatoes and things, but not a fish and chip shop.

'"You go over there and you have some fish and chips for your supper and you'll have a real night out," he said. "It won't cost you much."

'Right, I went to the Bricks, upstairs there, and nearly fell over the front right up in the gallery trying to look over, because it's very high. There were acrobats on the stage, and impossible things going on that I'd never heard of or thought of in all my life. All for twopence! I did as he said and I went across the road. Of course up on the top of Sandgate, high up on the hills there was a tremendous soldiers' camp there and all the soldiers came down there to the fish and chip shop. I followed them, got my turn and there was little windows there where you had to go up to the girl and order your fish. They were all saying two and one, two and one, two and one.

'So when it came to my turn I said two and one and then I said, "How much is it?"

'She swore at me, didn't half swear at me, this girl. I suppose she thought I was stupid or having her on. I didn't know a two and one meant a twopenny bit of fish and pennyworth of potatoes. She did lead off at me.

"Give us your money. I haven't got time with all these people waiting."

'I gave her 3d. and couldn't believe my eyes. I went and sat down and watched all the others and what they did with the two forks that you picked up and I done the same. God, that was a day of days in my life if ever there was. That was absolutely smashing. The end of a perfect day. I went back and told the porter and he laughed. They all laughed when I told them about the fish.

'Well, first thing in the morning I had to take the old cook, she was Irish, I had to take her a cup of tea up at seven o'clock into her room and then she'd get up, eventually, come down and do the breakfast. There was all these thirty people having all sorts of things, egg and bacon and fried sole, liver, kippers, all different things. The waiter came down to the kitchen and gave you an order and you had to cook it quick. She used to come down after her cup of tea and I had to help her. It was all right, but she drunk like a fish. After a week or two she began to drink more and when I got up there with the tea she'd say, "I can't come down. I can't come down. You'll have to do it." As I say, I'd been helping her, dishing it up and cooking a lot of it on this tremendous big stove there. I suppose I thought, well, I can do it. The only thing was I didn't have anybody to run about after me like she did. She had me to run about after her to get this and get that. I not only had to cook it, but I had to get it. First of all, if anybody wanted fish you had to go outside the hotel to the fish shop next door and buy it, well not pay for it, get in the order and come back and cook it, so it was fresh. Anyway I got on and I done this and I got on marvellous there doing the cooking. No one else knew only the waiter I was doing it with. She just lay idling up there. Cor, she was a big fat thing. Then we all had our own breakfast after that breakfast was settled and we had whatever we wanted. No one ever queried it. Smashing food, the same as they had in the dining room. That was where I started to have butter and jam on my bread not just one or the other. You could never have the two together at home. And butter and cheese. That used to be smashing.

'Well, I used to have a cigarette now and again. I started having a cigarette. And I used to go down the Bricks every week and the fish shop. Then I used to go to Folkestone on the bus which was only a penny. They had the horse trams running then. Sometimes I used to go to Hythe for a change. I used to get around. And I used to put me 5s. in the Post Office regular every week then draw it all out again because I wanted to spend it. I got my bank book full in no time. Nothing in there. Just put it in and took it out more or less. I went home one day and I said to me mum,

"Look at that, mum, nearly a bank book full."

'She said, "Cor, how do you do it!"

'After a bit she tumbled that though. She's not stupid. I was being barmy and putting it in and taking it out again.

'But it was so unheard of and different to be able to go about free dressed up in nice clothes. I went home one day in white stiff shirt and no one had a white shirt on only at weddings and christenings or on a Sunday in Hernhill. Just special days you had a white shirt on, stiff shirt and stiff cuffs. I got this white shirt and I went home in it on a weekday. All the school kids was around and the chaps working on the farm.

"Cor, it's old Albert Packman come home and he's got a white shirt on too on a weekday," they said.

"Whatever job has he got? However did he get that job?"

'See, I was one of the first one ever to leave the village. They just stayed there on the farm.

'My cousin came down one day and he said, "I've got a better job for you up at the Grand Hotel at Folkestone. Assistant cellarman." Off I went and saw them and they said, yes, when can you start? I said I could start tomorrow. Well I hadn't told the other lady anything about it. So I went back down there, packed all my things into my box, wrote a note, put 5s. in it in lieu of wages—I'd heard somewhere or other that you'd got to leave a week's wages instead of notice. I said, "Dear Madam, I'm sorry. I've gone to another job. I'm leaving 5s. in lieu of notice." Then I come outside, shoved this box on my shoulders, scared stiff I'd run against her and she'd make me come back, got a four wheeler cab outside and away I went. I sat on the back seat and they had a little six inch window at the back with a flap and I opened the flap and watched all the time to see if I could see her come running after. They were nice to me really. It was a dirty trick.

'Anyway, I got up to the Grand and they said, "About the money. What are you getting in your other job?"

'I said I was getting 7s. 6d. a week. It was the under manager that engaged me. He was a nice man.

'He said, "Oh, I'm sorry. We can't pay more than 7s. 6d. We'd like to give you more but we'll see how you get on."

"Well," I said, "I'll start at 7s. 6d. then."

'I was down in the cellars under the hotel there. They started having ice refrigerators then, tremendous things about the size of this living room. I was in charge of that. Well, you've seen the old ice blocks coming round on the old Italian ice carts. Haven't you seen those, even in your time? They were blocks of ice weighing a hundredweight and they used to come round on horse and cart and they had great big pincers to pull them around. They used to go to fish shops and such like all over the place. Well, this man used to have to bring down about half a ton to me downstairs. Then he had to break it a bit into smaller lumps and I had to break it all up into a bucket and go up some steps and tip it down into a great tank up there. Tip all this broken ice into this tank. Well, in this refrigerator there we kept all the fresh fruit, peaches, grapes, butter, goodness knows what. Everything you could think of all in rows and rows. My cousin used to come there and he had the order for fresh fruit. He made a bomb out of the hotels too. He didn't half used to charge. Anyway I had all that to see to.

'Then I had to dish out the wine and beer to the men. At eleven o'clock in the morning all the men, waiters and chefs, they were all Italian and French and such like, all foreigners, they were allowed a bottle of red wine each which I had to dish out to them. Englishmen had a pint of beer. I don't know how I did it. We had these fifty, six gallon hogsheads down there and I had to get them up on to a trough laying along there and they'd got to stand there. But the man that was over me, I was the assistant and he was the boss, he showed me. You just kept rocking them and eventually you could get them up. It was simple really when you got the knack of it. Of course, you know the old trick. I was only a boy. "Albert, can't you slip us another one? Go on Albert. You can manage that." "No," I said, "I can't do that. How am I going to account for it?" Anyway, there was a chef and I did used to give him some. He'd come in with his big white apron and he'd say, "When you come in dinner time, lunch time, night time or whatever, don't go and get your dinner off the staff chef, you come and see me." I used to go and see him. I had the tip-top food. So he had an extra bottle of wine and the pastry cook had an extra bottle of wine. I went to him for my pudding. Oh dear, oh dear, the things I had while I was there. I lived like a lord. You see, the Grand Hotel was such a marvellous big place there was a staff chef, oh, he was a dirty old man too, he used to cook all the staff food in the hotel. His job was just for the staff. It was awful the stuff really they dished down there.

'Oh, another thing. I had a place upstairs I was in charge of. A wine bin right along all in little pigeon holes, not too small, one would hold two or three bottles perhaps. The Grand Hotel, they wouldn't give it a liquor licence so the big wine merchants about a hundred yards down the main road at Folkestone—I thought of the name just now, Brooke's—they had a fleet of boys on bikes with baskets. If anybody was having dinner and they wanted a bottle of wine, they'd tell the waiter and he would come to me and I would have to ring up Brooke's, we had a straight line through to Brooke's, a bottle of this and a bottle of that. The boy would be up almost as soon as you put the phone down with this bottle. I had to keep it in this cubby hole. They were all numbered these cubby holes, you see, the person's number of his or her room was there and I dare not give a bottle to anybody without a chit from the waiter. Everything in the way of wine and spirits I was in charge of. Well then, two or three times a week perhaps, they'd have a ball there. Tremendous ballroom in those days where people used to come for dancing. I had a tremendous great press and I had a whole crate of lemons I had to cut in half and put in this machine, turn this heavy handle round and it came down and squashed the lemons into a big bowl underneath. All this lot I had to squash and then made lemonade for the ballroom. Real lemonade with lemons. Then when that was on, either me or the man above me had to stay until the last person was gone. Even if it was three or four in the morning, you were on duty until then in case they might need a drink. They couldn't have it unless you were there to hand it out with a chit. There was this head waiter and this under manager and two or three more and the still room maid. She was a nice girl too. She said, "I'm not calling you Albert. I'm calling you Cecil. Albert doesn't suit you. You're Cecil." Anyway they used to come of a night time, larking about near my place there away from the ballroom, you see. They came down there, jumped through the door—the bottom half closed and it had a shelf on it—and they helped themselves with these different wines. I was only the servant. He was the under manager and the head waiter. I said, "There will be trouble over this, you know. I'm not going to stand for it." "Don't you worry about that." They put it back again after they helped themselves to it. So it went on so often but nothing was ever said or found out.

'Then we had—oh, what was the big singer's name?—Tosky or whatever his name was. He would only have an apple. It had got to be perfectly red all over and polished. I polished this blimmin' apple up for him. If it wasn't just so he'd send it back. That wasn't right. In those days they could do as they liked.

'The accommodation we had was wicked. It wasn't in the hotel, we had to go across to a mews about 150 yards away, outside the hotel and across the main road and round the back. There we went upstairs over where they kept the carriages. People started to have cars then but not many. Over the top was this one long room and there was the whole of us men, boys whatever, all sleeping in like a—what do you call it?—dormitory, that's the word. All these different nationalities. The majority of them were Italians and there were some German waiters. In those days they used to come over to learn English. They worked for practically nothing, you see, to learn English, then they went back to their own country and they could speak English and got tremendous high jobs. The chefs came over just the same. They could do the French cooking but they wanted to learn the English language so they stayed over working for less money. The hotel owners was making money out of it because they were having them cheap while they learnt their English. I was sleeping next to a German and he started learning me German. Making me say . . . well, one or two things I've forgotten. Anyway, they'd go out drinking and they'd come in there, oh, there was blood and everything flying there. Fighting and carrying on. Well, all these foreigners, you know what they're like, especially if they go out drinking. I didn't like it at all. But I didn't get hurt.

'At the end of this long room was one part as big washing part partitioned off. Hot water was supplied by the man in charge of the garage. He had room free there. It was a big wash house. Plenty of bowls and hot water and shaving mirrors. What used to make me laugh, the cooks, or chefs as they called themselves, used to come over here and they'd start unwinding. They'd unwind yards and yards of wide material, belly belt I used to call them, this wide linen or flannel. When they came over from the kitchen they'd unwind all this stuff, put on their outdoor clothes and go out. Because in the kitchens they only wore a white coat over white trousers, thin white trousers, and I suppose that was to soak up perspiration. I never did know. I know I used to see my mother do that when she'd had a baby, wind up all this narrow white stuff all round that she used to be bound with.

'Anyway I used to have every other afternoon off and every other evening unless there was a ball on. Then I had to stay. I used to go walking down Folkestone looking in the shops. The shops had tremendous windows. Our little shops in Boughton High Street was tiny little windows and these were massive. I thought it was wonderful. One afternoon I was down there and there was a girl looking in there so I said hello and she said hello. We went for a walk and I took her home. We used to meet every other night and every other afternoon. She took me home to her people and I used to have a cup of tea there. They were very good to me.

'Then one afternoon she said, "Oh, wait here a minute. I won't be long. I'm going to the agency."

'I said, "Agency? What do you mean?"

'In Rendezvous Street it was.

"I'm looking for a job," she said. "You go up there and put your name down, name and address, and you pay a shilling and they find you a job."

"Well," I said, "what sort of job?"

"Anything. Any job you like."

'I was getting tired and I was afraid of getting found out too over the wine and stuff that I was giving out and shouldn't do. I was getting a bit nervous if they came to check things. And I was still wanting my buttons. I hadn't got my buttons there. I'd just got ordinary clothes.

"Could they get me a job as a footman, do you think?"

"Oh yes," she said, "they've plenty of footmen's jobs."

'So I went up with her, paid my shilling and the woman said, "What's your address?"

'I said, "Grand Hotel. I live over the stables."

"That's funny," she said. "We've got a gentleman staying there. He wants a footman but it's down in Marlow on the Thames in Buckinghamshire."

"That's all right. That'll be fine.

'So we got the room and we come down and I flew off and went in the hotel, and I went to this room to see this gentleman and his butler. He started looking me up and down.

'Then he started asking me, "Can you clean shoes?"

"Yes."

"Can you varnish shoes?"

"Oh yes."

'I thought what the hell's varnish shoes, but still.

"Lamps. Can you do lamps?"

'I'd never done a lamp in my life. So I said, "Yes, I can do lamps."

'On and on and on. Can you do this? How about hunting things? Can you clean those? Eventually I thought to myself, you're going a bit far, Albert.

'So I said, "Well sir, I maybe can't do everything but I'm very willing to learn. You'll find I'm very willing to learn anything and quickly."

"Well," he said to his butler, "what do you think? He sounds good. When can you start?"

'So I said a week's time, next Monday, and he said that would be just right. So I got the job. Thing was, I couldn't go and leave at a minute's notice in this place. I'd got to do something proper by giving notice. I rushed all round the hotel looking for Mr Knowle, the under manager, and eventually I ran up against him and I said,

"Sorry sir, I want to give a week's notice to leave next Monday. I've got another job."

'Shortly after he comes down to and he said, "You silly devil. Why did you do it? If you'd seen me and told me you weren't satisfied we would have asked you where you wanted to go, what position you wanted, and we would have helped you. Look, you go, but if you don't like it come straight back here and we'll talk it over and whatever position you want you can have."

'So I said, "Thank you very much sir."

'And that was it.'

Select Bibliography

There is no shortage of literature on Kentish history but there is little which attempts to portray the lifestyles of the people and little too on the twentieth century. Most of the information for this volume came from the oral recollections of the older generation, and the reader should not expect to find similar material in standard historical works. The purpose of this bibliography is twofold: first, to guide the reader to those books and articles which will provide more information on Kent in the thirty years leading up to the First World War, and secondly, to pick out a few works, not necessarily Kentish in content, which deal with some of the lifestyles portrayed. Most of the works listed should be relatively accessible to the general reader but government publications can be consulted at the Public Record Office or at university libraries.

T. Bavington Jones, *Kent at the Opening of the Twentieth Century* (1904), provides the most complete survey of the county in the period under review. G. F. Bosworth, *Kent* (1909), and G. Clinch, *Kent* (1903), also contain useful, although sometimes erroneous information. For a wider historical perspective Frank Jessup, *A History of Kent* (1958), and *Kent History Illustrated* (1966), are hard to beat. W. Page (ed.), *The Victoria History of the County of Kent*, vol. III (1932), is a mine of information for the intrepid reader, while M. Roake and J. Whyman (eds.), *Essays in Kentish History* (1973), is a valuable collection of articles on various aspects of the county's past. Kelly's directories for Kent (various years) contain potted histories of every town and village and details of their population, landowners, industries, and occupations. The *Census Returns* for the county (1891, 1901, 1911) are snapshot pictures full of intricate details.

Agriculture has always been a popular subject with both authors and their audiences. Kent's general development is concisely presented by G. H. Garrad, *A Survey of the Agriculture of Kent* (1954), and by C. W. Sabin in *The Victoria History of the County of Kent*. Detailed studies of the late nineteenth and early twentieth centuries include A. D. Hall, *A Pilgrimage of British Farming* (1913), chapter 8; A. D. Hall and E. J. Russell, *A Report on the Agriculture and Soils of Kent, Surrey, and Sussex* (1911); D. W. Harvey, 'Aspects of Agriculture and Rural Change in Kent, 1800–1900' (Cambridge Ph.D. Thesis, 1961, microfilm in the University of Kent library); C. Whitehead, 'A Sketch of the Agriculture of Kent', *Journal of the Royal Agricultural Society*, 3rd series, x (1899). Among the government enquiries which covered Kentish agriculture the following are of particular interest: the *Royal Commission on Agricultural Interests* (1879–82); *Royal Commission on Labour: The Agricultural Labourer* (1893–4); *Royal Commission on the Agricultural Depression* (1893–6); and *Board of Agriculture and Fisheries Report on the Decline in the Agricultural Population of Great Britain 1881–1906* (1906). T. W. Fletcher, 'The Great Depression in English Agriculture, 1873–1896', *Economic History Review*, 2nd series, XIII (1961), is a salutary reminder that government enquiries do not always portray events accurately.

The flavour of labouring life in the period can be tasted in some of Richard Jefferies' books: *The Toilers of the Field* (1892), and *Hodge and His Masters* (1880); also of interest are E. N. Bennett, *Problems of Village Life* (1914); G. Sturt, *Change in the Village* (1912); F. E. Green, *A History of English Agricultural Labourer 1870–1920* (1920); B. S. Rowntree and M. Kendall, *How the Labourer Lives* (1913); and F. G. Heath, *British Rural Life and Labour* (1911). 'The Kentish Waggoner' is the title of a very readable chapter in Richard Heath, *The English Peasant* (1893), while J. Boys, *A General View of the Agriculture of Kent* (1794), and Mr Marshall, *The Rural Economy of the Southern Counties* (1798), give some glimpses into earlier ways of life. The best general book on the work of the horseman is George Ewart Evans, *The Horse in the Furrow* (1960), although his information relates to East Anglia. Written material on higglers and horse dealers is virtually non-existent while oxen are more likely to be discussed by medieval historians: see for example, J. Moore, 'The Ox in the Middle Ages', *Agricultural History*, xxxv (1961). Threshing practices feature in several books on farming techniques, such as E. J. T. Collins, *Sickle to Combine* (1969), T. Hennell, *Change in the Farm* (1934), and W. Fream, *Elements of Agriculture* (1892). Information on the men who operated the machines can be found in the literature devoted to traction engines, e.g. Harold Bonnett, *Farming With Steam* (1974), R. Whitehead, *The Age of the Traction Engine* (1970). The reception accorded to their introduction into Kent is well related in E. J. Hobsbawm and G. Rudé, *Captain Swing* (1969), and T. L. Richardson, 'The Agricultural Labourers' Riots in Kent in 1830', *Cantium*, vi, no. 4 (Winter 1974). S. Macdonald, 'The Progress of the Early Threshing Machine', *Agricultural History Review*, xxiii (1975), traces its adoption throughout England.

Not unexpectedly, there is a voluminous literature dealing with hop picking, the most recent book being A. Bignell, *Hopping Down in Kent* (1977). Probably the most rewarding is Mary Lewis (ed.), *Old Days in the Kent Hop Gardens* (1962), a collection of essays published by the West Kent Federation of Women's Institutes. Good short articles include Caroline Baker, 'Hop Picking in the Weald before the First World War—Preliminary Findings of a Study in Oral History', *Cantium*, vi, no. 4 (Winter 1974), and M. W. L. Berry, 'Hand Picking of Hops', *Faversham Magazine*, vol. 1, no. 4 (1968). 'The Gay Invaders' is the title of a chapter in Charles Warren, *A Boy in Kent* (1939), a nostalgic portrayal of the hoppers' sojourn in 'Fladmere' at the turn of the century. John B. Marsh, *Hops and Hopping* (1892), is an attractive, over-glamorised view based on a season's picking. C. Whitehead, 'Hop Cultivation in Kent', *Journal of the Royal Agricultural Society*, 3rd series, iv (1893), gives a detailed account of the extent and practices of hop growing. R. Grover, 'A Great Depression in Kentish Hops?', *Cantium*, iii, no. 3 (1971), discusses their significance for the county's farming economy.

Fishing is less well documented and most of the information must be culled from contemporary sources such as the *Sea Fisheries Commission* (1866); *Board of Trade Report on the Herne Bay, Hampton and Reculver Oyster Fishery Company* (1876); *Annual Reports by the Board of Trade of their proceedings under Part III of the Sea Fisheries Act 1888* (1889–1913); *Board of Trade/Local Government Board, Investigation of the Fishing Apprenticeship System* (1894); *Board of Agriculture and Fisheries Departmental Committee on Inshore Fisheries* (1914). The history of oyster cultivation in the Thames is told by R. H. Goodsall in 'Oyster Fisheries on the North Kent Coast',

Archaeologia Cantiana, LXXX (1965). A. O. Collard, *The Oysters and Dredgers of Whitstable* (1902), published by the Whitstable Oyster Company, gives a detailed, but glowing account, of the activities of the company. Articles in the *East Coast Digest* contain much interesting, technical information on various practices around the coast, but Edward Carpenter, 'Kettlenet Fishing', *Kent Life* (May 1975) is the only attempt to document this particular activity.

Almost every town and village in Kent has its own 'History', and although many of these studies stop short of the present century and tend to concentrate on the physical features of the area rather than on social life or work practices there are significant exceptions such as J. Preston, *Industrial Medway* (1976). Careful use of trade directories and town guides can yield much interesting information, especially when the buildings referred to are still standing. The Sittingbourne brick industry is the subject of Frank Willmott's excellent little book, *Bricks and Brickies* (1972), while John Cadman, 'Faversham's Brickmaking Industry', *Faversham Magazine*, vol. 2, no. 1 (1970), is the only written piece of work dealing with this town's once-important activity. The seaside towns have attracted more attention. J. A. R. Pimlott, *The Englishman's Holiday* (1947, reprinted 1976), remains the best introduction to seaside holiday-making although A. Hern, *The Seaside Holiday: The History of the English Seaside Resort* (1967), is a readable account. J. Whyman, 'A Hanoverian Watering Place: Margate before the Railway', in A. Everitt, *Perspectives in English Urban History* (1973), is a revealing study of early nineteenth-century Margate, while his 'Kentish Seaside Resorts before 1900' (unpublished manuscript University of Canterbury library) is the best summary of the developments in the county. The various guides of the period still yield the most information (and provide the best entertainment!).